THE RESHAPING OF WEST EUROPEAN PARTY POLITICS

COMPARATIVE POLITICS

Comparative Politics is a series for researchers, teachers, and students of political science that deals with contemporary government and politics. Global in scope, books in the series are characterized by a stress on comparative analysis and strong methodological rigour. The series is published in association with the European Consortium for Political Research. For more information visit <http://www.ecprnet.eu>

The series is edited by Emilie van Haute, Professor of Political Science, Université libre de Bruxelles; Ferdinand Müller-Rommel, Director of the Center for the Study of Democracy, Leuphana University; and Susan Scarrow, John & Rebecca Moores Professor of Political Science, University of Houston.

OTHER TITLES IN THIS SERIES

Party Reform
The Causes, Challenges, and Consequences of Organizational Change
Anika Gauja

How Europeans View and Evaluate Democracy
Edited by Mónica Ferrín and Hanspeter Kriesi

Faces on the Ballot
The Personalization of Electoral Systems in Europe
Alan Renwick and Jean-Benoit Pilet

The Politics of Party Leadership
A Cross-National Perspective
Edited by William Cross and Jean-Benoit Pilet

Beyond Party Members
Changing Approaches to Partisan Mobilization
Susan E. Scarrow

Institutional Design and Party Government in Post-Communist Europe
Csaba Nikolenyi

Representing the People
A Survey among Members of Statewide and Sub-state Parliaments
Edited by Kris Deschouwer and Sam Depauw

New Parties in Old Party Systems
Persistence and Decline in Seventeen Democracies
Nicole Bolleyer

The Limits of Electoral Reform
Edited by Shaun Bowler and Todd Donovan

The Challenges of Intra-Party Democracy
Edited by William P. Cross and Richard S. Katz

The Reshaping of West European Party Politics

Agenda-Setting and Party Competition in Comparative Perspective

CHRISTOFFER GREEN-PEDERSEN

UNIVERSITY PRESS

Great Clarendon Street, Oxford, OX2 6DP,
United Kingdom

Oxford University Press is a department of the University of Oxford.
It furthers the University's objective of excellence in research, scholarship,
and education by publishing worldwide. Oxford is a registered trade mark of
Oxford University Press in the UK and in certain other countries

© Christoffer Green-Pedersen 2019

The moral rights of the author have been asserted

First Edition published in 2019

Impression: 1

All rights reserved. No part of this publication may be reproduced, stored in
a retrieval system, or transmitted, in any form or by any means, without the
prior permission in writing of Oxford University Press, or as expressly permitted
by law, by licence or under terms agreed with the appropriate reprographics
rights organization. Enquiries concerning reproduction outside the scope of the
above should be sent to the Rights Department, Oxford University Press, at the
address above

You must not circulate this work in any other form
and you must impose this same condition on any acquirer

Published in the United States of America by Oxford University Press
198 Madison Avenue, New York, NY 10016, United States of America

British Library Cataloguing in Publication Data
Data available

Library of Congress Control Number: 2019931800

ISBN 978–0–19–884289–7

Printed and bound in Great Britain by
Clays Ltd, Elcograf S.p.A.

Links to third party websites are provided by Oxford in good faith and
for information only. Oxford disclaims any responsibility for the materials
contained in any third party website referenced in this work.

Preface

This book is the result of 20 years' interest in two topics, namely party competition and agenda-setting. Bringing my research on these two topics together in a book has been my ambition for many years. Beyond the satisfaction of finally achieving this ambition, the publication of this book is also a fantastic opportunity to thank the many people who have helped me in doing so.

My interest in party competition has been with me since my PhD dissertation. My interest in agenda-setting is actually just as old. In 1998, I took a graduate course in agenda-setting at the University of Bergen with the late Richard Matland and Frank Baumgartner. At that time, agenda-setting was not on my agenda, but the course opened my eyes to the agenda-setting literature, and I was sure that agenda-setting was on my future research agenda. The course in Bergen was also my first meeting with Frank and his approach to research. My own work on agenda-setting really picked up when John Wilkerson from the University of Washington was a visiting scholar in Aarhus in 2001 and put me in touch with his colleague Bryan Jones. A grant from the Danish Social Science Research Council then allowed me to collect the first data for what was to become the Danish policy agendas project. The grant also allowed me to spend a semester at the University of Washington in the spring of 2004. The close interaction with John and Bryan allowed me to push the project beyond the data collection phase. Over the years, working with Bryan, Frank, and John has been a source of enormous inspiration. Seeing what social science looks like at its best taught me what to strive for. Thanks to the three of you for all the support over the years.

My interaction with the scholars behind the American Policy Agendas Project was part of what later developed into the Comparative Agendas Project known as CAP. CAP is not really a project, but a network of scholars with an interest in agenda-setting. Through an annual conference and many other activities, the CAP community has become an open academic family whose influence on this book is hard to overestimate. Thanks to all the people who have contributed to the CAP community over the years.

My more focused work on this book began in 2012. I had just obtained the Danish higher doctoral degree partly based on a book focused on Denmark, and I wanted to expand the idea into a comparative book. Grants from the Danish Social Science Research Council and the Aarhus University Research Foundation allowed me to set up the POLIS research group. The grants also made it possible for me to have two research stays at UNC Chapel Hill with my family in 2012 and 2014. These two stays were unforgettable for us and gave me the time and environment to lay the foundation for this book. Thanks again to Frank Baumgartner for all his help in making these two stays both possible and so rewarding. Thanks also to the UNC Political Science Department and the Centre for European Studies and its director John D. Stephens for hosting me.

From 2012 to 2016, the POLIS research group was a flourishing context for discussing the ideas that I was trying to develop for the book. Thanks to the members of the group: Flori So, Thomas Leeper, Henrik Seeberg, Gunnar Thesen, Peter B. Mortensen, Rune Slothuus, and Rune Stubager for their contribution to the many meetings and discussions of the group.

My alma mater, the Department of Political Science at Aarhus University has always been a fantastic place to work. When POLIS ended, I had an almost endless number of fantastic colleagues I could approach for comments on drafts of chapters. Thanks to Kees van Kersbergen, Carsten Jensen, Rune Slothuus, Henrik Seeberg, and Peter B. Mortensen for reading their way through often several versions of the same chapter. Also thanks to Kim Sønderskov for showing all the smart things STATA can do, which saved me hours of work.

A number of people outside the University of Aarhus have also influenced this book and in different ways helped me complete it. While at Chapel Hill, Herbert Kitschelt from the neighbouring Duke University not only invited me for niche lunches, but also commented intensively on my ideas. I am not sure this book will convince him that party politics should be studied in this way, but his criticism forced me to think much more clearly about my arguments. Over the years, I have also had the great pleasure of discussing my work with Hanspeter Kriesi. In some ways, this book is a criticism of his work, but discussing with him is always both a pleasure and highly rewarding. Also thanks to Tarik Abou-Chadi, who had a small role in the POLIS project, for reading large parts of the manuscript and providing excellent feedback. The two reviewers at OUP also deserve my thanks for careful and critical, but also constructive engagement with the manuscript.

When I began this book project, CAP coding of party manifestos was not available for all the countries I was interested in, so I needed the help from other people to code the manifestos. Thanks to Nina Liljeqvist for cooperation on coding the Swedish manifestos. Thanks to Isabelle Guinaudeau for setting up the coding of the German manifestos and also for providing me with the updated version of the French data. Furthermore, thanks to Simon Otjes for organizing the coding of the Dutch manifestos. We also co-authored an article (Green-Pedersen and Otjes 2017) on which Chapter 8 is partly based. Finally, thanks to Jeroen Joly for answering all my questions on the Belgium data and to Catherine Froi for proving the UK data. Thomas Pogunkte and Thomas Saalfeld were very helpful in my struggle with environmental politics in Germany, and Andrew Jordan and Roman Senninger helped me with the EU data, which, in the end, however, did not find their way into the book.

Over the years, I have been fortunate to have the opportunity of presenting parts of this book to a number of institutions. This includes the University of Strathclyde, the University of Gothenburg, the University of Southern Denmark, the Berlin Graduate School of Social Science, the University of South Carolina, and the University of Bamberg. Thanks to the participants on all these occasions for their many valuable inputs.

An additional factor that makes the Department of Political Science at Aarhus University such a great place to work is the friendly and efficient administrative staff. Thanks to Helle Bundgaard, Annette Andersen, and Helle Hornemann Møller for their careful work with references and language editing.

Last, but not least, thanks to those at home, my wife Lone and my kids Jacob, Kasper, and Lea who have put up with all my frustrations during the project and accepted the Saturdays when I was buried in the manuscript. I could not imagine a better base at home.

I dedicate this book to my three children. When this began, they were still kids. Now they have grown into something else, but for me they will always be my small kids. Please remember that height is a social construction.

Table of Contents

List of Figures   xi
List of Tables   xiii

1. What Has Happened to Party Politics in Western Europe? New Parties, New Issues, and New Conflicts   1

2. Bottom-Up or Top-Down? Theoretical Approaches to the Content of West European Party Politics   10

3. The Issue Incentive Model of Party System Attention   24

4. Data Sources for the Study of the Party System Agenda   41

5. The Development of the Party System Agenda in Western Europe: An Overview   52

6. The Dynamics of the Party System Agenda   71

7. Expansion from the Right: The Growth of Immigration on the Party System Agenda   82

8. An Ever-Sleeping Giant? European Integration on the Party System Agenda   99

9. Up and Down with the Environment   114

10. Attention to Education in the Post-Industrial Society   135

11. Everyone Really Loves Health Care   153

12. The Issue Content of West European Party Politics: The Central Role of Large, Mainstream Parties, but for How Long?   169

References   189
Index   207

List of Figures

5.1	Average length of party manifestos in quasi-sentences in seven countries from 1950 and onwards	53
5.2	Average length of party manifestos in quasi-sentences in five countries from 1950 and onwards	54
5.3	Attention to left–right related issues in seven countries from 1950 and onwards	55
5.4	Attention to left–right related issues in five countries from 1950 and onwards	55
5.5	Number of subtopics used in Denmark and Germany from 1953 and onwards	56
5.6	Attention to economic issues (macroeconomics, business, and labour) in seven countries from 1980 and onwards	58
5.7	Attention to foreign policy and defence in seven countries from 1980 and onwards	59
5.8	Attention to 'new politics issues' (immigration, European integration, environment, crime and justice, and personal rights) in seven countries from 1980 and onwards	60
5.9	Attention to the environment in seven countries from 1980 and onwards	61
5.10	Attention to European integration in seven countries from 1980 and onwards	61
5.11	Attention to immigration in seven countries from 1980 and onwards	62
5.12	Attention to crime and justice in seven countries from 1980 and onwards	63
5.13	Attention to personal rights in seven countries from 1980 and onwards	63
5.14	Attention to health care in seven countries from 1980 and onwards	65
5.15	Attention to education in seven countries from 1980 and onwards	65
5.16	Attention to social policy in seven countries from 1980 and onwards	68

xii *List of Figures*

6.1 Two-dimensional MDS configuration for Denmark ... 74
6.2 Two-dimensional MDS configuration for Sweden ... 74
6.3 Two-dimensional MDS configuration for France ... 75
6.4 Two-dimensional MDS configuration for the UK ... 76
6.5 Two-dimensional MDS configuration for Belgium ... 76
6.6 Two-dimensional MDS configuration for Germany ... 77
6.7 Two-dimensional MDS configuration for the Netherlands ... 77
7.1 Party system attention to immigration in seven countries from 1980 and onwards ... 88
8.1 Party system attention to European integration in seven countries from 1980 and onwards ... 106
9.1 Party system attention to the environment in seven countries from 1980 and onwards ... 120
9.2 The development of the general environmental index (Jahn 2016) ... 123
10.1 Party system attention to education in seven countries from 1980 and onwards ... 140
10.2 Party system attention to education divided into subcategories in Denmark, 1981–2015 ... 145
10.3 Party systems attention to education divided into subcategories in Sweden, 1982–2014 ... 147
10.4 Party system attention to education divided into subcategories in the UK, 1983–2015 ... 149
10.5 Party system attention to education divided into subcategories in Germany, 1981–2013 ... 150
11.1 Party system attention to health care in the seven countries from 1980 and onwards ... 158
11.2 Party system attention to health care divided into subtopics in the UK, 1983–2015 ... 164
11.3 Party system attention to health care divided into subtopics in Germany, 1980–2013 ... 166

List of Tables

4.1	Twenty-three main policy issues	46
4.2	Parties defined as large, mainstream parties	51
5.1	Percentage of elections in which the issue has been in top three from 1980 and onwards	67
6.1	Kruskal Stress Measure for different numbers of dimensions in the correlation of attention across the 23 issues in the seven countries from 1980 and onwards	73
7.1	Percentage of parties mentioning immigration in their election programme across decades	88
7.2	Immigration as a top issue	89
7.3	Regression estimates of party attention to immigration	90
7.4	Party attention to immigration in Denmark, 1984–2015	94
7.5	Party attention to immigration in the Netherlands, 1982–2012	96
8.1	Regression estimates of party attention to European integration	107
8.2	Percentage of parties mentioning European integration in their election programme across decades	109
8A	Overview of Eurosceptic parties	112
9.1	Percentage of parties mentioning the environment in their election programme across decades	120
9.2	The environment as a top issue	121
9.3	Regression estimates of party attention to the environment	122
9.4	Party attention to the environment in Germany, 1980–2013	126
9.5	Party attention to the environment in Sweden, 1982–2014	128
9.6	Party attention to the environment in the Netherlands, 1982–2012	130
10.1	Percentage of parties mentioning education in their election programme across decades	140
10.2	Education as a top issue	142

10.3	Regression estimates of party attention to education from 1980 and onwards	143
10.4	Party attention to education in Denmark, 1981–2015	145
10.5	Party attention to education in Sweden, 1981–2014	146
10.6	Party attention to education in the UK, 1983–2015	148
11.1	Percentage of parties mentioning education in their election programme across decades	159
11.2	Health care as a top issue	159
11.3	Regression estimates of party attention to health care	160
11.4	Party attention to health care in the UK, 1983–2015	165
11.5	Party attention to health care in Germany, 1980–2013	166

1

What Has Happened to Party Politics in Western Europe?

New Parties, New Issues, and New Conflicts

It is widely recognized that party politics in Western Europe has changed profoundly over the last decades. Long gone are the times when class-based political parties with extensive membership dominated politics. Instead, party politics has become issue-based. Political parties compete by presenting their views on the issues presently dominating the political agenda. This implies increased importance as to how political parties present their views in the media, a more volatile electorate, and many new political parties, often formed around particular issues.

The empirical examples of this development are plentiful. The clearest examples are probably the electoral success in the 2010s of parties like the AFD in Germany, the Sweden Democrats, and the PVV in the Netherlands. The consequences of the electoral growth of these parties are massive. The forming of coalition governments has become highly challenging in several West European countries. The Euroscepticism of these parties has also led to a concern for the stability of the European Union.

While there is broad agreement that a transformation of West European party politics has taken place, there is more divergence in terms of how to analyse and understand this development. Some studies focus on the new political parties, especially the niche parties that have emerged around particular issues (Adams et al. 2006; Meguid 2008). Rahat and Kenig (2018) study how this developmet has led to personalization of politics. Other studies focus on how the internal structure of political parties has changed, and how this has affected the linkage with the electorate (Katz and Mair 2018; Mair 2013). Finally, a rich literature has investigated how the transformation of party politics is related to changes in the social conflicts of West European countries (Hooghe and Marks 2018; Kriesi et al. 2008, 2012).

Surprisingly few studies have focused on how the issue content of West European party politics has developed over the past decades. There is an extensive literature around specific issues like immigration, European integration, the environment, or education. However, very few studies focus on the issue content of party politics in general. Basic questions like which issues have attracted party attention, which have not, and how this varies over time and across countries have only partially been answered. This book therefore offers a comprehensive analysis of the issue content of West European party politics.

To do so, the book develops a new theoretical model labelled the 'issue incentive model' of party system attention. The aim of the model is to explain how much attention issues get throughout the party system, which is labelled 'the party system agenda'. To explain the development of the party system agenda, one needs to focus on the incentives that individual policy issues offer to large, mainstream parties, i.e. the typical Social Democratic, Christian Democratic, or Conservative/Liberal parties that have dominated West European governments for decades. The core idea of the model is that the incentives that individual policy issues offer these vote- and office-seeking parties depend on three factors, namely issue characteristics, issue ownership, and coalition considerations:

- Issue characteristics refer to stable characteristics of the relevant policy problems, e.g. solubility and scope, and to problem information like the development of environmental problems.
- Issue ownership refers to whether the electorate on a stable basis sees one of the large, mainstream parties as most competent in dealing with the issue.
- Coalition considerations depend on whether party positions on the issue differ from the general left–right structure that determines coalition building. Large, mainstream parties can use a focus on a particular issue to build a coalition with a niche party or pursue wedge issue competition against a competing coalition.

The issue incentive model explains many of the empirical developments identified in the book. The limited party attention to European integration, even in times when it is expanding, is the result of the (lack of) incentives that the issue offers to large, mainstream parties. There is no constant stream of 'problem information'. When a party is in government, it is also difficult to deliver on promises of the direction in which the European Union should develop.

Another example is the rising party system attention to education in most countries. This can be explained by the increasing importance of education for the labour market, which leads to a debate about the 'knowledge society'. Large, mainstream parties respond to such a debate. One manifestation of this is the intense debate in many countries about the quality of primary schools, in some cases caused by PISA scores.[1] This has led to increasing party system attention to education in general and primary schools in particular.

---

[1] PISA is the Programme for International Student Assessment run by the OECD. It provides internationally comparable scores for the school abilities (reading, maths, etc.) of 15-year-old students.

Empirically, the book also offers a broader description of the development of the issue content of West European party politics. The rising importance of health care and education is often overlooked. Furthermore, the increased importance of new issues like immigration, European integration, and the environment can easily be overstated. The book also shows that the trajectories of these new issues differ considerably in terms of party attention. European integration remains an issue with limited party attention, and immigration has only become a top issue of party competition in some cases. In general, issues related to the welfare state also remain central to party politics. The issues that have declined, but far from disappeared in terms of party attention, are macroeconomics and the labour market.

The trends in attention to particular issues on the party system agenda are hugely important to explain for anyone interested in understanding the functioning of contemporary Western democracies. Once political parties focus on some issues rather than others, it is likely to affect their electoral support. This is the core of the idea of 'issue voting' (Bélanger and Meguid 2008). However, the issue content of party politics is not only important to study if one wants to understand the outcome of democratic elections. Which issues parties compete on has also significant consequences for the policies they implement. Political parties focus on issues by promising the electorate certain policies. In the autumn of 2015, Syrian refugees desperately tried to avoid having to seek asylum in Denmark and tried to make it to Sweden instead. This was a consequence of the substantial difference in asylum rules in the two countries. The very strict Danish asylum rules were introduced in the 2000s following intense party attention to the issue. In Sweden, immigration has played a much more limited role oin the party system agenda, and asylum rules are much less strict. Another example is how the general increase in party attention to health care has been accompanied by substantial increases in spending on health care.

THE CONTRIBUTION OF THE ISSUE INCENTIVE MODEL

The issue incentive model that will be developed and tested in this book is an attempt to increase our theoretical understanding of what shapes the issue content of West European party politics. Theoretically, two general perspectives on the issue content of party politics exist; a bottom-up and a top-down perspective (de Vries and Marks 2012).

From a bottom-up perspective, the issue content of party politics must be explained by the conflicts found within the electorate and the changes to this conflict structure. A clear example of the bottom-up approach is the work by

Kriesi et al. (2008, 2012), which is the most comprehensive attempt at analysing the issue content of West European party politics to date. The driving question for Kriesi et al. has been whether a conflict line has emerged around globalization involving particularly immigration and European integration. With regard to this work and other studies based on a bottom-up approach, the issue incentive model offers several contributions. One is the focus on the incentives of large, mainstream parties. This is in contrast to the focus of the bottom-up studies on niche parties which mobilize based on a new, second conflict (Beramendi et al. 2015; Hooghe and Marks 2018; Kriesi et al. 2008, 2012). The dynamics of party attention to issues cannot be explained by mainly focusing on niche parties. They are important, but primarily when they affect the coalition incentives of large, mainstream parties.

Another contribution of the issue incentive model is that it highlights the importance of studying party competition dynamics around individual policy issues rather than clusters of issues belonging to the second dimension. This is not to question the existence of a second positional dimension within the electorate and, also, at least partly, within party politics. The point is rather that to understand party competition dynamics, and why parties focus on certain issues, one needs to focus on individual issues. This does not imply that party positions are not structured by conflict dimensions. On the contrary, one of the factors shaping coalition considerations is exactly how party positions on a specific issue fit the more general left–right conflict. However, if one's research focus is to understand which issues political parties compete for, the findings in this book suggest that pooling different policy issues in broad categories, though mostly helpful in providing an overview, is problematic. The problem is that the issues that are pooled in fact vary considerably when analysed from the issue incentive model.

The other perspective on the issue content of party politics is the top-down approach. From this perspective, the content of party politics is determined by the strategic considerations of political parties and their competition with each other. The top-down perspective is the foundation of the extensive literature on issue competition among political parties that has emerged in recent years (e.g. Abou-Chadi 2016; Dolezal et al. 2013; Hobolt and de Vries 2015; Meyer and Wagner 2015; Spoon et al. 2014; van de Wardt et al. 2014). However, this literature typically focuses on specific groups of political parties like radical right-wing parties on particular issues like European integration, the environment, or immigration.

The issue incentive model builds on the top-down perspective and offers several important contributions to this literature. Studies within this literature typically analyse single issues and theorize from these issues. The issue incentive model developed in this book also explains individual issues, but the model explicitly includes issue characteristics and shows their importance. The issue incentive model thus offers an account of the general dynamics of party attention, and when and why some issues wax and wane on the party system agenda. A further contribution is the focus on the coalition considerations of large, mainstream parties. This factor is important for understanding party attention to different issues, not least cross-national variation in it. However, it has not received much attention in the issue competition literature, perhaps because the theoretical focus of this literature is mostly on the emergence of niche parties, whereas this book focuses on the incentives of large, mainstream parties. As for the latter, coalition building is crucial to win government power. Thus, the book does not argue that the growth of niche parties is unimportant. On the contrary, but rather than simply affecting the party system by their presence as competitors for votes, niche parties affect the party system and its agenda by affecting the opportunities for coalition building. The issue incentive model developed in this book is an attempt to develop a general top-down approach to the issue content of party politics. The literature on issue competition offers a plenitude of insights, but not a comprehensive model focused on the entire party system agenda.

The fact that the issue incentive model builds on a top-down approach does not imply that the bottom-up approach is mistaken or should be rejected. Quite the contrary. The work from the bottom-up approach such as Kriesi et al. (2008, 2012) points to changes within the West European electorate that are crucial from a long-term perspective. What the issue incentive model argues is that these long-term changes tell us much less about how the issue content of West European party politics develops in the medium term. The strategic interaction among political parties, which the issue incentive model theorizes, has greater consequences for the issue content of party politics than implied in the bottom-up approach.

From a broader theoretical perspective, the issue incentive model also has implications for how one understands the role of political parties as the key linkage between citizens and the political system (cf. Lawson 1980). How the profound changes to West European party politics have affected this linkage has been debated intensively (cf. Dalton et al. 2011; Katz and Mair 2018; Kitschelt and Rehm 2015). The bottom-up and top-down perspectives offer different views on this linkage. From the viewpoint of the bottom-up perspective, changes to the conflict structure of society are reflected rather directly in the party system through the emergence of new political parties (Hooghe and Marks 2018; Kitschelt and Rehm 2015; Kriesi et al. 2008, 2012). On the other hand, the cartel approach to political parties developed by Katz and Mair (1995, 2018) offers a clear example of a top-down perspective as to which established parties are able to control the issue agenda and keep new issues away. The message of the issue incentive model is that the degree to which the party system incorporates new issues depends on the incentives that large, mainstream parties face with regard to these issues, and these incentives vary.

In many ways, the issue incentive model is an elite perspective on the linkage between voters and parties, but one that includes much less elite control than the cartel approach. This is partly because elites, i.e. political parties, compete with each other for votes. Therefore, voters' attitudes and changes to them sometimes shape party behaviour. Partly this is because the development of real-world problems, or information on them, plays a crucial role. They are only controlled by political parties to a limited extent.

Empirically, the book draws on a new data set containing coding of party manifestos in seven West European countries (Germany, France, the UK, the Netherlands, Belgium, Sweden, and Denmark) from the early 1980s to the early 2010s, covering sixty-six elections. All party manifestos have been coded according to the policy agenda-setting coding system originally developed by Baumgartner and Jones (Baumgartner et al. 2019). Unlike the Comparative Manifesto (CMP) data set (Budge et al. 2001), which is based on similar documents, the policy agenda-setting coding scheme covers the entire policy agendas based on major topics/issues like health care, the economy, and immigration and subtopics like inflation, unemployment, and the public budget within economics. The coding scheme, which contains more than 200 subtopics, makes it possible to study issue attention in a much more detailed way than the CMP data set does. A further contribution of this book is thus to show how the data sets which are developed based on the Comparative Agendas Project (CAP) (cf. Baumgartner et al. 2019; Green-Pedersen and Walgrave 2014) can be used to study party competition. Moreover, the concepts and theoretical ideas of policy agenda-setting theory will be used in a number of ways to develop the theoretical argument and structure the empirical analysis. The book thereby demonstrates the usefulness of these ideas for studying party competition.

DEVELOPING AND TESTING THE ISSUE INCENTIVE MODEL: HOW THE BOOK PROCEEDS

To build support for these empirical and theoretical claims, the book proceeds in a number of steps. The first steps are theoretical, and they are presented in Chapters 2 and 3. Chapter 2 outlines the two dominant types of literature on the issue content of West European party politics in detail: the literature on the new, second dimension of West European politics, which is based on a bottom-up perspective, and the growing literature on issue competition, which builds on a top-down perspective. Chapter 3 outlines the issue incentive model, which further develops the top-down perspective. Theoretically, the issue incentive model combines two literatures which, though they both have attention to issues at their core, have lived rather separate lives, namely the policy agenda-setting literature (Green-Pedersen and Walgrave 2014) and the literature on issue competition, as laid out in Chapter 2. One key concept from the policy agenda-setting theory is the idea of a 'party system agenda' (Green-Pedersen and Mortensen 2010) that political parties influence but are also influenced by. Thus, the aim of explaining the issue content of party politics can be described more precisely as the aim of explaining the content of the party system agenda. Another key concept from the policy agenda-setting literature is the importance of issue characteristics for party system attention.

Next, Chapter 4 presents and discusses the data used in the book. It takes up questions about the use of party manifestos as a source for measuring party attention; it discusses the coding system used to code the party manifestos, the choice of countries, and finally what the data set has to offer in comparison with the CMP data set, which has mainly been used in the existing literature.[2] It thus explains how the issue content of party politics is analysed by studying party attention to twenty-three policy issues like the economy, health care, immigration, education, transportation, etc.

Chapter 5 and 6 are the first empirical steps in the book. Chapter 5 presents an overview of the development of the party system agendas in the seven countries using measures and concepts from the policy agenda-setting literature. It shows how the long-run decline of economic and class-related issues has opened up party competition in Western Europe where new issues have gained importance and made the issue content of party competition more complex. The literature typically argues that the new issues are 'new politics' issues, but this chapter shows that this is only part of the story. Issues like health care and education have also become central to party politics, and social policy issues remain central as well.

Chapter 6 explores general trends in the dynamics of the party system agenda. It first reports the findings from a multidimensional scaling (MDS) analysis of the party system agendas in the seven countries. A second dimension with a distinct and theoretically meaningful issue content has been clearly documented when focus is on issue positions (Kriesi et al. 2008, 2012). When focus is on issue attention, two or more dimensions are clearly found, but the issues that are argued to constitute the second dimension do not constitute a distinct group in terms of attention dynamics. Therefore, the chapter argues the need to focus on individual issues and discusses how they can be analysed based on the issue incentive model presented in Chapter 3. This includes reasons for choosing to analyse the following five issues: immigration, European integration, the environment, education, and health care.

---

[2] An online appendix presents the details of the coding of the party manifestos.

Chapters 7–11 explain, based on the issue incentive model, the waxing and waning of these individual issues. Immigration (Chapter 7) is characterized by a relatively limited increase in party system attention. In Denmark, party system attention has increased substantially, however, and the explanation is the coalition considerations of the large, mainstream right party in Denmark, the Liberals, from the early 1990s. Chapter 8 explains limited party system attention to European integration in all countries with a lack of incentives for large, mainstream parties to focus on it. Chapter 9 shows that attention to the environment generally rose until the early 1990s and then declined, but the issue has remained on the party system agenda. This trend partly reflects the development of the state of the environment. Still, substantial cross-national variation in party system attention to the environment also exists. This can largely be explained by the coalition incentives that the issue has opened up for Social Democratic parties. Education is analysed in Chapter 10. In most countries, party system attention to education has grown, but not in federal systems like Germany and Belgium where the national level does not control educational policy. This growth reflects the emergence of a 'knowledge society' which has increased the importance of the issue for large, mainstream parties. Chapter 11 looks at party system attention to health care, which has increased in all countries. All parties regardless of colour focus on health care. This reflects that health care is important for all citizens, but also that it is increasingly difficult for political parties to deliver all treatments and technologies that have become available because of medical-technological research. Furthermore, the organization of the health-care system seems to be important for the growth in party system attention to health care. The growth appears most pronounced in national health-care systems. Each of the issue chapters also discusses the often extensive literature on party politics and party attention that exists with regard to each of the five policy issues.

Finally, Chapter 12 summarizes the findings of the book empirically and theoretically. Empirically, it highlights the continuing importance of policy issues related to the welfare state and especially the increasing importance of health care and education. It also highlights the varying attention patterns found for issues like immigration and European integration that are both seen as belonging to the new, second dimension. Theoretically, the chapter summarizes the testing of the issue incentive model and discusses it further. This includes highlighting the importance of focusing on the incentives of large, mainstream parties rather than niche parties, which has been the dominant approach in the issue competition literature and the literature on the second dimension. This focus brings further attention to the importance of two factors that receive rather limited attention in these approaches, namely issue characteristics and coalition considerations.

The final question is whether the focus on large, mainstream parties is already obsolete because of their electoral decline in recent elections and the growing electoral strength of niche parties. The answer is NO, although it obviously depends on how much electoral strength large, mainstream parties actually lose. The foundation of their influence on the party system agenda is not only related to size, but also to government participation and their tradition for a broad issue appeal. As long as niche parties stay focused on their 'niche' issues and are reluctant to enter government, their impact on the party system agenda is more limited. The electoral growth of niche parties mainly affects coalition building. Large, mainstream parties can find it more attractive to approach niche parties by focusing on their issues. However, if this strategy is not likely to secure power, large, mainstream parties might cooperate with each other. The very long government formation process in Germany in 2017 and 2018 shows that this can be extremely challenging.

2

Bottom-Up or Top-Down?

Theoretical Approaches to the Content of West European Party Politics

As one would expect, the decline of mass political parties basing their support on class voting, and the growing importance of issue politics, have generated a quite extensive literature analysing different aspects of how party politics has developed. Part of this literature deals with broader questions as for instance the linkage between voters and parties (Dalton et al. 2011), the development of the internal organization of political parties (Katz and Mair 2018; Kitschelt 2000), and the future of political parties more generally (Bardi et al. 2014; Mair 2013; Rahat and Kenig 2018). Some of these broader questions will be addressed in the concluding Chapter 12. Focus in the following chapter is on the literature that deals directly with the issue content of West European party politics.

As argued by de Vries and Marks (2012: 187–8), there are basically two theoretical approaches to the struggle for the content of party politics: the first one can be described as a bottom-up or sociological approach that sees the issue content of party politics as a reflection of social conflicts. The starting point for this literature is where different social groups place themselves within these conflicts. The issue content of party politics reflects the mobilization of these groups around the issues constituting the social conflicts. Change in the content is typically the result of new political parties mobilizing social groups around new social conflicts. In continuation of the literature on 'new politics', Kriesi et al. (2008, 2012) thus focus on how the new social conflict around globalization mobilized by radical right-wing parties has become a new, second dimension of party politics.

The second theoretical approach can be labelled as a top-down or strategic approach in which the issue content of party politics reflects the strategic competition among political parties. Political parties try to attract attention to the issues they find attractive, and political parties that find the current issue content of party politics to their disadvantage try to introduce new issues. Schattschneider's (1960) idea of the 'conflict of conflicts' is the classic work within this tradition, which also emphasizes how political parties are able to structure social conflicts (Carmines and Stimson 1986). The strategic approach is fundamentally an elite perspective on the issue content of party politics. The bottom-up and top-down approaches offer quite different understandings of what drives change in the issue content of party politics. Is it driven by change in social conflicts or strategic elite behaviour? As two relatively distinct types of literature have emerged around them, they provide a useful way of organizing the discussion in the following.

The issue incentive model is an example of a top-down or elite approach. Therefore, the presentations of the two approaches differ slightly as the presentation of the top-down approach also presents a number of concepts and ideas which are used to develop the 'issue incentive model' in Chapter 3. Furthermore, the presentation of the bottom-up approach focuses on presenting the most recent, prominent examples of such an approach (Beramendi et al. 2015; Hooghe and Marks 2018; Kriesi et al. 2008, 2012). The presentation of the top-down approach is more fragmented as the literature within this approach mainly consists of journal articles in which different elements of this approach have been developed.

BOTTOM-UP APPROACHES TO THE CONTENT OF PARTY POLITICS

Lipset and Rokkan's (1967) classic work on how social cleavages shaped West European party systems when they formed in the late nineteenth and early twentieth century can be seen as the foundation of the bottom-up or sociological approach. The key idea of the original cleavage approach is that societal conflicts, like the one between workers and owners of capital, become institutionalized in politics through party systems organized along these conflict lines. Thus, what characterizes a cleavage—rather than just a conflict line in the party system—is that party conflicts are rooted in key social characteristics like status or religion and find an organizational expression through for instance a political party (Mair 2006: 373). The capitalist/worker cleavage is the most prominent example. Three points are worth highlighting further. First, the transformation of social characteristics into a cleavage is no automatic process. It is the result of mobilization by elites (Kitschelt 1994: 8–39). Second, once cleavages are established, people belonging to the same side of a cleavage, e.g. workers, not only share common interests but, more importantly, a common identity. From a cleavage perspective, being a worker is not so much a question of interest as it is a question of identity (Bartolini and Mair 1990: 212–49). Third, the idea of institutionalization plays a key role. The cleavages that were mobilized when most party systems were formed in the first decades of the twentieth century continued to dominate West European party politics throughout the century. Conflict lines in West European party systems are thus 'frozen' cleavages (cf. Mair 1997: 45–75). This is because cleavages are not just rooted in interests, but also in identity.

In recent decades, a new variant of the sociological approach has emerged focusing on how changes in the context of West European party politics have led to changes in its content. The starting point for this literature is exactly a sociological one: changes in social conflict due to the emergence of a new libertarian vs. authoritarian conflict in society change the issue content of party politics in Western Europe as political space becomes two-dimensional.[1] This implies new challenges for classic parties like Social Democratic parties (Kitschelt 1994) as well as the emergence of new political parties like Green parties (Kitschelt and Hellemans 1990) and radical right-wing parties (Kitschelt 1995). The latter two mobilize voters from both sides of the new conflict line. Green parties mainly mobilize from the libertarian side and radical right-wing parties from the authoritarian side. Compared to the more traditional cleavage literature (e.g. Bartolini and Mair 1990), recent literature on the new, second dimension pays much less attention to questions about identity. Focus is on political conflicts rather than on cleavages anchored in social identity (though see Stubager 2009).

The idea of a new second dimension of West European party politics, known as the 'new politics dimension', has been developed in several prominent theories of the change in West European party politics including its issue content. The most prominent example is the work of Kriesi et al. (2008, 2012). This represents an ambitious attempt at analysing party system change based on the general theory of change in the conflict structure of West European societies combined with a very comprehensive empirical investigation of changes in voter attitudes and party politics. The key element in Kriesi et al.'s approach is the emergence of a 'globalization' conflict between the winners and losers of globalization, leading to a conflict between integration vs. demarcation. This globalization conflict links itself to the cultural conflict dimension, which emerged in the 1960s and 1970s in Western Europe. Thus, the emergence of the globalization conflict does not add a new line of conflict, it rather transforms an existing one (Kriesi et al. 2008: 3–14). This process is driven by parties mobilizing the losers of globalization, in most cases populist right-wing parties, but sometimes also traditional right-wing parties that have transformed themselves in a nationalist direction (Kriesi et al. 2008: 19–20). At the same time, Kriesi et al. stay within a bottom-up approach. The question of change in the content of party politics is formulated as one concerning political mobilization

---

[1] The question of change in the dimensionality of party conflict could also be approached from a top-down perspective (discussed later in this chapter). However, the theories of the emergence of a new, second dimension of West European party politics all take a bottom-up approach.

of societal conflicts; political parties are analysed as mobilizing societal groups, in this case the losers of globalization (Kriesi et al. 2008: 9–14). Thus a new conflict line in the party system has emerged as a result of the emergence of a new societal conflict. This new conflict line consists of a number of policy issues of which immigration and European integration are the two most prominent ones.

Hooghe and Marks (2018) have recently presented a related version of a bottom-up approach arguing the emergence of a 'transnational conflict' containing the two issues of European integration and immigration. The conflict is one between a GAL (green/alternative/libertarian) pole and a TAN (traditional/authority/national) pole. Compared to Kriesi et al. (2008, 2012), the major difference is that Hooghe and Marks stress the importance of institutionalization as central to a sociological approach and highlight the stickiness of party conflict. Thus, major changes to party politics and its issue content happen through 'shocks' to party systems like the euro crisis after the financial crisis in 2008 or the migrant crisis in 2015. It is at such critical junctures that the content of West European party politics is reshaped.

Finally, Beramendi et al. (2015) have described this second dimension as a conflict between universalism and particularism with regard to social order. In this version of a bottom-up approach, which has a strong political economy focus, the occupational situation of different social groups shapes their preferences and thus the political conflicts around investment vs. consumption, which generate more attention to especially investment oriented issues like education (Beramendi et al. 2015).

No matter the exact conceptualization of this second new politics dimension, the underlying theoretical idea is the same. The emergence of a second dimension of conflict within the electorate allows parties, primarily new parties like radical right-wing parties, to mobilize around the issues constituting the second dimension such as immigration and European integration. Hence, the new parties become important actors in West European party systems. Three questions concerning the literature on the new second dimension deserve further discussion.

The first question has to do with the substantial character of this 'new politics' conflict. The original cleavages identified by Lipset and Rokkan (1967) all had a clear substantial content that linked the various issues together. The state vs. market conflict, for instance, manifested itself in relation to issues like macroeconomic policies, labour market policies, social policy, etc. In a parallel fashion, Kriesi et al. argue that the new, second conflict is about integration vs. demarcation in relation to globalization. This conflict manifests itself with regard to immigration and European integration, but also with regard to issues like law and order (security) and defence (army), but not the environment (Kriesi et al. 2008: 59–60; Kriesi et al. 2012: 109–13; cf. also Bornschier 2010). Other studies leave out European integration but include the environment (Stubager 2010). Hooghe and Marks (2018) link the 'transnational conflict' to immigration and European integration only. Beramendi et al. (2015) also link the second dimension to conflict over investment issues like education.

A relatively narrow understanding of the second dimension provides it with the substantial 'glue' that identifies the issues that belong and do not belong to it. However, the challenge when understanding the second dimension narrowly is to account for a rise in attention to an issue like the environment, which cannot be seen as part of a demarcation vs. integration conflict. Thus, it is unclear what the substantial content of the new line of conflict actually is. Furthermore, as will be demonstrated in the following, no matter how this second dimension is understood in terms of the issues constituting it, there is substantial variation in the party attention the various issues have received across time and countries. This challenges the bottom-up approach in the sense that it offers no clear argument for such variation. If attention to issues like immigration and European integration reflects mobilization of the same underlying social conflict, why does attention to them vary?

The second question concerning the literature on the new second dimension is that it builds on an argument about parallel conflicts within the electorate and the party system. The argument is that social conflicts within the electorate have in fact changed, and that this leads to a similar new conflict within the party system, i.e. a new, second dimension based on the authoritarian/libertarian, demarcation/integration, universalism/particularism, or GAL/TAN distinction. This first step in this argument is typically investigated by looking at how voters position themselves on issues like European integration and immigration and showing how these positions reflect an underlying dimension. At the level of the electorate, strong evidence suggests that such a new conflict has emerged, and that it correlates strongly with differences in education (Häusermann and Kriesi 2015; Stubager 2010; cf. also Langsæther and Stubager 2018). In terms of the next step, i.e. the party level, the evidence that party conflict is in fact structured along two dimensions is less clear. Van der Brug and van Spanje (2009) evaluate the existence of a globalization conflict as suggested by Kriesi et al. at the party level and do not find support for such a conflict line. Except for the issue of European integration, party positions on policy issues are structured by the left–right conflict only.[2] Hence, issues like the environment and immigration have become integrated in the left–right

---

[2] In the following, the left–right conflict refers to the basic conflict structure of the party system. Voters and experts are normally able to place parties on a general left–right scale without reference to any specific issue. The Chapel Hill Expert Survey, for instance, asks experts to place parties on such a general left–right scale (cf. Bakker et al. 2015). Party positions on state–market related issues (the economy, welfare state issues) are typically related to the left–right structure in the sense that party positions on the issues follow the left–right structure. To a varying extent, this may be the case for other issues.

Theoretical Approaches to Party Politics

conflict. Stoll (2010) points to a similar continuity in terms of conflicts at the party level despite the emergence of new conflicts within the electorate. Furthermore, Kitschelt (1994) also emphasizes that a 'rotation' of the main line of conflict in Western Europe has happened due to new issues. Thus, party competition retained a one-dimensional structure. Finally, the findings of Kriesi et al. (2008: 274–94) also show a tripolar conflict structure at the party level rather than a fully two-dimensional structure. The extent to which party conflict is in fact two-dimensional remains an open question.

Third, the mechanism linking the electorate and the party level within the literature on the new, second dimension also deserves discussion. The argument is that new political parties mobilize conflicts within the electorate. For instance, radical right-wing parties mobilize voters on the issue of immigration, and Green parties mobilize on the environment. However, the literature on the new, second dimension does not focus on particular issues, i.e. on the content of party politics. It focuses on the format of the party system, i.e. the number of dimensions. Focus has been on whether the party conflict has become two-dimensional rather than on the mobilization of new political issues. However, even if parties, to some extent, can be ordered along two dimensions, as one should expect from the literature, the question is how much explanation of party competition is actually provided by focusing on the format of the party system? A theory of party competition explaining the linkage between conflicts within the electorate and the party level presupposes studying individual policy issues. This is the level at which parties actually compete. Parties do not compete with each other on broad dimensions. Think about radical right-wing parties. If one, for instance, wants to understand their success and failure, an analysis based on dimensions will not tell us very much. Radical parties depend on attention to immigration, not on attention to the environment and only in some cases on attention to European integration. In other words, to understand exactly the success and failure of the 'agents' that are argued to mobilize the new, second dimension, one needs to go beyond dimensions and into the specific policy issues. For parties, attention to issues matters since their electoral fate is tied to particular issues, not to broad dimensions.

From the perspective of the literature on the new, second dimension, having to focus on individual issues might not necessarily be particularly problematic. Issues can be considered 'functional equivalents', and which particular issues receive attention is less important. This raises a more fundamental question, namely why issues as an analytical category are important in the first place. Does it matter whether immigration, European integration, or the environment receive attention as long as they represent the same underlying social conflict? The answer is 'yes' for two reasons. First, a significant rise in attention is likely to affect the behaviour of political parties; also in government. A significant rise in attention to European integration is, for instance, likely to cause governments to take Eurosceptic attitudes into account when deciding on matters related to European integration. As a consequence, the representational fit between parties and voters will be much tighter on issues with a high level of party attention and looser on issues like gender inequality that typically receives limited party attention (cf. Dalton 2017). Second, from an electoral perspective, the idea of issue voting also highlights how individual issues matter. A significant rise in party attention to European integration is also likely to make the issue more important to the electorate. Thus, neither from a policy perspective nor from an electoral perspective are policy issues functionally equivalent.

To sum up, the literature on the new, second dimension understands the content of party politics and thus also changes to it as a bottom-up process. The new, second dimension is a product of new social conflicts in society. The development of a two-dimensional conflict structure within the West European electorate has changed the format of West European party politics through mobilization of the issues linked to the new, second cleavage. New political parties like radical right-wing parties are the primary agents in this process. One challenge for the bottom-up approach is the definition of this second conflict line. Either it becomes a very broad label or, if it is defined more narrowly, the question is how to account for growing attention to issues that fall outside a narrower definition. More fundamentally, the weakness of the bottom-up approach is the link from social conflict to party behaviour. The content of party politics is formed by the issues that the parties pay attention to, and parties compete around issues rather than broad dimensions. The challenge is not the identification of new social conflicts; it is rather to present a satisfactory account of the party behaviour that brings these new issues into party politics.

It is important not to misunderstand the criticism voiced against the literature on the new, second dimension. The discussion focuses on whether the approach provides a strong theoretical account of the development of the issue agenda of West European party system in a medium-term perspective, i.e. which issues receive attention over, for instance, decades. To some extent, the bottom-up approach has a more long-term focus on how changes in social conflicts affect party politics. The question here is not whether such changes in social conflicts affect party politics in the long term. They clearly do. The question is how much such an approach actually tells us about party politics in the medium term, i.e. a decade.

Furthermore, it is important to remember that party politics in recent decades is fundamentally different from when party systems were formed as analysed by Lipset and Rokkan (1967) (cf. Hooghe and Marks 2018: 111–13). New parties were central in establishing the original cleavages, but of course there were no institutionalized party systems as there are today. The institutionalization of conflicts within the party systems means that the situation is fundamentally different. Rather than just focusing on the emergence of new parties, the starting point must be how existing party systems react to new issues including the entrance of new parties focused on these issues.

Besides the large literature that focuses on how new social conflicts have generated more party attention to new politics issues, it is also worth highlighting that a number of studies link the development of the issue content of party politics with broad societal developments like rising inequality (Tavits and Potter 2015) or increasing globalization (Ward et al. 2015). These studies are also examples of a bottom-up approach as they focus on the 'demand' side of politics, i.e. the preferences of the electorate as the main driver of the content of party politics. They also face some of the same challenges as the literature on the second dimension. For instance, Tavits and Potter (2015) explain party attention to two very general issue groups labelled 'redistributive' and 'non-redistributive/value-based' by how the level of inequality in society will make different groups in society demand different degrees of focus on redistributive issues. The challenge of this argument is basically the same as for the studies of the new second dimension discussed above. It lacks a theory of party behaviour explaining how issues related to redistribution become important to parties when redistribution is low. Voters have many demands; the question is which ones the parties have incentives to focus on. A parallel question is how much the finding that increased globalization generates more focus on non-economic issues (Ward et al. 2015) tells us about the issue content of party politics. Non-economic issues are all kinds of issues with very different party competition dynamics.

TOP-DOWN APPROACH

The other approach to studying the content of party politics is what de Vries and Marks (2012: 187–8) label a top-down or strategic approach. This approach goes back to e.g. Schattschneider (1960) and Riker (1996), but only a few studies within it spell out in theoretical detail how party interaction shapes the issue content of party politics. Studies of 'issue evolution' in the US like Carmines and Stimson (1986), Layman and Carsey (2002), and Lindaman and Haider-Markel (2002), and in a West European context Arndt (2016) and Stevens (2013), mainly focus on how the elite level, i.e. political parties, structures social conflicts. This provides a top-down perspective on the question of the dimensions of political conflict. However, the literature on issue evolution focuses less on the actual dynamics at the party level, whereas the literature on issue competition among political parties is the literature that has developed the understanding of the dynamics at the party level the most.

As mentioned above, the issue incentive model, which is presented in Chapter 3, is an example of a top-down approach, and it will draw significantly on the issue competition literature. Thus, the following presentation of this literature has a double aim of presenting the basic ideas of the issue competition literature while at the same time highlighting its most significant limitations. The issue incentive model is also an attempt to develop the issue competition perspective further.

The idea of issue competition as a theory of party competition is straightforward and has existed in political science at least since Robertson's work from 1976. In many ways, it was also the theoretical point of departure of the comparative manifesto project (CMP) (Budge and Farlie 1983; Budge et al. 2001). The underlying idea is that parties have preferred issues, and that they compete by trying to draw attention to these issues and avoid having to focus on the issues preferred by opponents. As Carmines argues (1991: 75): 'All successful politicians instinctively understand which issues benefit them and their party and which do not. The trick is to politicize the former and depoliticize the latter.' This, of course, raises the question of what it means that parties have preferred issues.

The idea of issue ownership typically provides the answer to this question within the literature on issue competition. Parties own issues in the sense that the electorate considers them most competent in dealing with these issues (Budge 2015; Petrocik 1996). Exactly what issue competition means, and how it can be studied empirically, has in itself been subject to a growing literature (Bélanger and Meguid 2008; Egan 2013; Green and Jennings 2017; Stubager and Slothuus 2013; Walgrave et al. 2015), but the underlying idea is widely accepted. Seeberg (2017) also shows quite stable and predictable patterns across time and countries of which parties the voters consider most competent at handling different issues. Still, parties can try to 'steal' issue ownership (Aragonès et al. 2015; Holian 2004), which explains why parties may want to address issues owned by their opponents. Whereas the basic theoretical components of the issue competition approach have existed for a long time, a literature that offers more in-depth analysis of the dynamics of issue competition has only emerged in recent decades. This new literature on issue competition has developed around a number of themes.

One central theme is issue overlap. If the idea of issue competition based on issue ownership is taken to its extreme, parties should only focus on their owned issues and ignore other issues leading to a very distinct issue profile for each political party. However, studies like Sigelman and Buell (2004), Green-Pedersen and Mortensen (2015), Dolezal et al. (2013), and Meyer and Wagner (2015) clearly show that issue competition is only partly about drawing attention to preferred issues. A considerable 'issue overlap' implies that parties actually do respond to each other and to some extent address issues preferred by opponents. Consequently, issue competition, as a model of party

Theoretical Approaches to Party Politics

competition, cannot be reduced to a relationship between the electorate and individual political parties trying to convince the electorate about the importance of their preferred issues. A central aspect of party competition is how political parties respond to each other and thereby come to have overlapping issues profiles, although they also have preferred issues to which they would like to draw attention. The latter is typically conceptualized based on issue ownership.[3]

Another central theme in the literature on issue competition is the effects of the emergence of 'niche parties'. Meguid's work on the electoral fate of niche parties in France and the UK, and the finding that this was dependent upon the strategies adopted by both mainstream left and mainstream right parties (2005, 2008), helped establish the central role of this concept in the literature on issue competition. One central discussion about niche parties has been the concept itself (Meyer and Miller 2015; Wagner 2012a). The core idea of niche parties seems to be that they primarily compete by emphasizing a few non-economic issues (Wagner 2012a). Classic examples are Green parties focusing on the environment and radical right-wing parties emphasizing immigration. As always, there are issues about borderline cases like small Christian Democratic parties, but the definition offered by Wagner seems to catch the core theoretical idea behind focusing on niche parties. Meyer and Miller (2015) suggest talking about 'nicheness' as a matter of scale, and Meyer and Wagner (2013) analyse when parties adopt a more mainstream or niche profile. They show that niche parties may develop a more mainstream profile—typically with a broader issue profile including economic issues—but mainstream parties rarely adopt a niche profile. In this way, the distinction between classic mainstream parties with a broad issue profile and newer niche parties that focus on very specific issues like the environment indicates a fundamental difference across political parties when it comes to issue competition (Adams et al. 2006).

The idea of 'issue entrepreneurs' launched by de Vries and Hobolt (2012; Hobolt and de Vries 2015) adds to this. Following the issue evolution literature discussed above, issue entrepreneurs are parties that are losers on the existing conflict line and therefore try to introduce new issues. Lack of government participation is a sign of being a loser on the existing conflict dimension. For example, issue entrepreneurs introduce the new issue of European integration to party competition and benefit from it electorally. Though niche parties like the German Greens have entered government, most niche parties have—more or less voluntarily—stayed away from office. The concept of issue entrepreneurs and the related idea of 'challenger parties'

---

[3] The recent idea of 'issue yield' launched by de Sio and Weber (2014), cf. also de Sio et al. (2017), offers a more empirical answer to the question of which issues parties find attractive. However, the study does recognize the fact that parties also pay attention to issues that do not appear attractive to them (de Sio and Weber 2014: 884).

(Hobolt and Tilley 2016) thus adds to our understanding of niche parties by pointing out that they typically weigh party goals like office and vote differently than mainstream parties.

Based on these fundamental differences between mainstream and niche parties, it is no surprise that a central discussion is about how mainstream parties respond to niche parties with a specific focus on immigration or the environment. This was, after all, the central question in Meguid's work. Spoon et al. (2014), Abou-Chadi (2016), and van de Wardt (2015) thus find that mainstream parties do respond to the emergence of niche parties with changes in issue emphasis or changes in position on issues, though the responses are clearly conditional on the more specific situation of the mainstream party in terms of issue competition. What further characterizes the studies of niche parties and the effects of their emergence on other parties is that they focus on the question of how mainstream parties react to the electoral threat from niche parties. Niche parties are primarily seen as new competitors for votes (cf. Ezrow 2007). They are not studied as potential coalition partners, and how mainstream parties react is not studied in light of the coalition implications of the emergence of niche parties.

The distinction between mainstream and niche parties is clearly important in terms of understanding issue competition in multi-party systems. However, in terms of the development of the issue agendas of West European party systems, the importance of niche parties remains a more open question. Is the rise in attention to political issues dependent upon 'niche parties' so that one only sees a significant rise in attention to 'new' issues in party systems in which niche parties emerge? Or does attention to new issues rise regardless of whether niche parties exist? Or is rising attention to new issues a general phenomenon whether or not niche parties exist, but more pronounced in party systems with niche parties? Answering these broad questions requires a broad empirical focus on multiple countries and issues to ensure that sufficient cases with and without niche parties are included. The literature on niche parties typically only focuses on cases (an issue in a given country) where niche parties exist.

Whereas the discussion about niche parties focuses on specific types of parties, other studies have focused on specific types of issues. Based on the idea of a 'wedge issue' from the study of American politics (Hillygus and Shields 2009), van de Wardt (2015) studies how issues that divide both coalitions and parties internally in multi-party systems are politicized—in this case European integration. Politicization is driven by opposition parties that rarely form coalitions with other parties, and therefore they are not affected by coalition cracks generated by wedge issues. Along the same lines, studies like Green-Pedersen and Krogstrup (2008) and Green-Pedersen (2007) show how coalition considerations are important for which issues parties try to draw attention to. For instance, attention to euthanasia in the Netherlands was driven by opposition parties trying to generate internal disagreement in the Dutch government consisting of a Christian Democratic and a secular party.

From a broader perspective, the findings on wedge issues and coalition considerations demonstrate that whether or not parties are interested in drawing attention to issues is not only a matter of electoral concerns in the form of whether parties hold issue ownership. In multi-party systems, coalition considerations matter as well. Coalition building is essentially a question of party positions. If parties, based on proximity on the general left–right scale, want to form a coalition to gain government power but take very different positions on one specific issue, they want to avoid attention to this issue as much as possible. In a broader perspective, this points to the interrelatedness of issue and positional competition. One cannot understand which issues are attractive to political parties without knowing their positions on them (cf. Wagner 2012b). The discussion of coalition considerations is the most systematic inclusion of positional logic in the literature on issue competition.

To sum up, the booming literature on issue competition presented here has provided a number of central insights going beyond the theoretical starting point that parties have preferred issues and try to draw attention to them. It is clear that parties do not only pay attention to preferred issues but also to issues preferred by the opponents—either because they are trying to 'steal' the electoral advantage on an issue, or because they consider the issue so important that not paying attention to it is worse than having to pay attention to an opponent's preferred issue. It is also clear that there is an important difference between mainstream parties with broad issue appeal and a focus on office and niche parties with focus on few, typically new, issues and less interest in office. Finally, the issue competition literature has shown that coalition considerations play a role for which issues parties focus on. Since coalition considerations are dependent on party positions on issues, the focus on coalition considerations also implies that one cannot understand the issue focus of political parties without knowing their positions on the issues. These insights are important building blocks for the issue incentive model presented in Chapter 3.

However, the literature that has developed on issue competition also has some significant limitations. Issue competition is about influencing the issue agenda of party politics, i.e. making your preferred issues dominant. Paradoxically, the outcome of issue competition—the issues that actually come to dominate party politics—remains an open question within the literature on issue competition (Tavits 2008: 51). Part of the reason is probably that the literature on issue competition has in fact been quite 'issue blind'. This is clear in studies of issue diversity, i.e. the number of issues that the parties emphasize, e.g. Greene (2016) and van Heck (2018). However, most other studies only focus on one or a few issues and study over-time variation in attention. Still, issue competition is about how some issues gain attention at the expense of others. Therefore, focusing on one or a few issues does not necessarily provide much information on the outcome of issue competition.

Some studies, e.g. Green-Pedersen and Mortensen (2010, 2015), do consider the entire issue agenda but only treat issues as panels within a regression analysis focused on explaining over-time dynamics, and thus they do not investigate which issues dominate party politics. Hence, focus is on the influence of the various actors, and cross-national variation in issue attention is often neglected. When studies include multiple countries (e.g. Abou-Chadi 2016), cross-national variation is handled statistically, but it is not a substantial focus point since the models again focus on explaining over-time dynamics.

A final aspect of the 'issue blindness' of the growing literature on issue competition is the limited attention to the character of the policy problems involved. A few studies include control variables to capture 'problem pressure' (e.g. Abou-Chadi 2016; Spoon et al. 2014), but little theoretical attention is paid to the character of the policy problems related to the issues. Consequently, the variation in issue competition that the difference in issue characteristics may generate receives little attention. The few studies like Abou-Chadi (2016) who studies more than just one issue, in this case two, also immediately find considerable issue variation.

In sum, despite its growth, the literature on issue competition has surprisingly little to say about the development of the issue content of West European party politics. What it offers is a series of important theoretical insights that can help build a theoretical framework for understanding how the issue content develops.

BOTTOM-UP VS. TOP-DOWN APPROACHES: HOW TO PROCEED?

The bottom-up and top-down approaches are not mutually exclusive. A top-down approach does not question the changes in social conflicts identified by the bottom-up approach, and a bottom-up approach also recognizes the importance of party competition. The importance of elite mobilization of social conflicts was central to Lipset and Rokkan (1967) and has continued to play a crucial role in the bottom-up approach (e.g. Kitschelt 1994: 8–39). However, from a top-down approach, changes in social conflicts are not the most fruitful starting point for explaining the issue content of party politics. To explain this, one needs a theoretical approach that focuses on the dynamics of party competition rather than seeing party conflict as a reflection of social conflicts. Social conflicts were a highly fruitful starting point when analysing the formation of party systems in the early twentieth century. Today, the question is how existing party systems are reacting to changes in social conflicts (cf. Hooghe and Marks 2018).

An approach focused on the dynamics of party competition needs to pay further attention to issues as the analytical starting point rather than party position on conflict dimensions. The reason is that issue attention is more dynamic than positions. Parties can change attention to issues rather quickly and are expected to do so. They are expected to address the problems facing any given society. When an economic crisis sets in, a terrorist attack happens, or environmental problems are discovered, parties are expected to change their attention in the direction of the problems. The real world is what makes politics dynamic, and it is what makes a general equilibrium in a political system impossible (Baumgartner and Jones 1993). Focusing on attention also allows the inclusion of real-world problems or information on them.

This is quite different with regard to party positions. Party positions are expected to reflect party ideology, and changes in party positions are therefore potentially dangerous for political parties. Voters might see parties giving up their ideology, and internal changes in positions often generate conflict, which is something parties want to avoid (Schumacher et al. 2013). Issue attention is thus the most dynamic aspect of party competition and therefore the best analytical starting point for understanding party competition. This is not an argument for the fact that party positions are less important for parties than attention, but rather that attention is a better starting point for unravelling the dynamics of party competition. Furthermore, it does not imply that party positions are not structured into a few dimensions—primarily the left–right dimension. However, how this format of party competition affects attention to issues can only be understood if one analyses the specific issues. Just because party positions on two issues are structured similarly, it does not imply that party competition on the two issues cannot develop differently. As demonstrated later in this book, party competition has developed differently on issues like immigration, European integration, and the environment.

To sum up, the bottom-up approach provides compelling evidence for changes in social conflicts, i.e. the emergence of a second conflict dimension. However, it does not provide a compelling theory of party behaviour. Therefore, the issue competition literature is the starting point for developing the issue incentive model in Chapter 3. The ambition is to develop further the issue competition literature. Until now, it has mainly focused on studying specific issues and actors or developing specific issue concepts. It still lacks a comprehensive theoretical framework that provides an answer to the question of why some issues receive party attention rather than others.

3

The Issue Incentive Model of Party System Attention

This chapter presents the 'issue incentive model of party system attention'. This model provides a theoretical framework for studying the issue content of party politics and thus for answering the question why some issues rather than others receive party attention. Chapter 2 outlined the two dominant theoretical approaches to studying the issue content of party politics, namely the bottom-up and the top-down approaches. The issue incentive model explains the issue content of party politics through the incentives that different issues offer for large, mainstream parties. Thus, it is clearly an example of a top-down or an elite competition approach, and it is an attempt to develop this approach further. A broader theoretical framework that can explain the development of the content of party politics has not been developed based on a top-down approach.

To achieve this, insights from policy agenda-setting theory will also be included (Baumgartner et al. 2017; Green-Pedersen and Walgrave 2014). The policy agenda-setting perspective offers a number of important insights into the dynamics of political attention to policy issues that complement the literature of issue competition very well. Combined, these two perspectives provide a platform for building a theoretical framework with individual issues as analytical points of departure, and at the same time they focus on explaining the entire issue agenda and not just individual issues.

POLICY AGENDA-SETTING THEORY

The policy agenda-setting perspective is developed from the American tradition of studying how political attention affects policy decisions. Kingdon (1995 [1984]) and Cobb and Elder (1983 [1972]) were the first seminal publications within this tradition, which gained substantial momentum with Baumgartner and Jones' (1993) book *Agendas and Instability in American Politics*. Compared to earlier studies of policy and agenda-setting, this book focused more on the agenda-setting or attention aspect rather than on policy decisions. In particular, it focused on mapping medium- and long-term patterns of attention, and thus on agenda-setting developments rather than on policy developments.

Baumgartner and Jones' (1993) first book and many later publications (e.g. Baumgartner et al. 2002; Baumgartner and Jones 2015; Jones and Baumgartner 2005), make up the foundation for what has become known as the 'policy agenda-setting theory' (Baumgartner et al. 2017; Green-Pedersen and Walgrave 2014). The core of this perspective is to study political attention in different venues as a way of understanding the workings of political systems and politics more broadly.[1] Based on this, various concepts and ideas about how to study attention to policy issues have developed.

At the most fundamental level, the starting point for the policy agenda-setting perspective is that attention is important for politics because it is consequential and, at the same time, scarce. It is consequential because fluctuations in attention to an issue change the political dynamics around the issue (Baumgartner and Jones 1993; Kingdon 1995). As Schattschneider argued many years ago (1960: 3–4), politics is about getting the uninterested interested because this will change the nature of political conflict. A political actor wanting to change the status quo may try to do so by generating more attention to an issue in order to get a broader set of actors involved. For instance, increasing attention to an issue may imply that public opinion becomes crucial for how political parties behave.

Since attention is scarce, more attention to one issue implies less attention to other issues. Agendas may expand somewhat, but no political system or actor can pay equal attention to all issues. Thus, agenda-setting is a question of the relative allocation of attention across issues. The combination of consequential and scarce implies that allocation of attention is politically conflictual. Political actors know that it matters which issues get attention, and they have preferences in that regard. Knowing that attention is consequential, trying to generate more or less attention to issues is a way for actors to try to achieve their policy preferences.

Another central premise of the policy agenda-setting perspective is that attention to issues implies attention to policy problems. When actors pay attention to health care, they usually express their views on problems in the health-care system and what should be done about them. Politics including party competition is rarely an abstract debate about whether parties are more to the left or the right. Rather, parties argue about how to deal with economic

---

[1] Venues refer to institutional structures in which political decisions are made. For instance, different branches of government, parliamentary chambers, referendums, or courts (cf. Baumgartner and Jones 1993: 31–8).

problems, how to secure a well-functioning health-care system, or whether pesticides should be allowed. This does not, by any means, imply that politics should be understood as 'rational problem solving', but attention should be studied by focusing on attention to specific policy issues like health care, the economy, etc. because this is what political attention is about. Two issues like, for instance, health and crime and justice contain very different political dynamics because the substantial problems involved are very different. Health is about how to provide health care and medication to citizens as well as managing hospitals, preventing diseases, etc. Crime and justice involves, for example, fighting criminals and deciding the right level of punishment.

To sum up, from a policy agenda-setting perspective, politics is an elite struggle over which issues should receive attention because the level of attention determines the nature of political conflicts. Furthermore, political actors pay attention to issues by discussing the nature of the policy problems involved and their possible solutions. Finally—as also argued by the issue competition perspective—political actors like political parties have issue preferences in the sense that they would rather see some issues getting more political attention than others. The basic theoretical ideas of the policy agenda-setting perspective are thus similar to those of the issue competition literature presented in Chapter 2. The biggest difference is the focus within the policy agenda-setting perspective on how policy problems drive attention to issues. The issue competition literature has largely neglected this aspect.

ISSUES AND THE PARTY SYSTEM AGENDA

The purpose of this chapter is to present the issue incentive model of party system attention in detail, including its theoretical foundation drawing on both the issue competition literature as well as the policy agenda-setting literature. Still, before turning to the model itself, it is necessary to explain the concept of the 'party system agenda', i.e. what the model explains. This requires discussion of two key concepts within the policy agenda-setting literature, namely issues and agendas.

The definition of an issue has received limited attention both within the policy agenda-setting literature and within the issue competition literature. Part of the reason is that there is empirical agreement that a list of policy issues should include the environment, transportation, defence, etc. However, a theoretical definition of an issue is also warranted. The best way to understand what an issue is, is to contrast the concept with two related concepts, namely 'policy problems' and 'conflict dimensions'. Policy problems are specific problems like organization of railway transportation, regulation of nuclear energy, or public pensions. Policy issues are bundles of policy problems that fit together in two related ways. First, they all relate to one overall policy problem. For instance, policy problems like the management of hospitals, which drugs should be allowed, how to prevent contagious diseases, etc. belong to health care because they all relate to people's health and involve professionals with medical training, etc. Second, political actors, especially political parties, tend to position themselves similarly on all policy problems relating to a policy issue. A left-wing party would favour public solutions to all health-related problems. Which policy problems are related to a certain issue is, of course, something that is open to reinterpretation and political struggles. For instance, in the US, tobacco was redefined from being an agricultural product to a health question (Baumgartner and Jones 2009: 264–81). However, a policy problem cannot be linked to any issue. For example, tobacco is not easily related to defence or energy.

Conflict dimensions are also policy issues to which parties position themselves similarly. For instance, the left–right dimension typically comprises economic and welfare issues to which parties position themselves similarly. However, in terms of policy problems, issues do not necessarily go together just because parties take similar positions on them. Although parties might take similar positions on European integration and immigration, the two issues are very different in terms of policy problems. European integration is about how the European Union should develop or whether new countries should join the union, whereas immigration is about the rules for obtaining citizenship or how to integrate refugees into the societies. From a policy agenda-setting perspective, policy problems are crucial in terms of understanding attention, and conflict dimensions are therefore to aggregate a level of analysis. Analytically, aggregation is necessary, and therefore policy issues are studied rather than policy problems. However, further aggregation into conflict dimensions solely based on party positions means aggregating across policy problems and thus the risk of conflating different attention dynamics.

Policy issues as a level of aggregation are also found in real politics, which in many ways is organized around policy issues. Ministries or departments are most often organized along defined issues (Minister of Defence, Agriculture, Health, Transportation, etc.), and the same is the case for committees in legislatures (health committee, defence committee, etc.). In other words, the idea of policy issues consisting of a series of policy problems belonging together in terms of both party positions and policy problems is also found in real-world politics.

Of course, this theoretical discussion of what a policy issue is does not identify which policy issues actually exist at a given time in a given country. However, this is not necessarily a theoretical question. New issues emerge, or issues are redefined, which is often reflected organizationally in the structure of ministries/departments or in the system of committees in legislatures (e.g. Baumgartner et al. 2000; Mortensen and Green-Pedersen 2015). In other words, the usefulness of issues as an analytical category for understanding party politics does not presuppose that the number of issues and their delimitation are fixed. How to create an issue coding system that allows comparison over time and countries is a methodological question addressed in Chapter 4.

Going back to the policy agenda-setting perspective, this perspective has also developed the concept of an agenda and its dynamics (cf. Dearing and Rogers 1996). The idea of studying allocation of attention to issues as an agenda-setting process implies that attention is scarce, and the allocation of attention is a relative process in which more attention to one issue implies less attention to another. Thus, an agenda is a hierarchy of attention to issues existing at a given time. Implicit in the focus on agendas is also an argument against focusing on attention to individual issues without comparing to attention to other issues. The idea of an agenda implies the relative comparison to other issues. Hence, the agenda-setting tradition has developed a number of concepts like the capacity, diversity, and volatility of an agenda (McCombs and Zhu 1995) as well as entropy which measures an agenda's concentration on specific issues (Boydstun et al. 2014).

The policy agenda-setting tradition has traditionally never focused specifically on political parties, but they have come more into focus in recent years (cf. Green-Pedersen and Walgrave 2014). From a policy agenda-setting perspective, Green-Pedersen and Mortensen (2010, 2015) have developed the concept of a party system agenda that can be used in the study of issue competition among political parties.[2] Political parties are strategic actors that pay close attention to each other. They never face the electorate alone but always have competitors who also have preferences in terms of the party system agenda. That political parties thus interact strategically with each other, and that the same type of party may behave differently depending on its competitors, is the core idea of a 'party system' rather than a set of parties (Bardi and Mair 2008). This idea has long been central in the study of party politics (cf. Kitschelt 2007). In terms of agenda-setting and issue attention, it means that political parties try to influence the party system agenda, while at the same time they are influenced by it. At any point in time, a hierarchy of issues that influences party attention exists, while parties try to influence the future content of this hierarchy. Parties therefore often pay attention to issues they would rather avoid but feel forced to address (Green-Pedersen and Mortensen 2010, 2015).

---

[2] In parallel, Steenbergen and Scott (2004) speak of 'systemic saliency'.

PARTY MOTIVATION AND LARGE, MAINSTREAM PARTIES

The issue incentive model explains the content of party politics, i.e. the party system agenda, through the incentives that various issues offer political parties. A necessary first step in developing the model is therefore to consider what motivates political parties; otherwise, one cannot understand the incentives that the issues offer them. Strøm's (1990) well-known article distinguishes between policy, office, and votes as basic motivations for political parties. The issue competition literature builds—though not necessarily explicitly—on the idea that votes are the most important motivation for political parties. The following is built on Beramendi et al. (2015: 2–3), and the premise is that parties—at least mainstream parties—are motivated by winning office. This does not mean that parties do not care about votes and policy. All parties want and need votes, and issue competition is one way to achieve this. Gaining votes is one way to achieve office, but in many countries gaining office also implies entering a coalition. Therefore, the focus on winning office as the basic motivation implies that parties are sometimes willing to sacrifice votes to gain office. In terms of issue competition, this means that they will sometimes avoid certain issues because paying attention to them will damage coalition building. In terms of policy, parties are interested in gaining office as a way to gain policy influence. However, their focus on winning office means that they are sometimes willing to give up their ideologically preferred policy position; either to enter a coalition or to win the votes necessary to win government power.

Not all parties are alike. As argued in Chapter 2, the distinction between mainstream and niche parties has come to play an important role in the literature on issue competition, and for good reasons. Niche and mainstream parties face a fundamentally different situation with regard to issue competition. Niche parties have emerged around a particular policy issue: Green parties around the environment, radical right-wing parties around immigration, the Parties for Animal Rights (PVDD) in the Netherlands around animal rights, etc. As these parties grow and become more established, they develop a broader policy profile, but their *raison d'être* are these issues. Due to their history, they are not expected to have a broad issue profile and can, to some extent, avoid other issues. In terms of issue competition, their behaviour is relatively easy to predict as they will focus on one particular issue and less on other issues. Furthermore, niche parties are typically rather hesitant to enter government as highlighted by the concept of challenger parties (Hobolt and Tilley 2016). Entering government makes it more difficult to keep focus on one particular issue. Therefore, policy and vote-seeking rather than office-seeking is the most applicable assumption about niche parties, and coalition considerations play a much more limited role for such parties. Likewise, policy and vote-seeking are also very closely linked. Voters expect niche parties to stay focused on their particular issue. A radical right-wing party will focus on immigration and demand a strict immigration policy because this is what the party wants, and also because this is the main expectation that voters have of the party. As shown by Green-Pedersen and Mortensen (2015), the issue focus of niche parties is more stable than that of mainstream parties.

Mainstream parties are different. Though they have preferred issues, for instance Social Democratic parties want attention to the welfare state, they compete by offering a broad issue package to the electorate (van Heck 2018). This also implies that they are more flexible in terms of issue focus. Furthermore, winning government power is often part of their *raison d'être*, which implies that they also judge the question of their issue focus from a coalition perspective. This adds to their flexibility in terms of issue focus. When it comes to mainstream parties, their issue focus is not just a matter of wanting to draw attention to one particular issue as it is for niche parties; they compete by offering a broad issue portfolio (Bertelli and John 2013).

Recent studies of general party competition have developed the idea of party differences further by focusing on the size of parties in terms of their electoral support (Klüver and Spoon 2014; Spoon 2011; Wagner 2012b) and their office aspirations (Schumacher et al. 2015). These studies indicate that the niche/mainstream distinction is too simple to theorize party behaviour. Most importantly, an important precondition for office-seeking becoming the dominant motive of mainstream parties is a certain size in terms of number of seats in the legislature. If parties become too small, they need to focus more on votes. Therefore, the focus in the following will be on large, mainstream parties.[3]

To sum up, the strategic issue considerations of niche parties are relatively simple. It is about drawing attention to the issue around which the party was formed in order to win votes. For large, mainstream parties, the strategic considerations are much more complex. It is about which of several issues to focus on. At the same time, the public expects a broad issue profile from these parties, which means that their possibility of avoiding certain issues is more limited. Finally, a third group of parties exists. This group consists of parties that historically have not been tied to a particular issue like niche parties, but they are smaller in electoral terms than the large, mainstream parties. This means that their behaviour is less driven by office-seeking. These parties may have been in office but rarely, if ever, held the position of Prime Minister. For large, mainstream parties, the expectation is mainly that winning government power also means holding the position of Prime Minister. Thus, the three groups of parties: niche parties, large, mainstream parties, and small, mainstream parties, weigh

---

[3] See Chapter 6 for a more precise discussion of what 'large' means here.

policy, vote, and office differently. Office is a much more important consideration for large, mainstream parties. The other two types of parties are more focused on vote-seeking, but for niche parties, vote-seeking means focusing on the particular issue that constitutes the parties' *raison d'être*, e.g. Green parties need to focus on the environment to win votes. Small, mainstream parties are more interested in office than niche parties, but their size implies that they are worried about electoral losses and thus prioritize votes higher than the large, mainstream parties do.

The different strategic situation of the parties in terms of issue competition has implications for their interaction and what shapes the party system agenda. Large, mainstream parties become key actors here because they have the flexibility to focus on one specific issue rather than another. Niche parties can do little else than focus on their preferred issue, but this is also mainly what the party wants. Niche parties emerge around particular issues and see that as their *raison d'être*, whereas large, mainstream parties are focused on government power and traditionally define governments because they hold the position of Prime Minister. This implies that the media will typically focus on the latter in their coverage of politics, and it is the conflicts among the large, mainstream parties that have shaped party politics and thus issue competition. Therefore, the key to understanding which issues get attention in the party system is to study the incentives that different issues offer large, mainstream parties. This is what shapes the party system agenda.

THE ISSUE INCENTIVES OF LARGE, MAINSTREAM PARTIES

Based on both the policy agenda-setting perspective and the issue competition literature, the next step is to map the incentive structure of large, mainstream parties when it comes to issue focus. The issue incentive model argues that three factors shape the incentives of large, mainstream parties with regard to a particular issue. These are the three factors that determine what vote- and office-seeking means with regard to a particular issue, namely issue characteristics, issue ownership, and coalition considerations. Each of these three factors needs further elaboration.

The importance of issue characteristics builds on the policy agenda-setting perspective and its emphasis on the importance of policy problems. From this perspective, two issues like immigration and European integration are fundamentally different. For example, the policy problems involved, the type of media stories they generate, the actors involved, how the public is affected by the problems, etc. are all fundamentally different features, but at the same time they are crucial to understanding attention dynamics. This also implies that theorizing about general attention dynamics based on single issues can be highly deceptive because issues vary so much in characteristics.

Cobb and Elder (1983: 94–109) pointed to such issue characteristics as the degree of complexity and the number of people affected. Baumgartner and Jones (1993: 150–72) talked about the special dynamics of valence issues. Soroka (2002) further developed an issue typology based on the concept of obtrusiveness of issues. However, as argued by Grossmann (2012), attempts at developing such typologies have largely failed as the grouping of issues within the typologies is typically much too open to interpretation. Rather, Grossmann (2012) recommends focusing on general patterns of attention dynamics across issues while at the same time studying how the characteristics of individual issues may make them deviate from the general trends in some, but far from all ways. Following this approach, the role of issue characteristics for party system attention can be theorized by having first a general approach highlighting the issue characteristics that may matter and, second by then discussing how these general characteristics apply to specific issues.

In terms of a general 'checklist', one can divide issue characteristics into two related but distinct aspects, namely 'problem information' and 'problem characteristics'. The problem information is variable over time as the content of information changes, whereas problem characteristics are stable. Likewise, it is the interaction between problem information and problem characteristics that matters for the party system agenda. Policy information is abundant (Baumgartner and Jones 2015), so new problem information is only attractive for political actors if the policy problem in question has certain characteristics. This is what the notion of issue characteristics refers to in the following.

Problem information is crucial because any political actor wanting to draw attention to an issue needs an 'occasion'. Parallel to what Kingdon (1995) labelled policy windows, political actors need 'attention windows' to draw attention to issues. A political party wanting to draw attention to health can try to generate its own occasion by, for instance, presenting a new programme on health care, but will find it much easier to react to new 'problem information' in the form of media reports on bad services or new statistics showing that waiting lists have become longer. The policy agenda-setting literature shows how problem information comes in different forms. Based on Kingdon (1995) and Jones and Baumgartner (2005), Liu et al. (2011: 406–7) highlight the role of problem indicators and focusing events. Problem indicators may either come in the form of personal experience with policy problems, e.g. a family member becoming unemployed, or in the form of statistics, e.g. unemployment statistics. However, problem indicators often have greater impact if they are accompanied by focusing events (Birkland 1997). Indicators of deteriorating environmental performance may not lead to more political attention unless a focusing event happens that draws additional attention to the problem. In that case, indicators showing a more general problem beyond the event are likely to be important. However, problems vary both in the extent to which they generate focusing events, and in terms of which problem indicators they generate. Problem information cannot be theorized independently of problem characteristics.

Problem characteristics refer to stable features of issues that shape their developments. The literature on problem characteristics provides a long list of potentially important characteristics (cf. Peters 2005). In this context, the important characteristics are those likely to affect whether parties pay attention to an issue. Here, four characteristics are important.

The first problem characteristic is typically referred to as 'solubility' (Peters 2005: 356–8). It is well known that many policy problems are wicked problems with no real solution (Rittel and Webber 1973). Still, some problems can, at least to some extent, be solved. This implies that the problem information on them begins to be positive, e.g. falling unemployment rates, and focusing events become less likely. Other problems may become 'chronic'. They provide information about a continuing problem, which implies that actors wanting to draw attention to the issue have continuous occasions to do so.

The second problem characteristic is the 'scope' of the problem in terms of the number of people affected (Cobb and Elder 1983: 94–109). This characteristic must be seen in combination with whether the issue is obtrusive, i.e. whether or not people have personal experience with the issue (Soroka 2002). Dealing with an obtrusive issue with a broad scope, the personal experience people have with the policy will be an important source of problem information. When it comes to issues that are either not obtrusive or have a limited scope, personal experience with the policy problem is not likely to be an important source of problem information.

The third problem characteristic is whether the issue is a 'valence' problem (Abou-Chadi 2016; Baumgartner and Jones 1993: 150–72). Concerning valence problems, the political disagreement is typically not the policy problem that should be addressed, but how to address it. Thus, with non-valence or positional issues, political actors may question whether an indicator is an indicator of a problem. This is not the case with a valence issue.

The fourth problem characteristic is the 'type' of policy typically involved. In broad terms, is one talking about a service like health care or education, a transfer like unemployment benefits, a regulation like of pollution, or an institutional question like regional autonomy? The type of policy involved will affect which problem indicators are available. Services are typically complex, and therefore a single indicator is rarely accepted as covering the entire issue. Which single indicator summarizes the service delivered by an entire health-care system? Institutional policies typically also deal with 'problems' to which no indicator is available. Which problem indicator is relevant in terms of European integration? Furthermore, different types of policies also vary in terms of the opportunities they offer to political actors for credibly addressing the problem. For instance, services are complex to deliver because they involve an extensive workforce and often also other political actors in the governance. This may provide political actors at the national level with less incentive to focus on them because it is more difficult to deliver promised solutions to the citizens.

In sum, the policy agenda-setting literature highlights how issue characteristics, i.e. the interaction between problem information and problem characteristics, shape political attention to issues. At the same time, this literature has also struggled in terms of how to incorporate this insight into the study of attention dynamics. The development of typologies of issues, or the problems related to them, has often proved unsuccessful. Following Grossmann (2012), the approach above is to generate a general 'checklist' of problem characteristics that can then form the basis for discussing the most important issue characteristics of individual issues later on. The aim is not to develop a typology that allows one to group all issues into a few types.

As discussed in Chapter 2, 'issue ownership' has been the central concept within the issue competition literature in terms of specifying which issues political parties prefer to focus on. The underlying idea is that voters consider certain parties more competent than others in dealing with a certain issue. Focusing on large, mainstream parties, the question is whether voters consider one particular large, mainstream party more competent than the other large, mainstream parties in dealing with the issue. Ceteris paribus, a large, mainstream party wants attention to an issue it owns because it expects that this will imply electoral gains compared to other large, mainstream parties. Furthermore, as shown by Seeberg (2017), patterns of issue ownership are relatively stable across time and countries, so the incentive for large, mainstream parties based on issue ownership is relatively stable and predictable.

Finally, the role of coalition considerations emerges from the fact that large, mainstream parties are office-seeking rather than vote-seeking. In most cases, coalition building for government power is based on how parties place themselves on the general left–right dimension. In addition, the patterns of coalition building are typically stable from election to election, i.e. in the medium term. These are integrated into the dynamics of the party system (Laver 1989: Mair 2006). However, they are also dynamic to some extent because parties gain and lose electoral strength, and new parties merge, and the purpose of coalition building is to win a majority. With regard to a specific issue, a large, mainstream party will judge the coalition implication of an issue by comparing it to the general left–right dimension. Any coalition would like to present itself as being in broad agreement. Therefore, large, mainstream parties prefer issues on which they agree with the parties that support them on the general left–right dimension and avoid issues on which they disagree with their 'usual' left–right coalition partners. Increasing the focus on an issue that is important to a potential coalition partner is also a way to signal agreement and cooperation to the electorate. Finally, based on the wedge issue logic presented in Chapter 2, focusing on issues into which an opposing coalition is internally divided compared to a 'normal' left–right situation may also be attractive for a large, mainstream party.

Mapping coalition considerations is the way to study how the existence of a niche party will affect the incentives of large, mainstream parties with regard to a particular issue. If a niche party is a potential coalition partner, its growth is not necessarily a problem for a large, mainstream party, especially if the niche party can gain votes from other large, mainstream parties as well. In that case, the large, mainstream party is likely to promote the issue around which the niche party has developed. For instance, a Social Democratic party may focus on the environment to win office based on a coalition with a Green party. The focus on the environment may strengthen both parties electorally or maybe just the Green party. However, what matters for the Social Democratic Party is that together the coalition gains electoral strength from focusing on the issue since this will enhance the chances of the party winning office. Thus, including coalition considerations in the framework leads to different implications in terms of how large, mainstream parties react compared to the studies discussed in Chapter 2. These studies only see niche parties as electoral competitors to large, mainstream parties (cf. Ezrow 2007).

In sum, the incentives that large, mainstream parties face in terms of focusing on a particular policy issue can be mapped by looking at three factors:

(1) Issue characteristics in terms of the interaction between problem information and problem characteristics.
(2) Issue ownership: Whether or not a large, mainstream party is considered more competent than other large, mainstream parties in dealing with the issue.
(3) Coalition implications: Can more focus on a given issue strengthen the coalition that will most likely bring the large, mainstream party to power, or can it undermine a rival coalition?

FURTHER ELABORATION OF THE ISSUE INCENTIVE MODEL OF PARTY SYSTEM ATTENTION

Before moving on, a number of aspects of the issue incentive model deserves further elaboration. The purpose of the model is to explain party system attention as outlined above. A number of points about this concept are worth emphasizing before applying it empirically. The concept of the party system agenda draws on the idea that to understand what shapes the dynamics of a given agenda, one needs to consider the interaction among the actors generating it.

The agenda of an electorate, or the public agenda for instance, refers to which issues a large number of people find important without paying particular attention to what other individuals find important. Voters, of course, interact with other voters, but not on a strategic level and only with a very limited number of people. The public agenda is thus likely to be affected by events or media stories to which the public is exposed. Likewise, the public agenda emerges when members of the public answer a survey question. The public agenda is not the result of interaction between strategic actors with clear issue preferences. It is basically the sum of a large number of personal agendas.

The media agenda is another example of an agenda with distinct characteristics. News media typically work through news criteria, which assist journalists and editors in deciding what is newsworthy. Thus, the media agenda is driven by the institutional features of the news media as described by Cook (1998). Even though news media systems are complex, all media involved are aware of what other news media pay attention to, and they all work through the same basic journalistic criteria. They are also competitors for consumers of news. Thus, unlike the public agenda, the media agenda is a structural phenomenon. It is not just the sum of the agendas of the individual news media, but the result of their interaction structured by news criteria and competition for consumers as well as by common sources like news agencies.

In the same way, the party system agenda has its distinct characteristics. Political parties are strategic actors who pay close attention to each other. They never face the electorate alone but always have competitors, who also have preferences in terms of the party system agenda. Therefore, perceptions and expectations play a key role for the dynamics of the party system agenda. If parties expect certain issues to be addressed by other parties, they will find it necessary to address them too. This generates considerable inertia in the party system agenda, and the best predictor of the party system agenda at time t is typically the party system agenda at time t−1 (Green-Pedersen and Mortensen 2015; Liu et al. 2011: 407).

Second, like the media agenda, the party system agenda is a structural phenomenon. Parties interact and are aware of which issues other parties pay attention to. In this way, the concept of a party system agenda explains the repeated findings of issue overlap. Though political parties have preferred issues and in principle would like just to focus on them, they end up also talking about issues they would rather avoid, but which their opponents prefer. This is an effect of the interaction between political parties in the mass media, in legislatures, and other political fora. Unlike interest groups that focus on selected issues, the nature of a political party is to focus on the entire agenda. Thus, when it is natural for an interest group not to have an opinion about a policy question that does not relate to their domain, a political party is expected to have a view on whatever policy question emerges. The concept of a niche party presented in Chapter 2 implies that some parties focus particularly on one or a few issues, but even niche parties will be questioned by the media and other political parties about their position on other issues. For instance, a niche party like a radical right-wing party cannot argue that it does not have a position on health care or education when asked. To sum up, the idea of a party system agenda provides a conceptual foundation for studying the issue agenda of party politics. Theoretically, one needs to focus on factors that shape the party system agenda.

One further implication of this logic is that no single political party controls the party system agenda; partly because other political parties also try to influence the agenda, and partly because it is also influenced by the real world through problem information. As argued above, problem information may have a major impact on attention. Some types of problem information, like the release of new statistics, may be predictable, but their more specific content is not, and many events are unpredictable.

Another central insight is that attention can be quite fluctuating in the short run. Events may influence attention dramatically in the short run as Kingdon (1995) points out. Thus, when agenda-setting dynamics are studied in a short-term perspective, they often appear chaotic and unpredictable. However, Baumgartner and Jones (1993) show how a medium- or long-term perspective on attention produces much more predictable patterns. But despite the difficulties in predicting attention in the short run, attention to issues in the medium or long run is more likely to be driven by predictable political forces than by specific events.

The policy agenda-setting tradition emphasizes how issue attention among political parties is a struggle over the relative attention to an issue that political actors try to influence but cannot control—especially not in the short run. Furthermore, from the policy agenda-setting perspective, struggles over attention is an elite dynamic. The public agenda discussed above is primarily reactive. If the public begins to consider certain issues as more important than before, it is either because it is responding to information about policy problems presented in the media, or because political actors, especially political parties, begin to pay more attention to these issues. It is hard to imagine that the general public on its own will begin to consider certain issues as more or less important without responding to other agendas. This is because the public agenda is generated by a large number of individuals, who generally do not interact strategically with each other.[4]

---

[4] From a methodological perspective, this implies that whereas problem indicators are crucial to include when explaining elite attention to policy issues, measures of public attention are less

The policy agenda-setting tradition also highlights the importance of the distinction between government and opposition when understanding party competition dynamics. This is an implication of the focus on policy problems as the substance of issue attention. When policy problems are debated, policy responsibility is often a crucial part of the debate, and policy responsibility largely rests with the parties in government. Whether a government is in fact to blame for policy problems, it is expected to be able to offer solutions to almost any problem in society. As shown by Green-Pedersen and Mortensen (2010), the government is therefore often reactive when it comes to agenda-setting. Whereas opposition parties can focus on the issue they find attractive from an agenda-setting perspective, policy responsibility forces government parties to respond to the issues brought up by the opposition and the media (Thesen 2013). The government parties' policy responsibility thus gives the opposition parties a strategic advantage in terms of influencing the party system agenda (Green-Pedersen and Mortensen 2010). Seeberg (2013a, 2013b) furthermore shows how the opposition's agenda-setting advantage can make government parties implement policies that move the policy status in a different direction than the government parties would otherwise have wanted.

In terms of studying variation in party attention to issues both over time and across countries, the policy agenda-setting perspective emphasizes that variation over time and issues is as likely as cross-national variation. Thus, when it comes to understanding the issue content of West European party politics, an important strength of the policy agenda-setting tradition is that it highlights factors that one would expect to generate similar attention patterns across countries, but variation in attention across time and issues. Issue characteristics are often quite similar across countries, partly because problem characteristics are quite similar, and partly because problem information on many issues like macroeconomic developments or climate change often follows relatively similar patterns across countries. Of course, this need not be the case, and problem information may also be a source of variation across countries.

THE ISSUE INCENTIVE MODEL OF PARTY SYSTEM ATTENTION

The issue incentive model, which is the theoretical framework used in this book to study the development of the issue content of party politics in Western Europe, can now be summarized.

relevant because public attention will reflect problem indicators as well as being affected by elite attention.

The concept of the party system agenda is a key element in the framework as it is the dependent variable. The development of the content of West European party politics will be studied by analysing the party system agenda in a medium-term perspective. Hence, the framework is not focused on explaining party attention at a particular time as for instance during an election campaign; focus here is on attention in the medium term such as a decade. The concept of the party system agenda highlights the interaction among political parties and their shared perceptions of which issues are important. The theoretical focus is thus on political parties as a group of strategic actors competing with each other, and because they interact, they generate a common agenda that can be mapped and tracked.

The next step is to explain the pattern of party competition underlying the attention to different issues on the party system agenda. Here the incentives for large, mainstream parties with regard to a particular issue are argued to be decisive; partly because large, mainstream parties are much more flexible in terms of issue attention than niche parties are, and partly because the largest parties traditionally dominate government formation and thus politics. Furthermore, three types of incentives are argued to be decisive for whether large, mainstream parties want to pay attention to an issue: issue characteristics, issue ownership, and coalition considerations.

In addition, this framework is an attempt to develop a more comprehensive top-down perspective on the content of party politics. Most of the literature within the top-down approach has focused on specific dynamics and political actors. This is in contrast to the bottom-up approach of especially Kriesi et al. (2008, 2012). One major contrast between this approach and the issue incentive model is what is seen as the driving change in the content of party politics. From the perspective of the bottom-up approach, it consists of changing social conflicts, i.e. changing attitudes among the electorate. In the issue incentive model, changes in policy problems provide the impetus for change. From the bottom-up perspective, on the contrary, the question becomes if and how such new social conflicts are incorporated into the party system. Within the top-down approach, the question is how political parties respond to new policy problems, and whether they have incentives to pay more attention to the relevant policy questions. Thus, a top-down approach does not imply that party politics is a closed system unaffected by changes in its context. However, the argument is that changes within the electorate are not the main driver of changes in the content of party politics. It is rather information on policy problems and the incentives that this information offers that make large, mainstream parties redirect their attention.

Finally, studying coalition incentives by looking at how party positions on new issues fit the existing conflict structure, namely the general left–right scale, is a way to take into account one of the key insights of the classical cleavage studies presented in Chapter 2. The conflict structure of most party systems is often 'frozen politics' from when the party systems emerged (Mair 1997: 45–75). In this context, the historical conflict structure comes to play an important role for attention dynamics today (Hooghe and Marks 2018). However, it also highlights the differences between studying the original building of party systems, as done by Lipset and Rokkan (1967), and the emergence of new issues today when a conflict structure is already in place in the party system.

4

Data Sources for the Study of the Party System Agenda

Applying the issue incentive model presented in Chapter 3 to the study of the party system agenda requires data on the issues that political parties emphasize in party competition. As already mentioned in Chapter 1, the following primarily draws on a new data source: party manifestos based on the CAP coding system. Two choices thus need further justification, namely the use of party manifestos as data source and the use of the CAP coding system rather than the CMP coding system (Budge et al. 2001). Further comments on the detailed use of the CAP coding system will also be provided in this chapter.

WHY USE PARTY MANIFESTOS TO STUDY THE PARTY SYSTEM AGENDA?

Studies of issue competition and issue attention of political parties have typically relied on one of following data sources: party manifestos, media data, parliamentary activities, or expert surveys. Party manifestos are the most widely used data source, partly due to the comparative manifesto data set (CMP) (Budge et al. 2001; Volkens et al. 2013). Other studies, like Kriesi et al. (2008, 2012), have used claims made by political parties in the media. A third group of studies draw on political parties' parliamentary activities like executive speeches, parliamentary debates, and questions to the minister (e.g. Green-Pedersen and Mortensen 2010; Vliegenthart and Walgrave 2011; Vliegenthart et al. 2011). Finally, expert surveys have also been used to study issue competition (e.g. Hobolt and de Vries 2015; van de Wardt et al. 2014). Given this diversity of data sources, a debate about the pros and cons of different data sources has also emerged (cf. Helbling and Tresch 2011).

All data sources come with pros and cons and measure party activities in different ways, and in general it is impossible to say which data source is the most appropriate. The right question is which data source is the most relevant for answering a specific research question. In addition, questions about data availability cannot be ignored. The focus of this study is on the content of party politics understood as medium- and long-term trends for which the political parties compete, i.e. the party system agenda. From this perspective, party manifestos are the most attractive alternative. They provide a direct measure of which issues each party prioritizes at relatively frequent intervals—typically four years—and they are typically easily available. Besides, a party manifesto represents the issue priorities of political parties as a unitary actor rather than the sum of media appearances of individual politicians who might be more newsworthy because they focus on issues that a party normally ignores.

Media data are very useful data sources for studying short-term trends in issue competition; for instance during an election campaign. Events like the flooding in Germany during the 2002 election campaign (Brettschneider 2004) or the conflict between the Netherlands and Turkey during the Dutch 2017 election campaign will be picked up by media data, not by party manifestos. However, though obviously important if one wants to understand the outcome of a specific election, such short-term dynamics are not what this book is about. It is about medium- and long-term trends in the issue content of party politics. The fact that media data are strongly influenced by short-term dynamics also implies that one should be careful using media data covering short intervals to discuss long-term trends. For such a purpose, media data on long-term intervals are needed although they are very demanding to collect, and even if such data were available, the role of the media as an institution governed by journalistic news criteria still need careful attention. Media data capture how the media covers party competition in terms of issue saliency rather than party competition as such. This distinction is less relevant if one focuses on party positions on issues because the media is unlikely to reflect party positions in a biased way. However, in terms of how much the media covers different issues, journalistic news criteria are likely to play a very important role. Helbling and Tresch (2011: 180) thus conclude that 'there might be a media bias with regard to the selection of topics, but not regarding the accuracy of content that is reported'.

Parliamentary data have also been used to study issue competition. Vliegenthart and Walgrave (2011) and Vliegenthart et al. (2011) all use questions to the minister as data source, and Mortensen et al. (2011) use executive speeches. However, parliamentary data have one central drawback; it is structured along the government/opposition divide. This is obviously the case for executive speeches, but also questions to the minister are primarily driven by opposition parties, though to a varying extent (Vliegenthart and Walgrave 2011). Even if it is possible to get data on both government and opposition parties by comparing attention in executive speeches to attention in parliamentary questions, it is potentially problematic as the parliamentary instruments may influence issue attention. If focus is on issue competition between government and opposition (cf. Green-Pedersen and Mortensen 2010), it is unproblematic, but the focus here is on issue competition among political parties rather than between government and opposition. Finally, data on the individual parties in a coalition government are a separate problem when for instance executive speeches are used.

As a final point, expert surveys have been used to study issue competition for particularly European integration (e.g. Hobolt and de Vries 2015; van de Wardt et al. 2014). Expert surveys have generally been a growth industry in political science; especially in terms of measuring party positions. The most developed example is the Chapel Hill Expert Survey (CHES) (Bakker et al. 2015). In addition to the more basic problem of expert surveys, i.e. they measure expert perceptions of issue importance for political parties rather than the parties' own prioritization of issues, even the CHES has two major limitations that make the data set not suitable for this study. The first one is simply the time period covered. The first version of the survey was launched in 1999, so it does not allow for a medium- and long-term focus. The other limitation is its measures of saliency. For most of the years covered, questions about saliency dealt with the relative importance of for instance European integration for a specific party.[1] However, the items asked about are a mixture of policy issues like the environment and broader ideological aspects like the importance of religious principles. Furthermore, many central policy issues like health, education, or the labour market are not covered. This makes it impossible to measure an entire issue agenda based on the CHES data, which has also never been the central aim of the CHES data.

To sum up, compared to the alternative data sources, party manifestos constitute the best data source available for investigating which issues parties focus on in party competition. Media data are highly suitable for investigating short-term dynamics, but this is not the focus of this book. Expert surveys are not available for longer time periods, and parliamentary data are typically structured along the government vs. opposition divide, which makes it difficult to measure the issues that the parties focus on in a way that is comparable across political parties. Additionally, it is worth stressing that the use of party manifestos does not imply that the aim is to study election campaigns as such. Party manifestos are not particularly well suited for this. However, the call for an election is an occasion for parties to step back and produce a document containing the issues that the party finds important to attend to.

Of course, party manifestos are far from the perfect data source. Two drawbacks are particularly worth mentioning. One is the fact that only an observation for typically every fourth year exists. Annual measures would have been preferable. For mapping long-term developments, this is less of

---

[1] See <http://chesdata.eu/1999-2014/1999-2014_CHES_codebook.pdf>.

a problem, but for investigating the dynamics of issue competition, the relatively limited number of observations even over a thirty-year period limits the analytical possibilities. The other drawback is the cross-national variation in the traditions of producing party manifestos. Some countries like the UK and the Netherlands have a strong tradition that all parties produce elaborate party manifestos at the beginning of each election campaign. A country like Denmark has no such tradition. However, parties typically produce documents stating their electoral platforms, which can then be used as functional equivalents of party manifestos. Nonetheless, identifying the appropriate documents is challenging in some countries especially back in time (cf. Hansen 2008). Furthermore, such alternative documents are typically shorter than elaborate party manifestos, which may affect the parties' issue profiles. This needs to be taken into account (discussed later in this chapter).

USING THE CAP APPROACH TO PARTY MANIFESTOS

The second major choice to be defended is the use of the CAP coding scheme rather than the CMP coding system to investigate which issues political parties emphasize. Given that the CMP data set already exists with a broad coverage over time and across countries, it would be tempting to base the book primarily on this data source. However, the drawback of the CMP data set for the purpose of this book is the coding scheme applied in the data set. Even though the CMP data set also draws on saliency theory (Budge and Farlie 1983; Robertson 1976), the main purpose of originally developing the CMP data set was to measure party positions. This was done from a saliency perspective, but the main purpose has never been to provide measures of entire policy agendas (Green-Pedersen 2019). This is visible from the coding scheme which contains categories for some policy issues like education and the environment, but it lacks specific categories for other central issues like health, the labour market, housing, and energy. Furthermore, when dealing with the issues that do exist in the CMP data set, the fact that the categories aim at capturing left–right attention rather than issue attention implies that not all aspects of the policy issue are in fact coded into this category. The main purpose of the CMP coding scheme is to capture the policy goal like inequality rather than the policy issue addressed (cf. Green-Pedersen 2019). Thus, if one wants to focus on issue agendas, the CMP data set has important limitations. In fact, this may be one of the reasons why the actual issue content of issue competition has received relatively little attention within the otherwise booming literature on issue competition. The CMP data set has made it possible to study issue competition for individual issues like the environment (Spoon et al. 2014) or immigration (Green-Pedersen and Krogstrup 2008) or broad developments like attention to economic issues vs. non-economic issues or redistributive vs. non-redistributive issues (Albright 2010; Green-Pedersen 2007; Tavits and Potter 2015; Ward et al. 2015). However, the CMP data set does not allow one to study individual issues as part of an entire issue agenda. Therefore, a different coding of the party manifestos has been necessary for this book.

This alternative coding scheme is known as 'the comparative policy agendas coding scheme' (Baumgartner et al. 2019)[2] and was originally developed by Frank R. Baumgartner and Bryan D. Jones (Baumgartner et al. 2002) to code various policy agendas in the US. This is done by coding congressional hearings, bills, newspaper front-pages, etc. Theoretically, the policy agendas coding scheme was developed as the empirical part of Baumgartner and Jones' (1993) punctuated equilibrium theory of policy stability and change, which has been the core theoretical element of the policy agenda-setting approach outlined in Chapter 3. The policy agendas coding scheme was thus developed to provide an empirical measurement of the entire policy agenda in order to measure both the development of the general agenda and the development of its individual issues. The coding scheme is structured around 19 major policy topics[3] and 230 subtopics.[4] Each coding unit (bills, hearings, etc.) is coded into only one subtopic and the corresponding major topic. The fact that all units are coded on the subtopic level means that the coding scheme has maximum flexibility in the sense that the subtopics can be reorganized into exactly the structure that fits a particular research question.

Inspired by the US policy agenda-setting data set, researchers in primarily other Western countries started to develop new data sets by coding parliamentary activities (bills, interpellations, questions to the minister, etc.), executive speeches, and party manifestos (Baumgartner et al. 2019). The latter provides the empirical foundation for this project. The policy agenda coding in non-US countries was based on the original US coding system, but all countries developed their own version by modifying the US codebook (Bevan 2019). These modifications were driven by two concerns: staying as close to the US coding scheme as possible and facilitating coding structured around the policy issues that were considered relevant in the given country. In general, few adjustments were made, and all national codebooks are quite similar to the original US codebook. Still, even though each national codebook deviated only slightly from the US code, the sum of deviations across all codebooks

---

[2] See https://www.comparativeagendas.net/pages/master-codebook.

[3] In relation to the CAP codebook, the term 'topic' is normally used rather than 'issue'.

[4] The exact number of subtopics has varied slightly over time due to adjustment of the coding scheme.

made comparison across a number of countries problematic. Therefore, a common master codebook with 21 major topics and 219 subtopics was created to ensure cross-walking across the different national codebooks. This also required limited recoding of the different national data sets (see Bevan 2019). Compared to the original US codebook, the most significant difference is the addition of two new major topics, namely immigration and cultural policies.

The data for this book draw on the master codebook, but 23 main issues were developed specifically for the book, and they are presented in Table 4.1. An online appendix available at agendasetting.dk presents the CAP manifesto dataset used in the book.[5] The main issues are very similar to those in the master codebook. The difference is that in this book the major topic of Foreign Trade and Public Lands do not exist, whereas a main issue for European Integration is added alongside one for Local and Regional Affairs, one for Politics,[6] and one for Territories/Former Colonies.

TABLE 4.1 *Twenty-three main policy issues*

Economy
Personal rights
Immigration
Health care
Agriculture
Labour
Education
Culture
Environment
Energy
Transportation
Crime and justice
Social policy
Housing
Business
Defence
Technology
Foreign affairs
European integration/EU
Local and regional affairs
Government operations
Politics
Territories/former colonies

---

[5] The online appendix (available at agendasetting.dk) also contains a more detailed description of the issues including which subtopics from the national codebooks belong to the various main issues.

[6] This refers to statements on the development of the political system, coalition opportunities, and political opponents.

To sum up, the CAP coding system with its focus on policy issues is well suited to study party competition and issue emphasis and better than the coding system embodied in the CMP. The limitation of using the CAP coding system is that data availability is more limited in terms of countries and time periods. The following thus includes data on seven countries during the period from the early 1980s and until the mid-2010s, covering one or two elections in the 2010s. The seven countries are the UK, Denmark, Sweden, France, the Netherlands, Belgium, and Germany.[7] In terms of the time periods, the data allow us to focus on issue competition over thirty periods, including the financial crisis. The drawback of the time period is that it provides limited possibilities of looking at long-term dynamics of party competition further back than 1980. However, for this purpose, the CAP data can be supplemented with CMP data which have a much longer time coverage. As argued above, the CMP can be used for broad issue developments because they are based on the same data source. Therefore, the CMP will also be included in some of the analyses in Chapter 5.

In terms of the countries included, this is partly dictated by data availability. However, the seven countries represent a strong selection of cases in two ways. First, the number of countries is sufficiently large to draw general conclusions about West European countries with some confidence. Of course, the choice of countries limits generalizability somewhat since Southern European countries are not included and the study has been limited to West European countries, i.e. East European countries are not included. In terms of the latter countries, the democratization process and the emergence of entirely new party systems in the early 1990s provide a very different context for issue competition. All the policy questions related to democratization and the transition to a market economy are highly likely to provide a very different 'problem environment' for these countries. This context clearly deserves attention, but also a very specific focus. The same is true for Southern European countries to some extent. Spain, Portugal, and Greece saw late democratization, and Italy experienced an extensive reconstruction of the party system in the early 1990s. The focus on party competition and the party system agenda presupposes a relatively stable party system in which parties compete with each other during several

---

[7] The data cover the following elections: Belgium 1981–2007, Denmark 1981–2015, France 1981–2012, Germany 1980–2013, the Netherlands 1982–2012, the UK 1983–2015, and Sweden 1982–2014. In the case of Denmark, the data set goes back to 1953, and in the case of Germany, it goes back to 1945. The additional data for these two countries will be used for analyses in Chapter 5. The Swedish data go back to 1976, and when dealing with the Flemish parties, the Belgian data go back to 1978. For the analyses in Chapters 7–11 that include a lagged dependent variable, existing data for the last election before 1980 will be included to avoid losing observation for the first election in the 1980s.

elections. What happens to the party system agenda when the party system is reconstructed is a highly interesting question in itself, but not the aim of this book.

Second, the countries vary on two key variables which, based on the theoretical framework presented in Chapter 2, can be expected to influence party competition for issues. The first is the pattern of coalition formation. Most of the countries, except the UK and to some extent France, typically have coalition governments, but the forms of coalitions vary. In the Netherlands, Belgium, and sometimes Germany, broad majority coalitions are the rule, whereas Denmark and Sweden are typically governed by bloc coalitions. The other key variable that varies across the party systems is the electoral system and thus how likely niche parties are to emerge. As discussed in Chapters 2 and 3, their role in issue competition is crucial, but to assess their impact one needs to compare cases in which they are present in the party system with cases in which they are not.

As outlined in Chapter 3, this book draws on the concept of a party system agenda in order to analyse how parties influence each other in issue competition. This concept raises the question of which parties to include in the measurement of the party system agenda. In other words, which parties' manifestos should be included? In the following, manifestos from parties that are considered relevant have been included as far as possible. Parties are considered relevant at a given election when they have won representation at the previous or the current election. It is important to stress that the question of relevance is considered from an issue competition perspective, not from a coalition-building perspective. Parties with which no other parties want to make a coalition, but which still play an important role in the political debate, may thus be included. For instance, a *cordon sanitaire* has kept Vlaams Belang away from coalition building in Belgium (Vangoidsenhoven and Pilet 2015), but the party is still highly relevant for understanding issue competition for immigration in Belgium. Representation in parliament provides any party with a platform from which to generate attention to its political views, which makes the inclusion for all parties represented in parliament logical. However, sometimes parties emerge between elections and become highly relevant for the political debate. To capture such parties, parties that have won representation at the current election are also included.

The online appendix presents an overview of all parties included in the study. Compared to the definition of relevant parties, the British and French data do not fully meet this definition. In the UK, only the major parties (Labour, Conservatives, and Liberal Democrats) were included in the data collection,[8] and in France only data on parties with more than 5 per cent of the votes were available.

---

[8] The UKIP is included in 2015.

The party manifestos for each country were collected and coded by different teams and, to some extent, with different purposes. The online appendix presents the details about each data set. All manifestos were coded by trained coders based on quasi-sentences (Sweden, the UK, France, and Belgium), natural sentences (Denmark and Germany), or paragraphs (the Netherlands). The use of different national versions of the codebook raises some issues of comparability, which are discussed in the online appendix.

Before turning to the empirical overview, a few comments on the exact measurement of the party system agenda are necessary. The idea of the concept, as developed by Green-Pedersen and Mortensen (2010, 2015) and presented in Chapter 3, is that, at a given time, all parties have a perception of a hierarchy of attention across issues to which they must attend while trying to influence the future content of this hierarchy. In other words, the party system agenda, on the one hand, constrains a party but opens up the possibility of 'constraining' other parties. This raises the obvious question whether some parties are more influential or less constrained than others. Answering this question is essential for understanding the dynamics of issue competition for a certain issue. It also has implications for how the measure of the party system agenda should be constructed. In the following, the party system agenda is simply calculated as the average across the relevant parties at a given election. In other words, first an agenda for each party is calculated which is the relative weight of each issue of the total manifesto. This relative measure is necessary to avoid that the varying length of the manifestos across parties influences the findings. At the next step, the average agenda is calculated across the parties.

This means that all parties count the same, and no weighing has been done. Weighing the parties according to party size in parliament, for instance, could have been an option. However, this would also mean that an assumption about party size equalling influence on the party system agenda would need to be defended. This book argues that large, mainstream parties are crucial for the development of the party system agenda (see Chapter 3). Yet, this claim needs to be defended by empirical analysis, and it should not be built into the measurement of the dependent variable from the outset. It is also worth noticing that Steenbergen and Scott (2004: 173) in their measurement of 'systemic saliency', which is similar to the idea of the party system agenda, also use an unweighted party average. A further problem of weighing by size is that, unless one uses a constant weight over the entire period, size changes over time. Thus, if one weighs by party size, it becomes unclear whether changes in the party system agenda in fact reflect changes in party attention or rather changes in party size.

The danger of using an average measure based on a relatively small number of cases is, of course, that the average can be strongly influenced by extreme values, i.e. individual parties that, for some reason, put a lot of emphasis on a certain issues. This is particularly problematic in countries like the UK,

France and Germany where the party system has few parties. Extreme values may furthermore be seen as especially problematic when they come from parties that are small in terms of size.

To judge how problematic such extreme values are, the data were inspected when, for example, an individual party spent 25 per cent or more of its manifesto on a single issue. There are examples of extreme values coming from small parties like the Danish Centre Democrats that spent 90 per cent of the party's 1987 manifesto on the economy, or the French Communist Party which spent 76.1 per cent of its manifesto on the issue of 'politics' in 1988. However, only in 81 cases, equal to 0.8 per cent of the cases, did a party spend more than 25 per cent of its manifesto on one particular issue,[9] and only six examples are from the three countries with very few parties (the UK, France, and Germany), and where such extreme cases influence the average strongly.[10] Furthermore, out of the 81, 39 are about attention to the economy, which in general is the top issue (discussed later in this book).[11] Finally, when high levels of attention to a particular issue come from a small party in terms of electoral support, this typically reflects the niche character of the party. An example is that the Dutch Party for the Animals (Partei voor de Dieren, PvdD) spent between 29 per cent and 38 per cent of its manifestos in the 2006, 2010, and 2012 elections on the issue of agriculture which includes animal rights. To sum up, extreme values from especially small parties driving the average values used to measure the party system agenda are generally not a problem. However, if focus is on a particular issue at a particular election, it is necessary to check whether the average is driven by extreme values.

Before the empirical analysis, the empirical grouping of parties into niche parties, large, mainstream parties, and small, mainstream parties needs further comments. In terms of niche parties, the focus on individual issues means that the status as niche parties will be determined with regard to the specific issue; in other words, parties that put special focus on this particular issue. This could be radical right-wing parties with regard to immigration or Green parties with regard to the environment. However, on other issues, e.g. Green parties on immigration, they are expected to behave like the group of small, mainstream parties discussed in Chapter 3.

---

[9] The data set has 10,465 cases. A case is how much attention a party pays to one of the 23 issues at a given election.

[10] Besides the French example from 1988, the other five examples are the following: the French Socialist Party spent 25.1% of its 2012 manifesto and 25.3% of its 1988 manifesto on the economy; the French Communists spent 26.9% of its 1981 manifesto on the labour market issue; the German CDU spent 25.8% of its 2005 manifesto on the economy; and the German Greens spent 25.3% of their 1983 manifesto on defence.

[11] Fifty-four cases were from the Danish manifestos, which probably reflect the nature of Danish manifestos in which the shorter documents imply a focus on fewer issues.

TABLE 4.2 *Parties defined as large, mainstream parties*

	Large, mainstream left	Large, mainstream centre	Large, mainstream right
Belgium	PS/SPA	CDH/CDV	MR/VLD
Netherlands	PvdA	CDA	VVD
France	Socialist Party		UPF/UMP/RPR
Germany	SPD	CDU/CSU	
UK	Labour		Conservatives
Denmark	Social Democrats		Liberals, Conservatives
Sweden	Social Democrats		Conservatives

As discussed above, large, mainstream parties have a broad issue focus as well as a strong focus on winning government power, and they traditionally hold the position of Prime Minister. Therefore, parties are defined as large, mainstream parties if they have held the position of Prime Minister in the period in question. The only exception is the Belgian case, in which the large socialist/Social Democratic parties are included despite all Prime Ministers in the period being either Christian Democratic or Liberal. Furthermore, parties from both the French and the Flemish party systems are included. This is done to secure comparability across countries. Table 4.2 presents an overview of these parties. Additionally, the parties are grouped into left, right, and centre based on their left–right orientation. The Christian Democratic Parties in Belgium, the Netherlands, and Germany are grouped as centre parties following the literature on these parties (van Kersbergen 1997).[12]

---

[12] The placement of the German CDU/CSU as a centre party is debatable, and therefore a placement of the CDU/CSU as a large, mainstream right party will also be analysed.

5

The Development of the Party System Agenda in Western Europe

An Overview

The first step in analysing the development of the party system agenda in the seven countries is to provide a general overview of how the issue content developed from 1980 and onwards. Which issues have grown and declined in the period, and how do these patterns vary across countries? This chapter provides an overview of the general patterns that the following chapters, which focus on particular issues, aim to explain. However, before turning to the medium-term perspective, a more long-term perspective is useful. Chapter 1 argues that the question of how the party system agenda has developed has become increasingly relevant during the last thirty to forty years. West European politics has moved away from its class-based nature and in a more issue-based direction. Party politics has become more issue-based parallel to the rising importance of issue voting. This generates a party system agenda that is more open in terms of its issue content. The development of the party system agenda after 1980 should thus be seen in a long-term perspective, which will be provided in the following.

LONG-TERM DEVELOPMENT OF THE PARTY SYSTEM AGENDAS IN WESTERN EUROPE

Looking at the long-term development of the party system agendas poses a challenge as the primary data of this book only go back to 1980, except for Denmark and Germany that go back to 1953 and 1945. Still, the CMP data set covers all relevant countries back to the Second World War. As argued in Chapter 4, the coding system used in the CMP makes it less useful for a detailed analysis of the party system agenda. However, more general aspects of the development can be analysed based on the CMP data set (cf. Albright 2010; Green-Pedersen 2007; Ward et al. 2015). Furthermore, the CMP data cover the entire group of northwestern European countries.

The Development of the Party System Agenda

As discussed in Chapter 3, the literature on agenda-setting policy offers a number of concepts that can be used to describe the long-term development of agendas. One concept is agenda capacity, i.e. the idea that agendas can expand and carry more issues to a certain extent (Baumgartner and Jones 2015: 114–37; McCombs and Zhu 1995). As argued by Green-Pedersen (2007), an expansion of the party system agenda is an expected consequence of the increased importance of issue competition and can be assessed by looking at the length of party manifestos.

Figures 5.1 and 5.2[1] show the average length of the party manifestos in the selected seven countries and five other northwestern European countries (Austria, Switzerland, Ireland, Finland, and Norway) from 1950 and onwards.[2] Both figures clearly show a considerable agenda expansion. This development is very pronounced in Germany, Norway, and Belgium and less pronounced in other countries. Still, even in Denmark, that has seen more limited agenda expansion (Figure 5.1), the party system agenda has expanded by a factor of almost 3. Switzerland is the only significant exception from the general trend as the average length of a party manifesto at the 2011

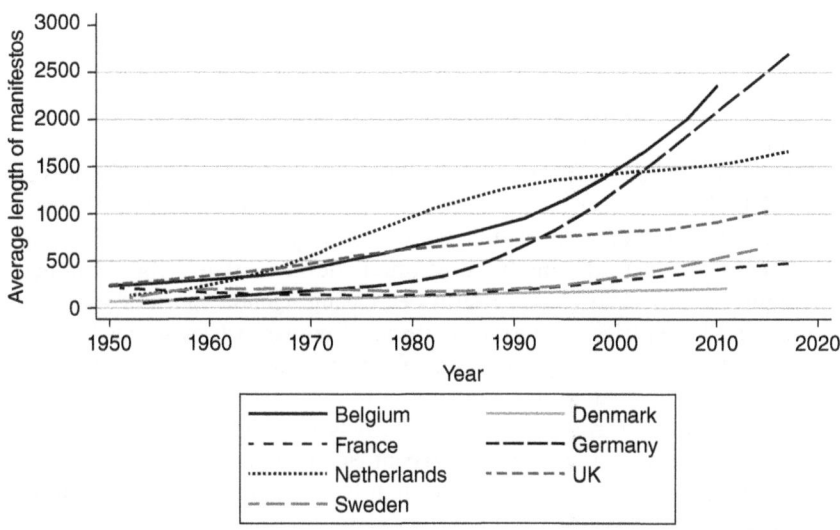

FIGURE 5.1 Average length of party manifestos in quasi-sentences in seven countries from 1950 and onwards

---

[1] Figures 5.1 to 5.4 are based on Lowess smoothing with a 0.8 bandwidth. This smoothing is done in order to focus on the trends in the data rather than on the individual observations.

[2] The length of each manifesto is taken from the CMP data set and is measured in quasi-sentences. The 2018a version of the data set was used (see <https://manifestoproject.wzb.eu/>). The parties included in the CMP data set may deviate slightly from the parties included in the CAP-based data set otherwise used in the book.

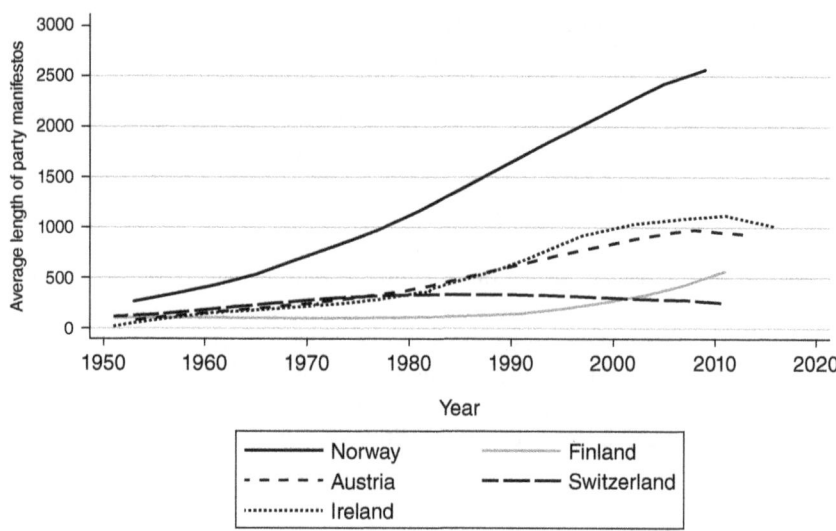

FIGURE 5.2 Average length of party manifestos in quasi-sentences in five countries from 1950 and onwards

election was the same as in 1951 after having been much longer for several elections. Thus, over the past sixty years, party system agendas have expanded, but to varying extents.

Naturally, agenda capacity says nothing about issue content, so Figures 5.3 and 5.4 look at the share of the party system agenda devoted to the categories in the CMP data set that concern economy and international affairs. These issues have traditionally constituted the general left–right conflict.[3] The figures clearly show a long-term decreasing agenda share of these categories in all countries. The exact pattern, of course, varies somewhat. For most countries, the decline has been relatively steady throughout the sixty years, though for France and Germany, it did not really pick up until about 1980, and some countries such as the UK, Belgium, France, and the Netherlands have seen an increase again in recent elections. In Finland, the agenda share of these issues has actually risen slightly since the 1980s, but not to the level of 1950.

In sum, as also argued by Green-Pedersen (2007) and Albright (2010) based on the CMP data set, the issue agenda of West European party politics has expanded and become less focused on the issues traditionally belonging to the general left–right conflict. Based on the CMP data set, Albright (2010) also

---

[3] This includes the following categories in the CMP coding scheme: 401–15, 101–7, 109, 701–4. Attention to European integration is not included (see <https://manifesto-project.wzb.eu/down/data/2017a/codebooks/codebook_MPDataset_MPDS2017a.pdf>).

The Development of the Party System Agenda

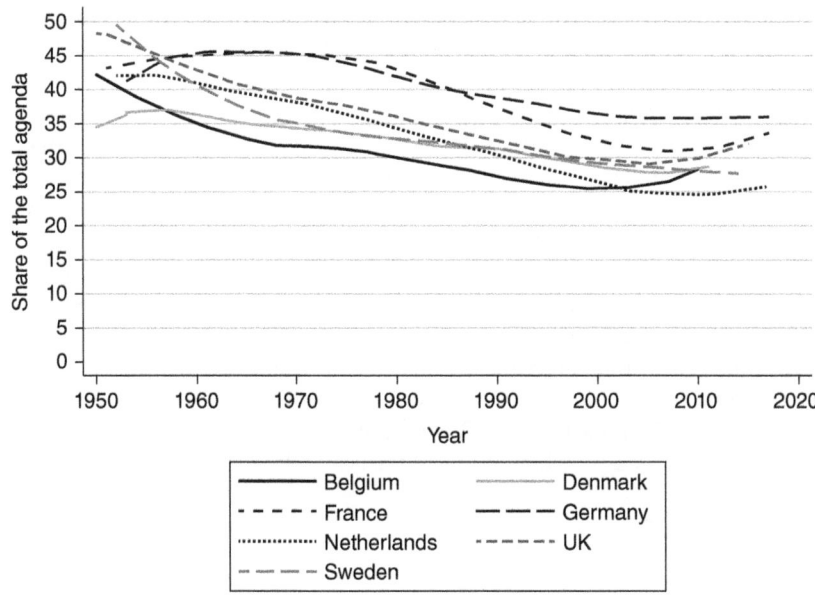

FIGURE 5.3 Attention to left–right related issues in seven countries from 1950 and onwards

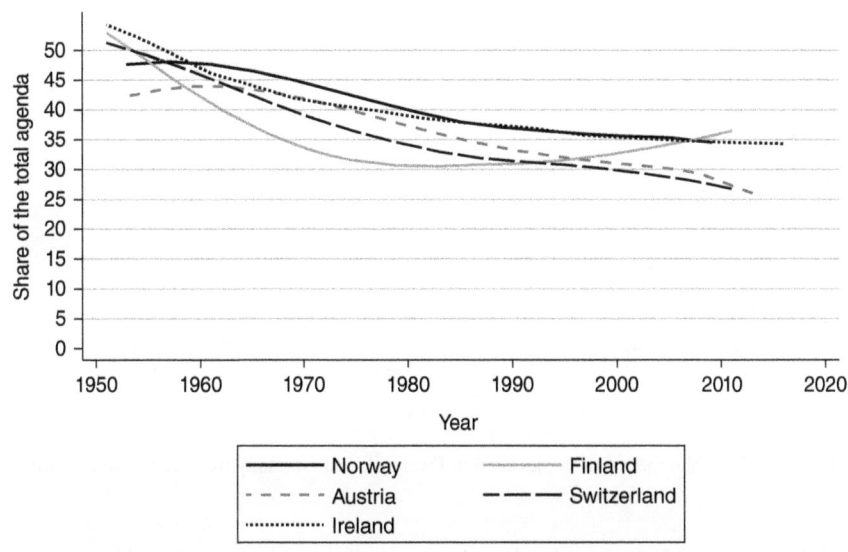

FIGURE 5.4 Attention to left–right related issues in five countries from 1950 and onwards

argues that West European party politics has become more complex as parties pay attention to more issues. However, the CMP data set is problematic for assessing agenda complexity because many of the coding categories do not really measure policy issues (Green-Pedersen 2019). Therefore, long-term rising agenda diversity is better studied by looking at Denmark and Germany, where policy agenda coding of party manifestos exists back to 1953 and 1945.

One way to examine the complexity of an agenda is to look at how many of the subtopic categories have been used to code the manifestos (cf. Baumgartner and Jones 2015: 118–20).[4] This shows whether longer manifestos imply that more policy questions receive attention from political parties.[5] This is shown for Denmark and Germany from 1953 and onwards in Figure 5.5. The figure clearly shows how the longer manifestos in both countries also imply attention to more subtopics.[6] This growth has been quite steady in both countries, though with a drop in Denmark in the 2000s. Thus, a more complex party system agenda has emerged on which political parties address more policy questions.

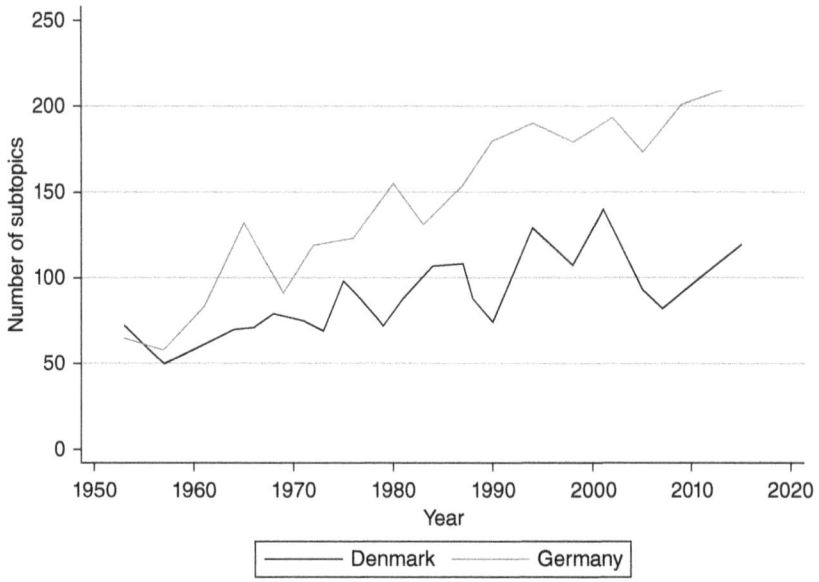

FIGURE 5.5 Number of subtopics used in Denmark and Germany from 1953 and onwards

---

[4] The German coding scheme has 232 subtopics; the Danish scheme has 231 subtopics.

[5] Subtopics in the CAP coding system resemble what was described as policy questions in Chapter 2.

[6] The correlation between the number of subtopic categories used in the policy agendas coding and the length of the manifestos as reported by the CMP data is 0.77 for Denmark from 1953–2011 and 0.75 for Germany from 1953–2013.

The Development of the Party System Agenda 57

This is in line with Albright's (2010) analysis based on the CMP data set. The party system agenda in Germany covers more policy questions than in Denmark. The most likely explanation is probably that party manifestos in Denmark are quite short and therefore likely to focus on fewer policy questions (see Chapter 4).

The analysis based on the CMP data set shows a long-term trend in which agenda capacity has expanded, while the relative share of traditionally left–right related issues has declined. The analyses of Denmark and Germany further show that this decline in left–right related issues also implies that far more policy questions receive party attention. In sum, the long-term development of the party system agenda is one of expansion of both agenda capacity and complexity.[7] These long-term trends in the party system agenda indicate a process of steady transformation of West European party system agendas away from a strong focus on a relatively limited number of mainly left–right related issues towards covering more issues. This is a process which began in the 1950s and 1960s and has continued after the 1980s, i.e. the time period in focus in this book. The question then is what this more open and more complex party system agenda looks like, i.e. which issues get attention. The purpose of the following analysis is to answer exactly this question focusing on the seven countries from the 1980s and onwards.

WHAT HAS BEEN ON THE AGENDA?

As a first step in analysing which issues have waxed and waned on the party system agenda in the seven countries since 1980, one looks at whether the long-term decline of the economy and international affairs as identified above can also be found in the seven countries after 1980.

Figure 5.6 shows[8] the development of economic issues in a broad sense, including macroeconomic questions, the labour market, and regulation of businesses.[9] In all the countries except Germany, attention to these issues has declined. Thus, the trend of the declining attention to such issues has

---

[7] Green-Pedersen (2006) provides a similar analysis and reaches similar conclusions based on parliamentary data on Denmark (parliamentary debates and questions).

[8] All the remaining figures in the chapter are based on Lowess smoothing with a 0.8 bandwidth. This smoothing is done in order to focus on the trends in the data rather than the individual observations.

[9] This refers to subtopics, which have been grouped under the three main issues of economics (1), labour (5), and business (15) (see online appendix).

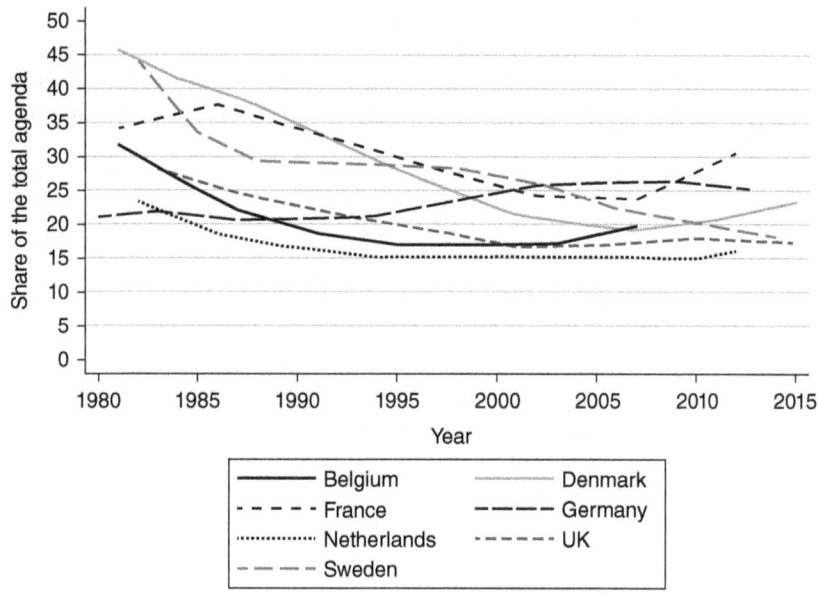

FIGURE 5.6 Attention to economic issues (macroeconomics, business, and labour) in seven countries from 1980 and onwards

continued after 1980. As Figure 5.6 shows, in Denmark, France, and to a lesser degree in the Netherlands and the UK, attention to these issues rose again in the end of the period, most likely in response to the financial crisis. The same tendency was not found in Sweden and Germany, which passed through the crisis relatively easily. Thus, the tendency towards a decreasing attention to economic issues is clearly not unaffected by 'problem information', i.e. how the economy is doing, and it is not an inevitable process. Economic issues still play a crucial role in the party system agenda. However, not even the financial crisis has brought the attention to these issues back to the level of the early 1980s.

Figure 5.7 provides information on international affairs, i.e. attention to defence and foreign policy, and the tendency is less uniform across the seven countries.[10] In Denmark, Germany, and the Netherlands, where attention to these issues was high in the 1980s, attention has declined significantly. Attention to international affairs was also high in the UK in the early 1980s, but it has declined less significantly and has actually been rising in the 2000s, reaching the same level as in the 1980s. In general, international affairs have not disappeared from the agenda in any of the countries. However, in all countries

---

[10] Defence refers to the main issue 16 in the CAP system, whereas foreign policy refers to main issue 19, though not including European integration.

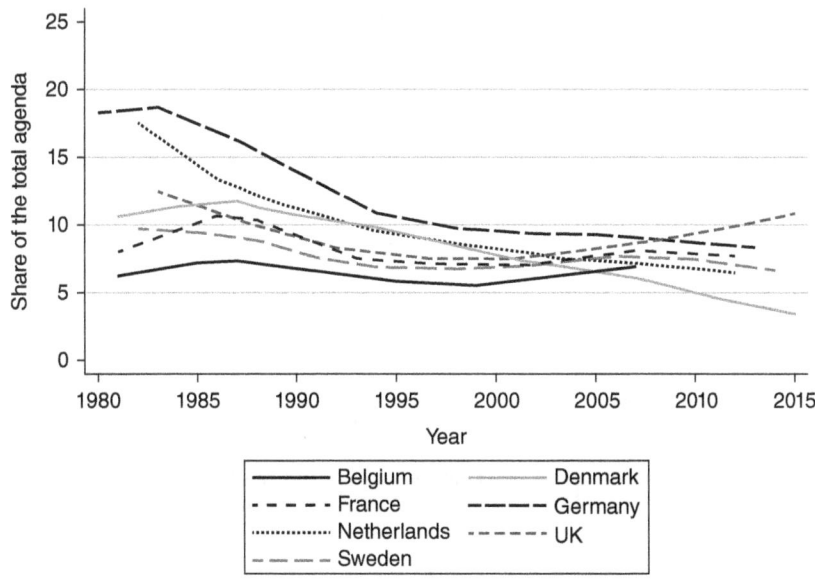

FIGURE 5.7 Attention to foreign policy and defence in seven countries from 1980 and onwards

except the UK, these issues occupy a lower share of the party system agenda today than they did during the 1980s.

The decline of the traditional left–right related issues opens up agenda space for other issues. The question is which other issues have taken up this space. As argued in Chapter 2, the most prominent answer to this question has been issues belonging to the new second dimension (Hooghe and Marks 2018; Kriesi et al. 2008, 2012), or 'non-economic'/'cultural' issues (Norris and Inglehart 2019; Ward et al. 2015). Exactly which issues belong to the second dimension is debated, as explained in Chapter 2, but five issues play the most prominent role in the discussion, namely the environment, immigration, personal rights, crime and justice, and European integration. Figure 5.8 shows how these five issues have developed over time in the seven countries. The general trend is clearly that these issues have taken up an increasing share of the party system agendas. However, in most countries the attention to 'new politics' issues levelled off around 2000 and even declined slightly. In Germany, the level actually dropped to the level of the early 1980s. Finally, it is also worth noticing that attention to this group of issues is typically lower in the UK and France where the electoral system in most cases generates single party majority governments, and where coalition considerations thus play a limited role for how the large, mainstream parties can gain office.

The next question then is whether party system attention to this group of issues is in fact driven by the same party competition dynamics. If this is the

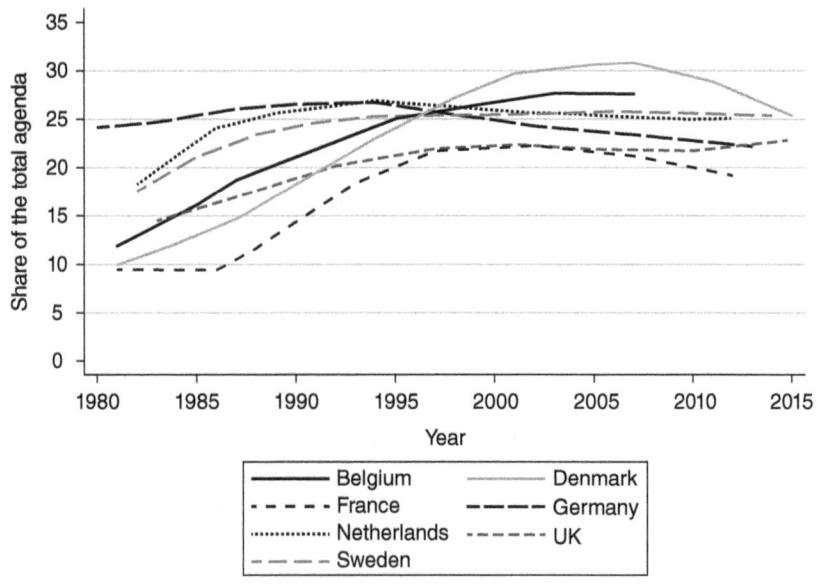

FIGURE 5.8 Attention to 'new politics issues' (immigration, European integration, environment, crime and justice, and personal rights) in seven countries from 1980 and onwards

case, they can be analysed together as is typically done in studies focusing on the new, 'second dimension' (e.g. Hooghe and Marks 2018; Kriesi et al. 2008, 2012). The first step in investigating this is to look at party system attention to the individual issues.

Figure 5.9 illustrates attention to the environment, which varied somewhat across the seven countries around 1980. The issue was already firmly established on the party system agenda in Germany, Sweden, and the Netherlands, but it was a marginal issue in Denmark, France, and the UK. Together with Belgium, the latter countries then saw a relatively rapid increase in attention to the environment. From around the mid-1990s, the issue lost some attention but without becoming a marginal issue in any of the countries. Attention to the party system agenda has stabilized somewhere between 4 per cent and 8 per cent.

Figure 5.10 looks at European integration which began as a very small issue with less than 2 per cent attention; then it increased to a maximum of 4 per cent and declined again to 2–3 per cent or even less. Compared to the environment for instance, European integration continues to be a marginal issue on the party system agenda in all countries.

Figure 5.11 looks at attention to immigration. In the early 1980s, this was also a marginal issue in all countries with 2–3 per cent attention. In most countries, party system attention has increased moderately to a level of 4–5

The Development of the Party System Agenda

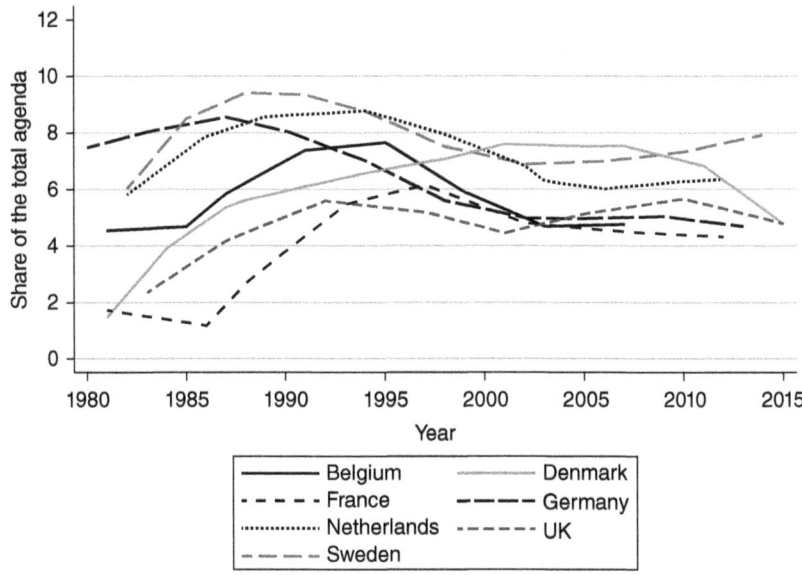

FIGURE 5.9 Attention to the environment in seven countries from 1980 and onwards

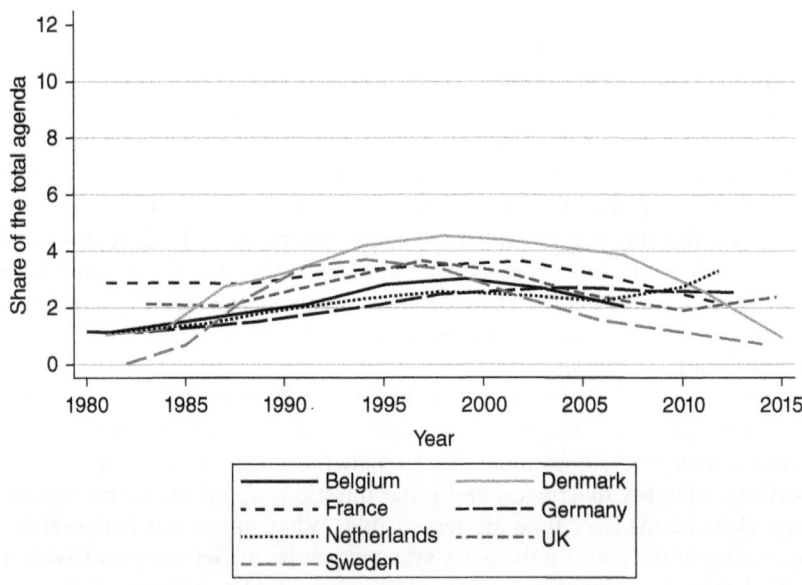

FIGURE 5.10 Attention to European integration in seven countries from 1980 and onwards

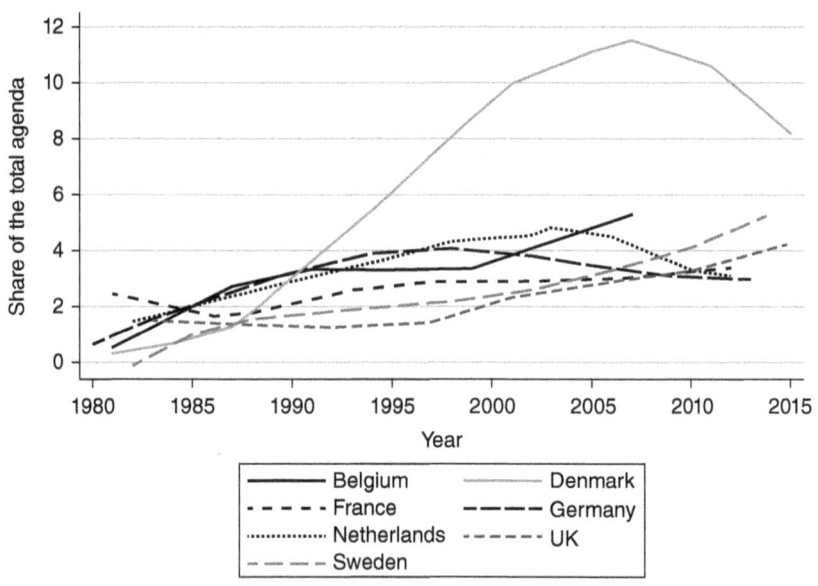

FIGURE 5.11 Attention to immigration in seven countries from 1980 and onwards

per cent. In Denmark it has passed 10 per cent, though somewhat declining in recent years.

Figure 5.12 shows attention to crime and justice. This was also a relatively marginal issue in the early 1980s, but it received some attention in the Netherlands and the UK. Since then, attention has risen significantly in all countries, but most pronouncedly in Belgium where it reached a level of more than 10 per cent after the mid-1990s. In Denmark, attention to crime and justice has also increased towards the end of the period. The development in Belgium reflects the intense party interest in reforming the entire criminal and justice system following the Dutroux crisis involving the arrest and escape of the paedophile Marc Dutroux in the period from 1996 to 1998 (Walgrave and Varone 2008).

Finally, Figure 5.13 shows attention to personal rights. This involves questions about personal liberties like freedom of speech and religion, protection against surveillance, questions about equal treatment of men and women, abortion, same-sex marriages, and other questions about sexual orientation. Here, clear trends over time are less visible. What stands out is the relative importance of the issue on the party system agendas in Germany and Sweden. In the latter case, attention to the question of equal treatment of men and women and women's rights has been central to this development (cf. Cowell-Meyers 2017).

The Development of the Party System Agenda 63

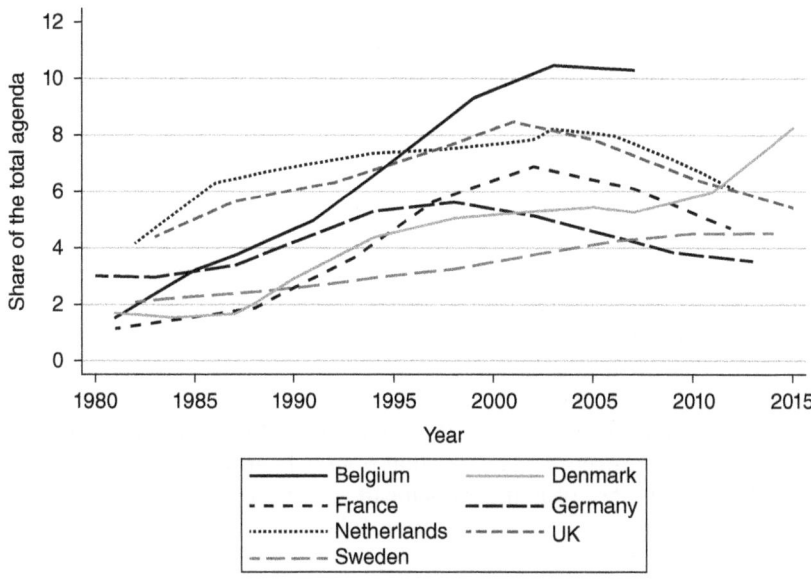

FIGURE 5.12 Attention to crime and justice in seven countries from 1980 and onwards

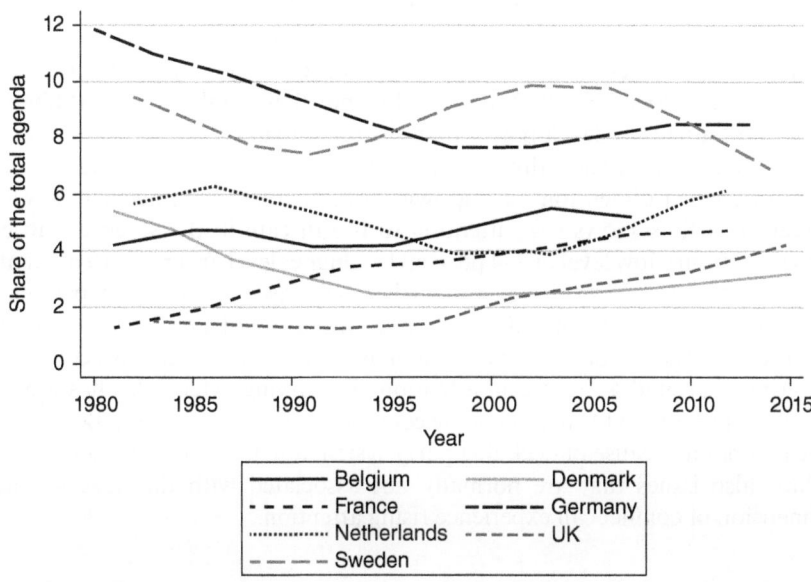

FIGURE 5.13 Attention to personal rights in seven countries from 1980 and onwards

Looking across the five issues, they do not appear to be driven by the same underlying dynamics of party competition. The environment has seen a rather similar development across the countries where the issue rose on the party system agenda and then declined somewhat without becoming a marginal issue. European integration saw a limited increase, then declined, and now it remains an issue with quite limited party system attention in all countries. Crime and justice and immigration are characterized by increasing attention, but with more cross-national variation. Denmark has thus seen a very substantial increase in attention to immigration, whereas Belgium has seen a very substantial increase in attention to crime and justice. Finally, attention to personal rights has been more stable over time, but with substantial differences across countries.

Thus, it is difficult to see party system attention to these issues as reflecting the same underlying party competition dynamics. Rather, it seems that each issue has its own trajectory. The fact that political parties position themselves similarly on a number of issues, which can then be seen as a conflict dimension, does not mean that party attention follows similar trends. In terms of the new, second dimension, the fact that parties position themselves similarly on issues like immigration, the environment, or crime and justice does not mean that these issues follow the same trends in terms of party system attention. This picture is further strengthened when the decline in attention to foreign policy and defence described above is taken into account. These issues are sometimes at least partly seen as part of the new, second dimension (Kriesi et al., 2008: 59–60, 2012: 109–13), but they exhibit a quite different pattern of attention development than the other issues.

Finally, other issues than those normally seen as belonging to the second conflict dimension have grown on the party system agenda as well. Figure 5.14 thus shows that attention to health care in the seven countries has risen from a low level of 2–4 per cent to a higher level around 7–10 per cent. In Germany and France, however, it has only risen to around 5 per cent. Attention to education exhibits quite similar tendencies as shown in Figure 5.15. Education did not begin as a marginal issue, but in most countries it received around 4–5 per cent attention. To varying extent, this has grown in all countries with Denmark and Sweden as the clearest examples. Belgium is the exception because of declining party system attention after the late 1980s. Thus, also issues that are normally not associated with the new, second dimension of conflict can experience rising attention.[11]

---

[11] Beramendi et al. (2015) argue that political conflicts over education are part of the second dimension in the sense that social groups with universal values would also support education as a long-term investment. This conflict over education could be argued to generate attention to the issue (see Chapter 10 on education).

The Development of the Party System Agenda 65

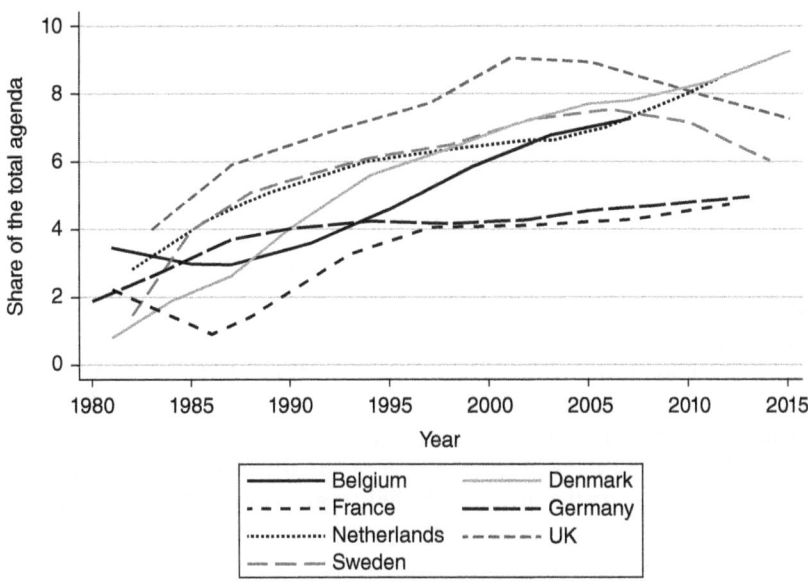

FIGURE 5.14 Attention to health care in seven countries from 1980 and onwards

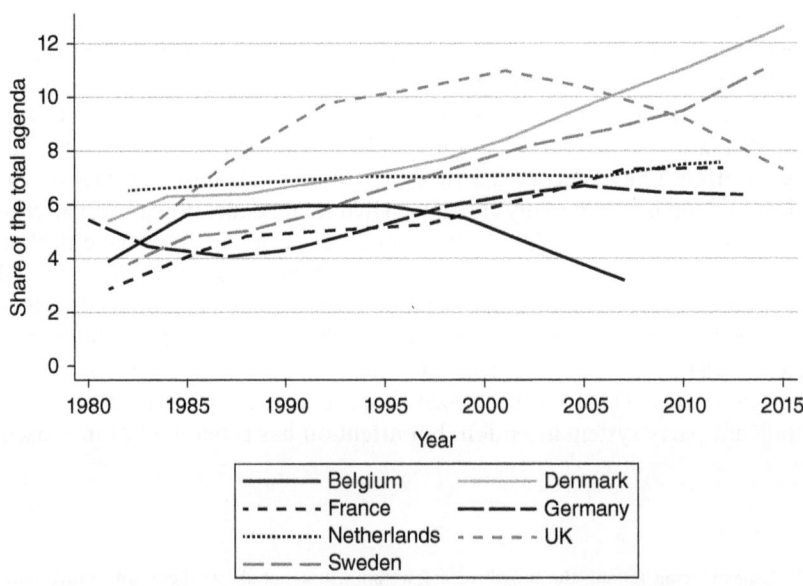

FIGURE 5.15 Attention to education in seven countries from 1980 and onwards

The above focus on the over-time trends of the individual issues has one significant drawback, namely that it looks at each issue in isolation, although agenda setting is fundamentally a relative process in which issues wax and wane at the expense of other issues. One thing is increased attention to an issue; another thing is whether the issue has come to be a top issue on the party system agenda. A relative look at the party system agenda is thus necessary. The question is what such a relative perspective should look like. Or to formulate the same question differently: When is an issue politicized? With regard to European integration, Hutter (2016: 306) suggests that the issue is politicized if it gets above the mean level of attention.

The analysis below mainly focuses on the top three issues on the party system agendas in the period. The reason for this relatively narrow understanding of when issues have played an important role is that simply looking at whether attention to an issue gets above the mean hides a lot of important change. For the 23 issue categories, the mean attention to an issue is 4.35. Hence, getting above the mean could hide a growth in attention from 5 per cent to 15 per cent. Furthermore, the purpose of focusing on the top three issues is to provide an overview of the development of the content of the party system agendas based on a comparison with other issues rather that a comparison over time with the issue itself. If one focuses on the development of individual issues, a less strict definition of politicization or 'top' issue may be more appropriate.

Table 5.1 shows the percentage of times an issue has been among the top three issues in the 66 elections included in the seven countries. The table is divided into before and after 1995 to capture the development over time.

The table generally confirms the tendencies described above. Left–right related issues, the economy, labour, and international affairs (defence and foreign affairs) have declined, although both the economy and labour continue to be top issues in many elections. Health and education as well as crime and justice have grown. The environment and personal rights have declined after being relatively prominent in the period before 1995. Finally, the EU and immigration continue to play a rather limited role.[12] The table also shows that social policy questions have increasingly been among the top three issues. Figure 5.16 therefore shows attention to the social policy issue over time in the seven countries. The issue has received quite stable and in many countries significant party system attention, but attention has generally not increased.

---

[12] Issues scoring among the top three a few times, but not shown here, are: Government operations, Business, Politics, Housing, and Agriculture. Culture, Energy, Transportation, Technology, Local and Regional Affairs, and Territories/Former Colonies have never been top three issues in any of the 66 elections covered.

TABLE 5.1 *Percentage of elections in which the issue has been in top three from 1980 and onwards*

	Economy	Labour	Foreign Affairs	Defence	Health care	Education	Social Policy	Crime/ Justice	EU	Immigration	Environment	Personal Rights	N
Before 1995	29%	17%	2%	5%	0%	2%	16%	1%	1%	0%	10%	8%	93
After 1995	19%	9%	0%	0%	10%	18%	24%	9%	0%	2%	3%	3%	105

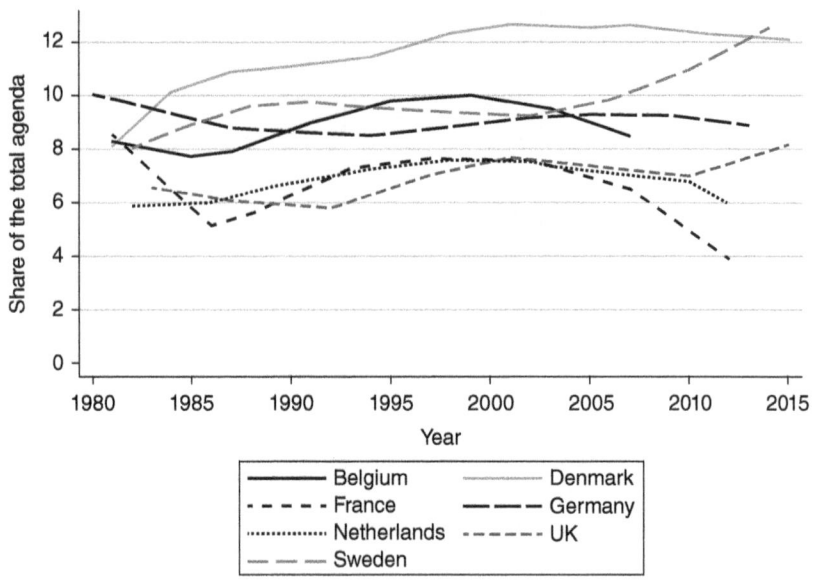

FIGURE 5.16 Attention to social policy in seven countries from 1980 and onwards

Table 5.1 therefore probably reflects the fact that the decline of attention to both the economy and the labour market has made it easier for social policy to become a top three issue without the level of attention actually increasing.

The development of social policy also raises the question of what has happened to the welfare state in terms of attention. The development of the welfare state in northwestern Europe is closely linked to the left–right conflict (Esping-Andersen 1990), and the decline of other traditional left–right related issues like the economy and defence could lead one to expect that attention to the welfare state would also decline. However, the analysis here rather indicates that the conclusion depends crucially on which welfare state issues one is looking at. Health care and education have seen increasing attention, the labour market declining attention, and social policy has seen a more stable attention (cf. also Green-Pedersen and Jensen 2019). This pattern further shows that conclusions about broad groups of issues like the decline of economic issues or the rise of non-economic/post-material issues are exactly too general. Economic issues, in the sense of the economy and the labour market, have generally declined. Material issues like health care, education, and social policy have grown or been stable on the party system agenda. At the same time, this points in the direction of a partly reshuffle of the left–right dimension. If focus is only on the format of the party system as discussed in Chapter 2, i.e. the number of conflict dimensions, this may be seen as a minor change. However, as will be discussed further on in the chapters on health care and education, these are distinct issues with distinct party competition dynamics. Therefore, the change in the composition of the left–right dimension is an important development in itself. At the same time, it is not recognized if focus is solely on the format of the party system, i.e. the number of dimensions.

HOW HAS THE PARTY SYSTEM AGENDA DEVELOPED?

This chapter has aimed at providing a broad description of the development of party system agendas in the seven countries with focus on the period after 1980. However, the development after 1980 should be seen in a more long-term perspective in which the decline of class politics has led not only to an expansion of the party system agenda as seen by the substantial growth in the length of party manifestos, but also to a more complex agenda on which more issues receive substantial attention. This development matches the idea of party politics becoming more issue-based. In terms of issue attention, traditional left–right related issues such as the economy, labour, and business, but also defence and foreign policy have seen declining attention, but they have not disappeared from the agenda. Other issues such as health, education, crime and justice, and to a more limited extent immigration have gained attention. Attention to the environment grew considerably in the beginning of the period, but then declined somewhat again. Attention to social policy has remained stable at a high level throughout the period, whereas European integration has remained an issue with limited attention.

The above analysis also provides a potential answer to the question of how similar the party system agendas of West European party politics actually are. To some extent, this is a question of whether the glass is half full or half empty. However, a number of striking similarities are worth highlighting: the limited attention to European integration, the relatively limited growth in attention to immigration in all countries except Denmark, the growth in attention to health care in all countries, and the continuing high attention to social policy in all countries. Thus, despite the differences in political systems and party system developments—especially the varying growth of new niche parties—there are important similarities in how the party system agendas develop. The argument in the following is that this is the result of the incentives that the large, mainstream parties face with regard to the varying issues. There are, of course, also important cross-national differences like the significant growth in attention to immigration in Denmark or the decline in attention to education in Belgium which needs explanation. However, when one looks at the entire party system agenda, the variation across issues is more striking than the variation across countries.

The aim of this description was double: to provide an overview of the issue developments to be explained in the following chapters and to evaluate the most common claim about the content of party politics, namely the growth of issues belonging to the new, second dimension at the expense of traditional left–right related issues (see also Kriesi et al. 2008: 935–7). The findings generally support this conclusion as issues related to the new, second dimension have grown when seen as one, whereas issues like the economy, labour, and business have declined. However, the analysis also shows that this only provides a very general and rough picture of what has happened to the content of party politics in Western Europe. The pattern identified was also not simply one of more or less growth of these issues. The issues that are typically seen as related to the new, second dimension such as immigration, European integration, the environment, personal rights, and crime and justice show very different patterns of variation across time and countries. At the same time, the findings also show important changes in attention to the state-market related issues that traditionally form the core of the left–right first dimension. Social policy issues remain an important and stable part of this, but health and education have grown and partly replaced economic issues in the sense of macroeconomics, the labour market, and business.

6

The Dynamics of the Party System Agenda

Chapter 5 presented a broad outline of how the party system agenda has developed over the past decades in the seven West European countries. The purpose of the chapter was to present shortly the long-term trends and then identify the medium trends in the party system agendas that the issue incentive model is supposed to explain. One key aspect of this model is that one needs to study individual issues to understand the party competition dynamics that shape the party system agenda. Before moving on to actually analysing individual issues, it is worth substantiating this focus on the individual issues by analysing the empirical patterns described in Chapter 5 further. This is the starting point for this chapter that will then move on to discuss the analytical strategy for the individual issues.

DIMENSIONS OF PARTY SYSTEM ATTENTION

The analysis of Chapter 5 described the development of individual issues on the party system agenda. However, the question is whether another approach would have been possible if the 23 issues were reduced to a few dimensions, and attention to these dimensions could then be studied. Such an approach would be very much in line with studies focusing on positional competition among political parties. The literature on spatial party competition (e.g. Adams et al. 2005) typically focuses on one dimension, whereas the emergence of a new, second dimension in terms of party positions has been a key question of the bottom-up approaches discussed in Chapter 2 (see Kriesi et al. 2008, 2012). Thus, an important question is whether issue competition could also be reduced to one or two dimensions which would then be the appropriate level of analysis in the rest of this book.

The analysis in Chapter 5 showed quite varying developments for the issues argued to belong to the new, second dimension of conflict. However, from this perspective the individual issues are less important. Which of the issues belonging to the new, second dimension that receive party system attention may vary across time and countries, but this is less important if the issues are manifestations of the same underlying party competition dynamics. From this perspective, whether parties pay attention to immigration or European integration is less important as they express the same party conflict. They can be seen as 'functionally equivalent' as discussed in Chapter 2. In terms of issue competition, this logic would imply that the same party competition dynamics generate attention to the issues belonging to the new, second dimension. Therefore, one would expect attention to the issues to correlate positively so they grow together, but perhaps with varying strength.[1]

A formal way to evaluate this logic is through a multidimensional scaling analysis. Inspired by Jones and Baumgartner (2005: 263–7), multidimensional scaling (MDS) has been conducted for each country based on the correlations of the 23 issues. MDS is a way of analysing whether groups of issues grow or decline together over time, which indicates that they are driven by similar attention dynamics. The MDS approach is well suited for such an explorative analysis (Borg and Groenen 1997: 4–6), so no a priori assumptions have to be made about the dynamics of the party system agenda. Kriesi et al. (2008: 71–3) also use MDS to document the existence of a second dimension in terms of the positions parties take on issues. Thus, the analysis in the following is an attempt to investigate whether positional dimensions are also reflected in issue attention. The purpose is not to contribute to the debate about whether party competition in terms of party positions is one- or two-dimensional (cf. Kriesi et al. 2012: 96–107; van der Brug and van Spanje 2009). The questions of positional dimensions and dimension of attention are two separate questions, and whereas the former has been the object of intense debate, the latter has not received much attention.

In the following, a metric, classical form of MDS has been performed on the correlations of attention across the 23 different issues (Cox and Cox 1994: 22–37; Jones and Baumgartner 2005: 263–7). Such an analysis raises two basic questions: First, how many dimensions are necessary to present the correlation across the 23 issues in a simple but still 'satisfactory' way, and second, what is the substantial interpretation of these dimensions? The latter depends on how the issues actually cluster on the dimensions produced by the MDS analysis (Borg and Groenen 1997: 36–8; Kruskal and Wish 1978: 48–52).

In terms of the first question, Table 6.1 presents the Kruskal Stress Measure for one, two, and three dimensions for each country. In terms of the number of dimensions, more dimensions produce less 'stress', so the question is how much stress declines by adding additional dimensions? Looking at Table 6.1,

---

[1] One could also imagine issues belonging to the same dimension to correlate negatively, so they grow at the expense of each other. Still, from the perspective of the increasing importance of the new, second dimension, one should not, for instance, expect attention to immigration to grow at the expense of attention to European integration. These issues should grow at the expense of issues related to the first dimension.

The Dynamics of the Party System Agenda 73

TABLE 6.1 *Kruskal Stress Measure for different numbers of dimensions in the correlation of attention across the 23 issues in the seven countries from 1980 and onwards*

	Kruskal Stress Measure		
	1 dimension	2 dimensions	3 dimensions
Denmark	0.22	0.13	0.09
Sweden	0.31	0.18	0.08
France	0.28	0.12	0.04
UK	0.26	0.15	0.09
Germany	0.25	0.14	0.04
Netherlands	0.28	0.12	0.04
Belgium	0.22	0.08	0.03

moving from one to two dimensions reduces stress substantially. Moving from two to three dimensions also reduces stress, but not to quite the same extent, although especially for countries like Sweden and Germany, there is a substantial reduction when moving to three dimensions. Thus, in most countries, it takes a third dimension to achieve a 'fair level of stress': <0.10. However, a two-dimensional solution generally provides acceptable results in the sense that stress is <0.15. Furthermore, the two-dimensional solution can easily be plotted as shown below, which greatly facilitates the substantial interpretation. Therefore, the two-dimensional solution is presented below for each country. In terms of the actual dimensions produced, no prior assumptions about possible dimensions are incorporated into an MDS analysis. This implies that there is no guarantee that the dimensions identified provide a clear, substantial meaning.

Figure 6.1 shows the two-dimensional configuration for Denmark. Dimension 1 distinguishes issues with declining attention like the economy, labour, and housing from issues like immigration, health care, crime and justice, the environment, and transportation for which attention has grown. Dimension 2 is more difficult to interpret, but it provides some indications of a difference between 'international' and domestic issues as the EU and foreign affairs cluster together on this dimension. In terms of the existence of a dimension similar to the new, second dimension identified with regard to party positions, the figure does not support this idea. Some of the relevant issues like immigration and crime and justice are placed together on dimension 1 indicating that they have grown together, but on this dimension, they are not distinct from issues like health care and transportation.

Figure 6.2 on Sweden provides a similar picture. Dimension 1 has a quite similar structure where issues like immigration, health care, transportation, and crime and justice have grown at the expense of traditional state-market issues

74   *The Reshaping of West European Politics*

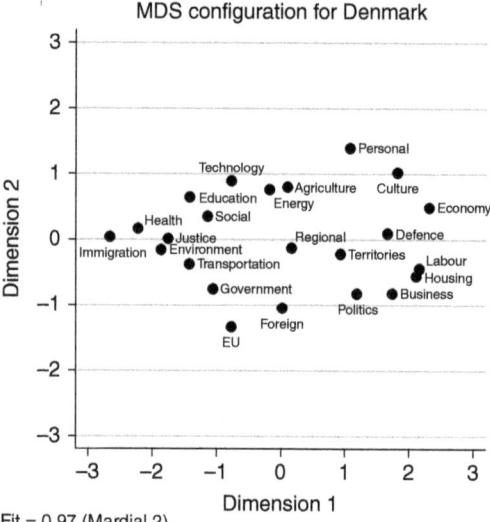

FIGURE 6.1 Two-dimensional MDS configuration for Denmark

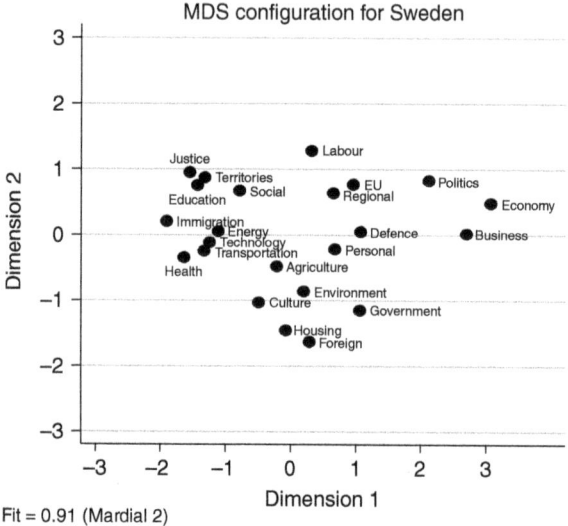

FIGURE 6.2 Two-dimensional MDS configuration for Sweden

like the economy and business. Like in Denmark, foreign affairs stands out on dimension 2. Along the same lines, the findings for France, shown in Figure 6.3, identify one dimension that separates traditional state-market issues like the economy, business, and labour from issues that have grown at their expense like

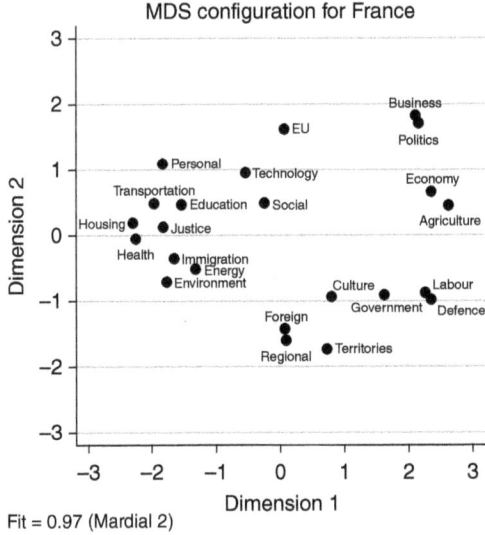

FIGURE 6.3 Two-dimensional MDS configuration for France

health care, crime and justice, transportation, the environment, and housing. Again, dimension 2 is hard to interpret substantially. The picture for the UK shown in Figure 6.4 is similar to the one found in the other countries. Traditional issues like housing, labour, and the economy cluster at one end of dimension 1, in this case also with defence, and new issues like health care and crime and justice cluster at the other end, in this case also with education. Dimension 2 is again difficult to interpret substantially. Figure 6.5 presents the Belgian case that resembles the four aforementioned countries. Dimension 1 separates the economy, which has seen declining attention, in this case clustered with government operations and local and regional affairs from issues that have grown like crime and justice, transportation, health care, immigration, and in this case also housing. As said before, dimension 2 is hard to interpret substantially.

The German case presented in Figure 6.6 presents a somewhat different picture. Dimension 1 distinguishes issues like the environment, personal rights, defence, and foreign affairs, which have declined during the period, from issues like local and regional affairs, technology, immigration, health care, and the EU. Dimension 2 contains a cluster of state-market issues like labour and the economy. The Dutch case presented in Figure 6.7 resembles the German case. A dimension distinguishing declining state-market issues from new rising issues is not found.

To sum up, the dimensions identified in the German and Dutch cases do not present a clear pattern. However, as for the other five countries, a dimension

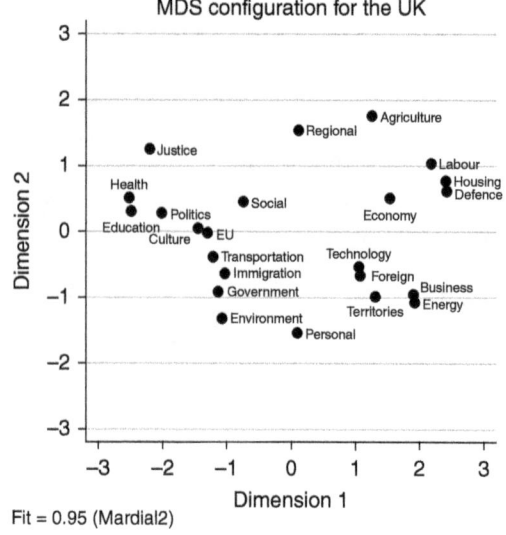

FIGURE 6.4 Two-dimensional MDS configuration for the UK

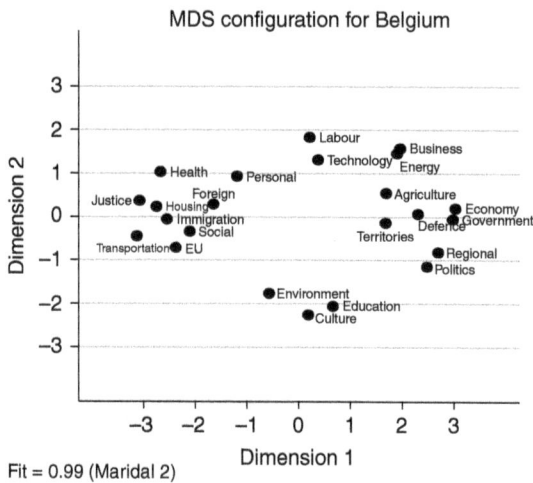

FIGURE 6.5 Two-dimensional MDS configuration for Belgium

that separates traditional state-market issues like the economy, labour, and business, which have generally declined, from 'new issues' like health care, crime and justice, immigration, and transportation, which have typically grown in attention, can be identified. This also implies that there is no clear evidence of a dimension of attention similar to the second dimension

The Dynamics of the Party System Agenda 77

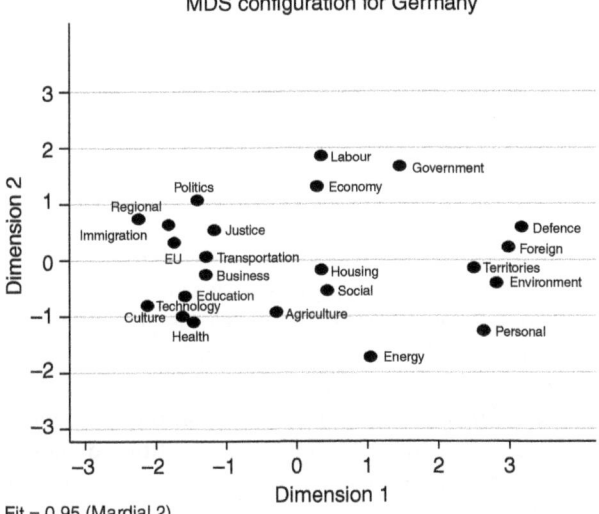

FIGURE 6.6 Two-dimensional MDS configuration for Germany

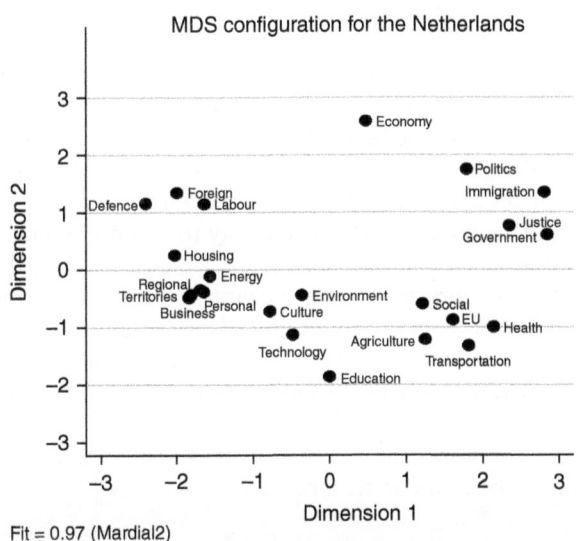

FIGURE 6.7 Two-dimensional MDS configuration for the Netherlands

identified when looking at party positions. In five of the seven countries, issues like immigration and crime and justice typically cluster relatively closely on one dimension, but they also cluster closely with issues like health care and transportation.

In many ways, the MDS analysis confirms the picture presented in Chapter 5 that in most countries the decline of left–right related issues has opened up the agenda for new issues. This includes some of the issues related to the new, second dimension, but the MDS analysis does not indicate that these issues constitute a distinct group driven by a distinct political logic. On the contrary, the MDS analysis shows that the dynamics of the party system agenda are not structured along dimensions with a clear substantial content. Therefore, when focusing on party attention, not positions, shifting the level of analysis towards dimensions consisting of a number of issues does not present itself as a promising way forward.

These conclusions from the MDS analysis thus provide further empirical support for the analytical focus of this book on individual issues rather than on broader dimensions. The incentives that structure party competition are found at the level of the individual issues, not on broad conflict dimensions bundling together issues with different party competition dynamics. This does not mean that party positions are not structured into left–right dimensions for instance, or a new, second dimension, nor that attention dynamics are unaffected by positional dimensions as discussed in Chapter 2. What it means is that one cannot simply group issues into a few dimensions when analysing their attention dynamics; one needs to study the individual issues.

The danger of focusing on individual issues is that one develops a theory of individual issues. Another option would be to try to bundle issues based on the issue typologies developed in the policy agenda-setting literature (e.g. Cobb and Elder 1983; Soroka 2002). However, as argued by Grossmann (2012), attempts at building such typologies have largely failed. Instead, Grossman suggests focusing on general attention dynamics and analysing how individual issues differ from such trends. This is the way to avoid building a theory for each individual issue.

This strategy structures the following chapters. Each chapter begins with a discussion of how the issue incentive model presented in Chapter 3 can be applied to the individual issues. To apply the model, one must analyse the three factors argued to shape the incentives of large, mainstream parties with regard to specific issues, namely issue characteristics, issue ownership, and coalition considerations. This is a way in which the specific issues can be analysed from a general theoretical perspective.

WHICH ISSUES TO STUDY?

Analysing all 23 issues individually is impossible within the framework of one book. Therefore, a selection of issues has to be made. Based on theoretical and

The Dynamics of the Party System Agenda

empirical concerns, the following five issues have been selected: immigration, European integration, the environment, education, and health care. Theoretically, the choice of issues has to allow for a test of the issue incentive model. As will be outlined in the analyses of individual issues, these vary considerably with regard to issue characteristics and issue ownership. In terms of issue characteristics, immigration and the environment are examples of issues for which new problem information is regularly published, which is not the case with European integration. There are examples of ownership by large, mainstream right parties (immigration), by large, mainstream left parties (the environment), and by none of the large, mainstream parties (education). Furthermore, the issues vary with regard to coalition incentives because they, to varying degrees, fit the left–right dimension. European integration fits the least (see Chapter 8).

The second concern about the choice of issues is empirical. The issue incentive model should explain the most significant empirical trends identified in Chapter 5. For instance, how can the general rise in attention to health care or the limited attention to European integration be explained? For the issue incentive model to provide a convincing analysis of the development of the party system agenda, it needs to be able to explain such trends. Additionally, most of the studied issues have been subject to a quite extensive literature because of their empirical importance. Thus, the findings of this literature can also be discussed based on the issue incentive model presented in this book.

HOW TO STUDY THE ISSUES?

Each of the five issues will be analysed following a similar structure. Each analysis will begin with a discussion of how the three factors of the issue incentive model, i.e. issue characteristics, issue ownership, and coalition considerations apply to this particular issue.

As argued in Chapter 3, issue characteristics refer to the interaction between problem information and problem characteristics, which needs to be discussed in relation to each particular issue. Issue ownership has received considerable attention in recent years. As laid out in Chapter 2, issue ownership concerns which parties are considered the most competent by the electorate to deal with an issue (i.e. competence issue ownership, Walgrave et al. 2012). Furthermore, focus in terms of issue ownership is on the large, mainstream parties. Other studies (e.g. Abou-Chadi 2016) focus on issue ownership by niche parties. However, issue ownership then becomes more of a question of 'associative' issue ownership (Walgrave et al. 2012), i.e. which parties voters see as the most interested in the issue. Moreover, issue ownership will be treated as constant over time. It is clear from a number of studies that parties can influence each other's issue ownership (e.g. Stubager and Seeberg 2016), and a party's issue ownership may suffer across a number of issues when, for instance, the party is in government (Green and Jennings 2012). However, there are few examples of permanent change of issue ownership, so from the medium-term perspective of this book, issue ownership can be considered constant over time (cf. Seeberg 2017).[2]

Coalition considerations are partly shaped by stable patterns of coalition building found in the countries where winning government power means forming coalitions. In these countries, cooperation for office is largely based on the parties' general left–right positions, and coalition considerations are shaped by the extent to which party positions on specific issues deviate from the left–right structure. Thus, evaluating coalition considerations concerning an individual issue requires knowledge of both the general and most frequent stable patterns of coalition building in a country as well as knowledge of party positions on individual issues.

After placing the issue within the issue incentive model, each chapter takes a closer look at attention to the issue following the analysis in Chapter 5. Especially the question of how the issue is placed on the party system agenda will be in focus. As discussed in Chapter 5, different criteria can be set up for evaluating the relative importance of an issue. Chapter 5 focused on whether the issue was among the top three on the party system agenda to provide a general overview of its issue content. However, this is a relatively limited definition of a 'top' issue suited for providing an overview. For the study of individual issues, a focus on the top five seems more appropriate. Still, this definition may also be problematic when one focuses on cross-national differences. The extent to which party system agendas concentrate attention varies over time and countries. In order to take this into account, cases will be identified in which attention to an issue on the party system agenda is one standard deviation higher than the mean. The standard deviation varies across elections between 2.15 (the Netherlands 1986) and 6.35 (Denmark 1984), reflecting the extent to which attention to issues on the party system agenda is concentrated on few issues or spread out more equally across the issues. At most elections, three to six issues fulfil the criterion of attention being more than one standard deviation above the mean of 4.35 per cent (given the 23 issues analysed).

The next step is to explain the trends in party attention found in Chapter 5. These trends will be analysed via a combination of regression analysis

---

[2] Exactly which of the large, mainstream parties, if any, has ownership of a given issue in a given country is an empirical question that will be further discussed in relation to each issue. Seeberg (2017) provides data on issue ownership of either the left or right on most issues in the seven countries covered. Seeberg draws on national election surveys.

explaining attention by individual parties to an issue and case studies of the development of the entire party system agenda. The logic of combining the two approaches is based on the 'nested analysis' approach suggested by Lieberman (2005) which focuses on combining the strength of both approaches. Combining the two types of analyses thus makes it possible to evaluate both the development of the general party system agenda and the behaviour of individual parties which structure the party system agenda. The idea of a party system agenda requires inclusion of both perspectives. The regression analyses focus on explaining the variation across time and parties. The variation across countries is expected to be driven more by coalition considerations. Such considerations also contribute to explaining variation over time, but they are difficult to investigate within the regression framework. It requires a focus on the entire party system rather than on individual parties, and the number of cases therefore becomes too limited given the election manifesto data.

Furthermore, the case studies will also allow for a more detailed look at the party competition dynamics for particular issues, i.e. when parties react to each other. The regression framework presented in the following is well suited to capturing stable differences across parties, e.g. the differences in attention to an issue between a niche party and other parties, but once parties begin responding to each other and changing issue focus, this is difficult to capture with the short time series following the election manifesto data. Moreover, parties are also quite likely to respond to each other in between elections. Thus, the evaluation of the theoretical framework needs to draw on a nested approach (Lieberman 2005) containing both the regression framework and the case studies. Finally, each chapter discusses how the findings of the book relate to the issue-specific literature that exists on many of these issues.

7

Expansion from the Right

The Growth of Immigration on the Party System Agenda

For both theoretical and empirical reasons, the development of immigration on the party system agendas deserves a closer look.[1] From the perspective of the issue incentive model, immigration is an attractive issue to focus on because the coalition considerations of the large, mainstream right-wing parties vary cross-nationally. Coalition considerations are a key element in this model, and their importance can be investigated empirically by studying immigration. At the same time, the issue has attracted attention as a case which allows one to study the impact of emerging niche parties on the other parties in the party system (e.g. Abou-Chadi 2016; Meguid 2005). This is due to the growing strength of radical right-wing parties with a clear focus on immigration. As their strength varies cross-nationally and over time, it is also possible to analyse their effect. Finally, immigration is perhaps the most central issue in the discussion about a new, second dimension of party competition.

Empirically, the rising number of immigrants and the public debates about integration, citizenship, etc. have also generated an extensive literature on the issue of immigration as such. This includes a literature on the party politics of immigration (e.g. Odmalm and Bale 2015; van der Brug et al. 2015; Grande et al. 2018). Like most works of literature that focus specifically on one issue, the drawback of this literature is that the immigration is rarely compared to other issues, which is exactly what this books does.

IMMIGRATION AS A POLICY ISSUE

As a first step, it is worth defining the issue of immigration. Like other studies of immigration (e.g. Berkhout et al. 2015: 20–1), one defines immigration relatively broadly as all policy questions relating to refugees and immigrants

---

[1] This chapter is partly based on Green-Pedersen and Otjes (2019).

as well as entrance, integration, and citizenship. The reason for this relatively broad definition is that the political debate typically treats these policy questions together. For instance, arguments for limiting entrance are often based on arguments about problems with integration. One also includes questions about ethnic and racial discrimination as they are typically also linked to the other policy questions.

The analysis of an individual issue first requires a discussion of how the issue incentive model applies to this specific issue. In other words, which incentives does the issue provide for large, mainstream parties? To evaluate this, one needs to discuss the three elements of the issue incentive model, i.e. issue characteristics, issue ownership, and coalition considerations with regard to immigration.

ISSUE INCENTIVES AND IMMIGRATION

In terms of issue characteristics, i.e. the interaction between problem information and problem characteristics, immigration is an issue to which media stories are a key source of information. The reason is that it is not an obtrusive issue with a broad scope. Of course, personal experience with the policy problems related to the issue exists, but the majority of the population does not personally encounter these problems on a regular basis. They primarily encounter the issue through media stories. Due to colour, race, etc., immigrants are often an easily identifiable group. Therefore, problems related to housing, education, crime, etc. are easily framed in the media as group-related even though they might just be examples of general social problems. Hence, crime in social housing areas involving immigrants is easily framed as immigration-related though it may be the result of poor social conditions. Thus, problem information comes through media coverage as immigration is an issue that easily catches media attention.

Immigration is furthermore an issue where statistics on the number of refugees, i.e. the number of people with immigrant background, etc., are relatively easily available. There are obviously important questions related to such statistics like what is the definition of an immigrant? However, the statistics are available and can be used by the media, political parties, and other political actors to raise the issue of immigration. Therefore, media attention to immigration and the number of immigrants are likely to be relatively closely correlated.

Immigration is also a positional issue. Political parties will disagree on whether immigration as such is a problem, or whether anything should be done to protect national identity in times of immigration.

Finally, many problems related to immigration, especially integration, are 'wicked problems' (Rittel and Webber 1973), i.e. problems without a clear definition and without clear solutions. This gives actors with an interest in generating attention to immigration good opportunities to point to immigration-related problems. Such questions are in reality impossible to 'solve'.

These issue characteristics of immigration imply that party system attention to immigration is likely to be affected directly by the number of immigrants. In a country with few immigrants, large, mainstream parties have very little to draw attention to. When the number of immigrants grows, a large, mainstream party wanting to draw attention to the issue finds itself in a good position. There is plenty of problem information, including news stories on the problem, and the problem is never solved. A large, mainstream party that wants to avoid the issue will find it hard once another large, mainstream party begins to focus on it. However, because of its positional character, immigration is an issue that a large, mainstream party may be able to avoid if no other large, mainstream party promotes it. The party may argue that immigration is not a problem and then not attend to it. In sum, party attention to immigration depends on whether one of the large, mainstream parties takes up the issue. If one of them does so, statistics and news stories that can be used as attention windows will be readily available. The question then is which other incentives a large, mainstream party faces.

In terms of issue ownership, Seeberg (2017: 482–7) finds that immigration is owned by the mainstream right in all countries investigated, and it is the issue with the strongest mainstream right issue ownership of all issues. Studies of public opinion on immigration (Ivarsflaten 2005; Sides and Citrin 2007) also show that public opinion generally favours a restrictive immigration policy that is more in line with the mainstream right than the mainstream left. Thus, it is the mainstream right that has the incentive to focus on the issue.

The issue incentives model implies that the third factor, coalition considerations of the large, mainstream parties, has to be understood by how positions on the specific issue fit the general left–right dimension which structures coalition formation in most West European countries. Even though immigration is often used as an example of the new, second dimension, van der Brug and van Spanje (2009) have shown how party positions on immigration are typically structured similarly to the left–right dimension since positions become less positive towards immigration and a multicultural society as one moves from the left towards the right.

One important complication to this general picture is the position of Social Liberal parties like the People's Party in Sweden (Odmalm and Super 2014) or the Social Liberals in Denmark (Green-Pedersen and Odmalm 2008). Whereas these parties position themselves more towards the right on economic issues, they are typically more left-wing oriented on an issue like immigration. Their position on immigration is often close to or even left of the Social Democrats' position. Thus, in terms of coalition considerations, the mainstream right may easily face a dilemma with regard to immigration. Coalition considerations may either make immigration very attractive to focus on for large, mainstream right parties, or it may make the issue unattractive. This will depend on the structure of coalition building, and how this is affected by the emergence of a radical right-wing party. In most countries, the way for the large, mainstream right to win government power has been to cooperate with centre parties of various kinds and often with Social Liberal parties. For such a cooperation, immigration is not necessarily an attractive issue exactly because such parties are often more left-wing oriented on immigration than on economic and welfare state issues.

The question then is whether the emergence of a radical right-wing party changes this (Bale 2003). Once/if a strong, radical right-wing party emerges, a large, mainstream right-wing party may find it attractive to cooperate with it in order to win government. A focus on immigration may strengthen the radical right more than the mainstream in term of votes, but in terms of building a majority behind a coalition, this may be less important. Focusing on immigration is thus an attractive strategy for a large, mainstream right-wing party in order to foster cooperation with the radical right. However, the dilemma for the large, mainstream right-wing party is that a strong focus on immigration is likely to generate a conflict with centre parties like the Social Liberal parties, which may then drop their support for the mainstream right. Thus, for a large, mainstream right-wing party the question is whether it is likely to benefit enough electorally from focusing on immigration to win government power when it may lose the support of centre parties. This, of course, depends on the electoral strength of the large, mainstream right as well as the radical right.

This theoretical discussion can be summarized in a number of expectations, which guide the analysis below. First, one should expect that an increasing number of immigrants generates more party system attention to the issue due to the stream of problem information on the issue as well as the attractiveness of the issue from a media perspective. This implies that even in countries like the UK and France where coalition politics normally does not play a role due to the electoral system, a rising number of immigrants also generates more party system attention to the issue. Furthermore, one would expect more attention from the large, mainstream right-wing parties due to issue ownership.

Second, one would expect that the growing strength of radical right-wing parties in itself leads to more party system attention to immigration. To radical right-wing parties, anti-immigration is their *raison d'être*, and therefore they will use any opportunity to focus on it. This will not automatically generate much more attention from the other parties, but it will make it necessary for all parties to pay some attention to the issue in order to make their positions clear to the electorate.

Finally, coalition considerations may make it attractive to the large, mainstream right parties to focus on immigration in order to gain government power based on support from the radical right. However, whether or not this is an attractive strategy for the large, mainstream right parties depends on the structure of coalition politics, especially the extent to which a right-wing governing majority without centre parties can be formed. Such parties are likely to find cooperation with the radical right and its extreme positions on immigration unattractive.

THE PARTY POLITICS OF IMMIGRATION

Before turning to the empirical part, it is worth briefly discussing some of the main findings from the growing literature on the party politics of immigration (e.g. Odmalm and Bale 2015; van der Brug et al. 2015). The literature examines how mainly mainstream parties have reacted to the growing strength of radical right-wing parties by looking at their positions on immigration or their broader strategies on the issue (e.g. Abou-Chadi 2016; Akkerman 2012; Alonso and Fonseca 2012; Meguid 2008; Schain 2006; van Spanje 2010). The main focus has been on the mainstream right (Bale 2008), but the mainstream left has also been studied (Bale et al. 2010). Generally, the findings are that large, mainstream parties have moved to the right on immigration. However, as argued by for instance Mudde (2013) and van Heerden et al. (2013), many developments ascribed to the emergence of radical right-wing parties may have other causes that might also explain the rise of radical right-wing parties. Their exact role can only be studied by comparing countries with and without significant radical right-wing parties.

A more recent theme in the literature on the party politics of immigration is internal party dynamics related to immigration, and how the parties approach the issue from an ideological perspective. For large, mainstream parties on the left and right, placing themselves on the issue of immigration is not straightforward and may be a cause of internal disagreement (Hinnfors et al. 2012; Odmalm and Bale 2015; Odmalm and Super 2014). As for the mainstream right, a business-friendly, liberal immigration policy with focus on the benefits of immigration for the supply of labour would be one position; a value-conservative, nationalistic approach would be another. The degree to which immigration becomes a source of internal disagreement within the large, mainstream right parties is also likely to depend on the type of large, mainstream right party. Parties with a clearly liberal business orientation like the Dutch VVD are likely to find it more difficult to agree with a nationalistic approach than with a conservative party like the British Conservatives. The same tension is somewhat relevant for large, mainstream left, i.e. Social Democratic parties (Hinnfors et al. 2012; Odmalm and Bale 2015; Odmalm and Super 2014). On the one hand, they may be sceptical towards immigration because they fear that it will undermine labour rights, but on the other hand, they typically take an international or universalistic approach in opposition to value conservative positions.

To sum up, the many recent studies of party competition for immigration provide a considerable understanding of how the issue has become an integral part of West European politics with a strong focus on the impact of radical right-wing parties as well as a more recent focus on the ideological challenges large, mainstream parties face when positioning themselves on immigration. However, the literature is unclear about the extent to which immigration has actually become a salient issue compared to other issues, and how this varies cross-nationally (Grande et al. 2018). The existing literature on the party politics of immigration also often lacks a clear cross-national perspective. Though studies like van der Brug et al. (2015) and Odmalm and Bale (2015) cover the politics of immigration in a number of West European countries, they do not focus strongly on mapping cross-national variation in the politics of immigration including its saliency. Finally, like most other works of literature with a single issue focus, the literature on immigration suffers from the weakness that it does not compare to other issues.

Thus, unlike the extensive literature on the party politics of immigration, this chapter provides a cross-national perspective on the question of the saliency of the issue. This perspective allows for a better understanding of the potential impact of the radical right. The expectation derived above, that the growing strength of the radical right would lead to some increase in party system attention, is thus in line with the recent literature on the party politics of immigration. What goes beyond the understanding of the impact of the radical right in the literature is the focus on the coalition impact of the radical right. The expectation that the growing strength of the radical right may change the coalition incentives of the large, mainstream right and thus make it attractive for these parties to focus on the issue was originally developed by Bale (2003) based on a study of immigration. However, the focus on coalition implications of the radical right has not received much attention within the literature on the party politics of immigration.

WHICH PARTIES PAY ATTENTION TO IMMIGRATION?

Before a detailed look at what drives party attention to immigration, a few words on the empirical definition of immigration are needed. In the above definition, the issue of immigration includes policy questions relating to refugees and immigrants such as entrance, integration, and citizenship. In terms of the policy agenda codebook (Bevan 2019), this means all sub-issues included in main topic 900 under general immigration and refugees questions and subtopic 201 about ethnic and racial discrimination. Policy questions related to migrant and seasonal workers (subtopic 529) are not included because of the temporary nature of their stay.

Based on this definition, Figure 7.1 shows that attention to immigration has risen in all seven countries since 1980 when the issue received limited attention in all countries.[2] Another approach is to look at the percentage of parties that mention the issue in their programme across decades as done in Table 7.1.

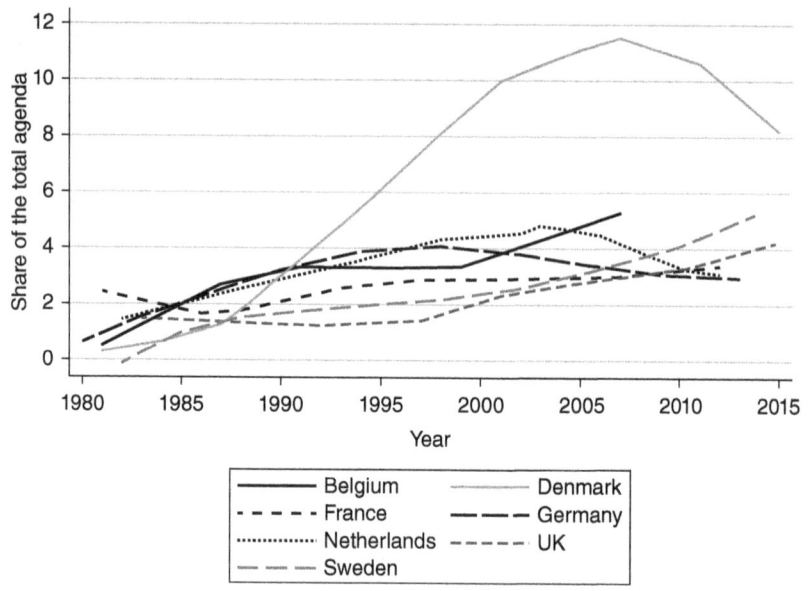

FIGURE 7.1 Party system attention to immigration in seven countries from 1980 and onwards

TABLE 7.1 *Percentage of parties mentioning immigration in their election programme across decades*

Decade	Percentage	N
1980s	68%	141
1990s	90%	131
2000s	97%	183

[2] The figure is identical to Figure 5.11.

In the 1980s, about one third of the election programmes did not mention immigration at all; in the 2000s, hardly any parties ignored the issue in their election programmes.

Figure 7.1 also reveals a significant difference between Denmark and the other countries in terms of the rise in party system attention to immigration. This rise has been much more significant in Denmark (cf. Lehmann & Zobel 2018). However, as discussed in Chapters 5 and 6, the development of party system attention to an individual issue needs to be compared to other issues, which can be done in different ways. One solution is to look at whether the issue has been among the top five issues in any election, and the other is to look at whether attention to the issue in any election has been more than one standard deviation higher than the mean of 4.35 per cent. The latter method takes into account that the party system agenda varies across elections with regard to how concentrated attention is on the top issues.

Table 7.2 shows elections in which immigration was a top issue based on any of the two definitions. The two definitions yield almost similar results. Based on the top five definitions, immigration has been a top issue in Denmark from 1998 and until 2015. Based on the definition of one standard deviation above the mean, the result is the same except that party system attention to immigration in the 1998 and 2015 elections in Denmark just fails to meet this criterion. The only other case meeting the top five criteria is the Dutch 2003 election, which just fails to meet the criterion of one standard deviation above the mean. Thus, the issue of immigration presents two general questions to the theoretical framework; namely why party system attention to immigration has generally risen, and why this trend has been much more pronounced in Denmark.[3]

To answer these questions, the first step is to analyse the attention of individual parties further. This is done by using OLS models explaining

TABLE 7.2 *Immigration as a top issue*

Elections with immigration as a top five issue (place in brackets)	Party system attention	4.35+1sd	Party system attention > 4.35+1sd
Denmark 1998(5)	8.1%	8.2%	
Denmark 2001(2)	12.1%	8.2%	X
Denmark 2005(4)	10.1%	9.0%	X
Denmark 2007(1)	16.6%	9.2%	X
Denmark 2011(4)	9.9%	8.9%	X
Denmark 2015(5)	8.3%	8.6%	
The Netherlands 2003(4)	7.4%	7.7%	

[3] Green-Pedersen and Krogstrup (2008) also find much more party attention to immigration in Denmark compared to Sweden when measuring party attention using parliamentary questions.

TABLE 7.3 *Regression estimates of party attention to immigration*

	Model 1	Model 2	Model 3
Immigration attention t−1	0.47(0.1)***	0.34(0.1)***	0.32(0.1)**
Radical right-wing party (=1)	2.81(1.35)*	3.44(1.35)*	3.39(1.37)*
Large, mainstream right party (=1)	1.15(0.57)*	1.37(0.62)*	1.39(0.61)*
Immigrant share		0.90(0.23)***	0.82(0.23)***
Unemployment		−0.37(0.1)***	−0.37(0.1)***
Strength of radical right-wing party			0.1(0.04)*
Government (=1)	−0.63(0.34)	−0.61(0.35)	−0.62(0.35)
Constant	2.87(0.58)***	2.05(1.12)	1.65(1.12)
N	398	356	356
Adj. R2	0.38	0.43	0.43

Note: robust standard errors in parentheses. * $p<0.05$, ** $p<0.01$, *** $p<0.001$. Estimated with country fixed effects (country dummies not shown). The drop in N in Models 2 and 3 are due to missing data on immigration share for France before 2005 and before 1984 for the other countries.

party attention to immigration as reported in Table 7.3. The models are all country-fixed effects models in order to centre the analysis on within country variation. The models are estimated with robust standard errors and a lagged dependent variable. The latter is included based on the theoretical discussion in Chapter 3. One would expect parties to show stability in their issue focus as this is partly driven by their expectations about which issues other parties focus on. Thus, one would expect that the share of party attention to immigration in the election before is positively correlated with party attention to immigration in the next election (cf. Green-Pedersen and Mortensen 2015; Liu et al. 2011: 407). This is also the case across all the models in Table 7.3.[4] Based on the discussion above, one would also expect that radical right-wing parties pay more attention to immigration than other parties, which is clearly the finding across all models.[5] A radical right-wing party typically spends about 3.4 percentage points more than other parties of its election programme on immigration. The discussion of issue ownership implies that large, mainstream right-wing parties should pay more attention to immigration than other parties. As expected, the models show a positive effect of the large,

---

[4] To avoid losing too many cases when including the lagged dependent variable, data on the last election before 1980 have been included when available. This is the case for Denmark, Sweden, Germany, and the Flemish parties in Belgium (see Chapter 4).

[5] Radical right-wing status is captured by a dummy variable in which the following parties are considered radical right: Belgium (Vlaams Belang, Front National); the Netherlands (the Centre Party, the Centre Democrats, LN, LPF, PVV); Sweden (New Democracy, the Sweden Democrats); Denmark (the Progress Party, Danish People's Party); France (Front National); the UK (UKIP).

mainstream right-wing status.[6] All models also control for government status, which has no effect on attention to immigration.[7]

Following the discussion of problem information, one would expect that the number of immigrants in society would affect party attention to immigration. Therefore, Models 2 and 3 include the share of the population with foreign background.[8] This variable has a clear effect on party attention to immigration which rises by 0.82 percentage point (Model 3) when the immigrant share of the population rises by one percentage point. Other studies (e.g. van der Brug et al. 2015: 180–3) have found a 'crowding out' effect of unemployment on party attention to immigration. So if unemployment increases, it crowds out party attention to immigration. This effect can also be seen in Models 2 and 3 in which the unemployment variable has a negative effect on party attention to immigration.[9] Model 3 includes the lagged vote share of radical right-wing parties.[10] The literature on the party politics of immigration has shown how other parties react to the growing strength of the radical right (e.g. Abou-Chadi 2016; Grande et al. 2018). Model 3 shows how a 1 percentage point increase in the voter share of the radical right increases

---

[6] Large, mainstream right-wing status is captured by a dummy variable in which the following parties are considered large, mainstream right (cf. Table 4.2): Belgium (MR, VLD); the Netherlands (VVD); Sweden (Conservatives); Denmark (Liberals, Conservatives); France (UPF/UMP/RPR); the UK (Conservatives). A broader definition that includes the German CDU gives the same result as Model 3, and the same is the case when the large, mainstream Christian Democratic Parties in the Netherlands and Belgium are categorized as large, mainstream right.

[7] Including both the radical right and the large, mainstream right, dummies in the same model imply that for instance radical right-wing parties are compared to all other parties except for the large, mainstream right-wing parties. The effect of radical right-wing status weakens but is still significant when compared to all other parties. This is not the case for large, mainstream parties when compared to all parties including radical right-wing parties.

[8] The data come from OECD's migration database, which contains the stock of foreigners based on nationality (data from OECD 2017a and OECD 2018). One could also have used a flow measure, i.e. the number of new immigrants, but numbers are often driven by events like the Syrian refugees crisis, whereas the stock measure better captures the stream of information related to immigration as understood in this book, i.e. including integration questions. The OECD data generally begin in 1984 apart from for France where it does not begin until 2005, except for 1990 and 1999.

[9] Data on unemployment come from Armingeon et al. (2018).

[10] This includes the vote share of the following parties: Sweden (New Democracy, the Sweden Democrats); France (Front National); the Netherlands (the Centre Party, the Centre Democrats, LPF, PVV); Denmark (the Progress Party, Danish People's Party); Germany (the Republicans, NPD); the UK (UKIP, BNP). To model the linguistic divide in Belgium, the votes of the Flemish Bloc/Flemish Interest (Vlaams Blok/Vlaams Belang, VB) relative to the other Dutch-speaking parties for the Dutch-speaking parties and the votes of the National Front relative to the other French-speaking parties for the French-speaking parties were included.

party attention to immigration by 0.1 percentage point in the next election.[11] Once a radical right-wing party enters parliament, this has a 'mechanical' effect on the party system agenda in the sense that the radical right-wing party is now included in the party system agenda, and such a party focuses more on immigration than other parties; about 3.4 percentage points. In this sense, immigration gets a voice in the party system. When a radical right-wing party becomes electorally strong, the other parties in the party system cannot completely ignore the issue, but the weak effect of the electoral strength of radical right-wing parties shows that it takes more to turn immigration into a top issue.[12]

To sum up, the theoretical expectations above are largely confirmed.[13] The rising attention to immigration across all countries seems to be generated by the increasing share of immigrants in the population and the growing strength of radical right-wing parties, though the latter effect is weak. The expectation that large, mainstream right-wing parties pay more attention to the issue than other parties was also confirmed.[14] The limitation of this analysis is that it fails to answer why attention to immigration has risen so much more in Denmark.[15]

The discussion at the beginning of this chapter implies an expectation that coalition considerations would be the main driver of cross-national variation in attention to immigration. However, this expectation is difficult to evaluate in an analysis focusing on individual parties. One needs to look at how parties react to each other over time to capture how coalition considerations shape the party system agenda. In terms of coalition considerations, the key question is whether a large, mainstream right party has an incentive to draw

---

[11] Alternatively (see Abou-Chadi 2016), one could run the models with party-fixed effects instead of country-fixed effects in order to focus on the change in attention by parties over time. This yields similar results for immigration share, unemployment, and radical right-wing strength.

[12] If one excludes the radical right-wing parties from the analysis, the effect is slightly higher: 0.13 percentage point.

[13] Two additional robustness checks were performed. First, to take the censoring of the data into account—party attention cannot be below 0 or above 100%—Model 3 was run as a Tobit model. The result was similar to those reported in Table 7.3. Second, to handle potential outliers in terms of party attention driving the results as discussed in Chapter 4, the models were also run excluding the four cases in which a party spends more than 25% of its manifesto on immigration. This did not alter the findings substantially except that the negative effect of government status is now significant.

[14] To test whether radical right-wing or large, mainstream right-wing parties respond more to the growth in the level of immigration than other parties, an interaction effect between the foreign share of the population and each of the two dummy variables was added separately to Model 3, but no significant effect of any of the two interaction terms was found.

[15] The country dummies included above (not shown) also show that attention to immigration is significantly higher in Denmark (between 1.5 percentage points and 4.1 percentage points) than in all the other countries.

attention to immigration in order to win government power with the support of the radical right, or whether it needs the support of centre parties and therefore would rather focus on other issues.

To investigate this claim, one needs to compare two countries with equally strong radical right-wing parties where the coalition incentives differ. Based on a most similar system logic, the two countries should ideally also be similar in other theoretically relevant respects. A comparison of Denmark and the Netherlands comes closest to fulfilling these requirements (Green-Pedersen and Otjes 2017). As will be argued, the coalition incentives of the Danish mainstream right after 1993 clearly point towards a focus on immigration. In contrast, in the Netherlands, even after the rise of first the LPF and later the PVV, the major Dutch right-wing party, the VVD, has always been forced to build coalitions with the centre and has therefore never had a strong coalition incentive to focus on immigration. The Netherlands and Denmark both have a multi-party parliamentary system and a relatively similar share of foreigners. Thus, one is able to control for important alternative explanations. The most obvious alternative to the Netherlands would be Sweden, but the late growth of the Sweden Democrats makes the comparison to Denmark, where the Danish People's Party already grew in the 1990s, less compelling. However, the five other countries will be examined below.

HOW IMMIGRATION BECAME A TOP ISSUE IN DANISH PARTY POLITICS

Starting with coalition incentives in Denmark, party positions on immigration typically follow the general left–right structure. The one significant exception to this rule is the Social Liberal Party which is placed at the centre on state–market related issues but is more left-leaning on immigration and more to the left than the Social Democrats (Green-Pedersen and Odmalm 2008). Moreover, the Social Liberals have often been in a position to decide which of the two blocs holds government power (Green-Pedersen and Thomsen 2005).

Though immigration to Denmark already began in the 1970s, it did not really emerge as a political issue until the second half of the 1980s when the share of people with foreign nationality began to increase. For the centre-right coalition government at that time, the issue may at first have seemed attractive because of right-wing issue ownership of the issue. However, from a coalition perspective it was not. From 1982 to 1993, Denmark was governed by the centre-right governments dominated by the Conservatives and the Liberals, the two large, mainstream right-wing parties. Until 1988, they governed with two small centre parties, the Christian Democrats and the Centre Democrats.

From 1988 to 1990 they governed with the Social Liberals, and from 1990 to 1993 they governed alone. However, these governments were mostly dependent on support from all non-socialist parties, i.e. the five coalition parties and the radical right-wing Progress Party.

From that perspective, immigration was a 'wedge issue' (van de Wardt et al. 2014) because of the Social Liberal position. They largely agreed with the other right-wing parties on state-market related issues, but on many other issues like immigration, the environment, and foreign policy, the Social Liberals cooperated with the left-wing opposition (Damgaard and Svensson 1989). As for the governments until 1993, immigration was therefore unattractive from a coalition perspective. As Table 7.4 shows, it was left to the radical right-wing Progress Party to focus on immigration, which it did specifically in the 1987 election.

In 1993, the Social Liberals, the Centre Democrats, and the Christian Democrats switched to the left-wing bloc and joined a government with the Social Democrats. The large, mainstream right-wing parties now found themselves in opposition. The Liberals had grown at the expense of the Conservatives and had become the dominant mainstream right-wing party in Denmark. In terms of winning government power, the two parties knew that regaining support from the centre parties was a long-term project, so the only realistic medium-term option was to try to gain voters and build a closer cooperation with the radical right. For this purpose, focusing on immigration was attractive because of the right-wing issue ownership. In policy terms, the focus on immigration implied demands for a stricter immigration policy. At the same time, the position of the Social Liberals made the issue difficult for the Social Democratic-led government. Parts of the Social Democratic party wanted a stricter immigration policy, but these demands led to internal

TABLE 7.4 *Party attention to immigration in Denmark, 1984–2015*

	Liberals	Social Democrats	Progress Party	Danish People's Party	Party system agenda
1984	1.0%	0%	0%		0.2%
1987	0%	0%	11.3%		1.7%
1988	0%	0%	Missing		0.7%
1990	0%	0%	1.7%		1.6%
1994	7.6%	0%	2.1%		4.9%
1998	20.4%	14.2%	5.4%	13.1%	8.1%
2001	8.2%	7.4%		33.3%	12.1%
2005	16.3%	12.5%		15.4%	10.1%
2007	25.9%	15.1%		19.5%	16.6%
2011	15.6%	3.8%		14.5%	9.9%
2015	20.7%	8.2%		21.2%	8.3%

disagreement within the government (Bale et al. 2010). In 1995, the Danish People's Party emerged as a splinter party from the Progress Party. After winning 7.4 per cent of the vote in the 1998 election, the party established itself in the party system with a strong focus on immigration and a demand for a stricter immigration policy.

As Table 7.4 shows, the focus on immigration by especially the Liberals was successful in the sense that it put the issue on the party system agenda. In the 2001 election, it played a central role and was decisive for the outcome of the election (Andersen 2003). The Liberals and the Conservatives were able to form a government based on the support of the Danish People's Party. This new government implemented various reforms of Danish immigration policies that, from a comparative perspective, became very restrictive (Akkerman 2012: 518–20). When in opposition, the Social Democrats tried to limit the importance of the immigration issue on the party system agenda by moving its policy position towards the right (Bale et al. 2010). In the 2011 and 2015 elections, the party was somewhat successful as the issue played a more limited role. The party won back government power in 2011, but lost it again in 2015. In sum, the Danish case clearly shows how the change in coalition considerations of the large, mainstream right parties in 1993 made the immigration issue much more attractive for them to focus on.

One alternative interpretation is that the focus on immigration was an 'automatic reaction' to the emergence of a strong radical right-wing party, in this case the Danish People's Party after the 1998 election. In other words, the emergence of a radical right-wing party with a strong immigration focus led the large, mainstream right parties to focus on the issue irrespective of coalition considerations. In this regard, it is worth noticing that the radical right-wing Progress Party already focused on the issue in the late 1980s as can be seen from Table 7.4 without the Liberals or Conservatives taking up the issue. As can also be seen from Table 7.4, the Liberals began to focus on immigration right after returning to opposition in 1993 and before the Danish People's Party had established itself in the party system, which happened in the 1998 election.

As argued above, a comparison with the Netherlands, which has different coalition considerations, but where a strong radical right-wing party has also established itself, demonstrates the importance of coalition considerations. In the Netherlands, the large, mainstream right-wing party the VVD is the major actor to focus on because it could potentially benefit from the issue playing a stronger role on the party system agenda (van Kersbergen and Krouwel 2008). However, in the Dutch case, winning government power means cooperation with centre parties, mainly the CDA or the Social Democrats (PvdA), across the left–right divide. While the VVD has historically governed with the CDA, it governed with the Social Democrats and the Social Liberal D66 from 1994 to 2002.

TABLE 7.5 *Party attention to immigration in the Netherlands, 1982–2012*

	VVD	PvdA	Party system agenda
1982	1.7%	1.8%	1.5%
1986	1.8%	1.6%	1.9%
1989	1.3%	2.5%	2.9%
1994	3.5%	1.1%	4.1%
1998	4.8%	1.4%	3.4%
2002	3.4%	1.5%	4.4%
2003	7.7%	6.8%	7.4%
2006	5.0%	4.3%	3.7%
2010	5.3%	2.6%	3.2%
2012	6.4%	2.4%	3.1%

The Netherlands had seen smaller radical right-wing parties before the radical right established itself in the Dutch party system in the 2002 election when the LPF (List Pim Fortuin) received 17 per cent of the vote. The LPF lost most of its support again in the 2003 election, but in the 2006 election, the PVV entered the Dutch parliament with 5.9 per cent of the vote under the leadership of Geert Wilders. The party, which is a splinter party from the VVD, grew to 15.4 per cent in the 2010 election and thus established itself as a major party in the Dutch party system.

However, as Table 7.5 shows, the VVD has not begun to focus strongly on immigration like the Liberals in Denmark. This is understandable considering Dutch coalition politics. As for the VVD, winning government power has continued to imply cooperation with the centre or with the left. Gaining a majority based on only the support of the PVV has not been a realistic strategy for winning government power. Cooperation across the centre has secured the VVD government power since 1994, except for 2006–10, and the position of Prime Minister since 2010. From 2010 to 2012, the VVD did govern based on the support of the PVV, but together with the CDA, and this coalition was unstable and short-lived. Thus, the VVD's coalition considerations are fundamentally different from those of the Danish Liberals.

In the Belgian case, the Vlaams Belang has established itself as a significant radical right-wing party in Flanders, and the National Front has established itself in Wallonia, though much less powerfully. However, the Vlaams Belang's strong support for Flemish nationalism has made the party unattractive as a coalition partner. Instead, the large, mainstream Belgian parties practise a *cordon sanitaire*, which has also implied a neglect of the immigration issue (Vangoidsenhoven and Pilet 2015).

In Sweden, the large, mainstream right-wing party, the Conservatives (Moderaterna), has traditionally stayed away from the immigration issue and focused on holding together an alliance with the centre parties which all hold a relatively immigration-friendly position (Green-Pedersen and Krogstrup 2008). This strategy was the backbone of the Swedish right-wing governments from 2006 to 2014. The Sweden Democrats established themselves in the Swedish party system in the 2010 election with 5.7 per cent of the vote and advanced to 12.9 per cent of the vote in 2014. However, from a coalition perspective, the incentives of the Conservatives have not changed. Winning a majority based on the Sweden Democrats is not a realistic option. Most of the gain of the Sweden Democrats in the 2014 election came at the expense of the Conservatives, and winning a majority without the more immigration-friendly centre parties is not within reach. Therefore, the Swedish Conservatives continue not to focus strongly on immigration.[16]

In France, Germany, and the UK, the limited parliamentary role of radical right-wing parties means that coalition incentives have never made immigration a very attractive issue to focus on for the large, mainstream right and thus not a central part of their strategy for winning government power as it has been for the Danish Liberals.[17]

THE ISSUE INCENTIVE MODEL AND IMMIGRATION

In terms of the issue incentive model, the issue of immigration shows the importance of problem information. The increased share of foreigners has, together with the growth of radical right-wing parties, generated more attention to the issue. In all countries, the issue has become an established issue

[16] The party grew to 17.5% in the 2018 election. This made the formation of a government coalition highly challenging and challenged the internal cohesion of the center-right bloc (Alliansen). The Conservatives and Christian Democrats suggested a center right government but supported by the Sweden Democrats as this was only way for avoid a Social Democratic led government. However, the Center Party and the Liberals deiced to support a Social Democratic government rather than having to rely on the support of the Sweden Democrats. This development might lead the Conservatives in Sweden to focus more on immigration to win government power based on the support of the Sweden Democrats, now that the Center Party and the Liberals have defected to the Social Democrats.

[17] In 2017, the AFD made it into the German Bundestag for the first time with 12.6% of the vote. Based on the issue incentive model, the crucial question in terms of party system attention to immigration is whether the CDU/CSU finds the AFD interesting from a coalition perspective. Given the formation of another 'grand coalition' with the SPD in 2018, there is no sign of this. This is also not surprising given that cooperation with the AFD would not provide the CDU/CSU with a majority in the German Bundestag. In the UK, the UKIP gained a seat in the House of Commons in 2015 but lost it again in 2017 and struggled for survival after the Brexit referendum. In France, Front National has never established itself as an important party in the French National Assembly despite success in the presidential elections in 2002 and 2017.

on the party system agenda. The chapter furthermore shows the crucial role of large, mainstream parties' coalition considerations in explaining how issues can make it to the top of the party system agenda. Only in Denmark has a strong focus on immigration been attractive from a coalition perspective. Denmark is thus the only country studied where immigration has become a central issue in the competition between the large, mainstream parties for office.

From the perspective of the literature on the idea of a globalization or transnational conflict (Hooghe and Marks 2018; Kriesi et al. 2012), the general increase in attention to immigration is not surprising. However, the literature does not offer an explanation for the difference between Denmark and the other countries. Furthermore, the strong focus on radical right-wing parties as the agent mobilizing the globalization conflict makes it difficult to explain why attention to immigration has also risen in countries like Germany and the UK where no strong radical right-wing parties emerged until recently.

8

An Ever-Sleeping Giant?

European Integration on the Party System Agenda

From a theoretical perspective, i.e. the issue incentive model, European integration is an attractive issue to analyse for several reasons: In terms of issue characteristics, it is distinct from most other issues. Due to the structure of party positions on the issue, coalition incentives are also quite different from other policy areas. Finally, it is also an attractive issue in terms of evaluating the impact of issue entrepreneurs. They try to push the issue on the party system agenda. The question is whether they are successful.

Empirically, European integration has attracted considerable attention because of the increasing importance of European integration for member countries. Hooghe and Marks' (2009, 2018) claim that European integration has been politicized has been debated by a growing literature (e.g. de Wilde 2011; de Wilde et al. 2016; Green-Pedersen 2012; Hoeglinger 2016; Hutter and Grande 2014; Hutter et al. 2016b). Politicization is typically defined more broadly than issue saliency on the party system agenda, but the latter is always a central component of politicization (cf. Hutter and Grande 2014). Thus, explaining the attention dynamics related to European integration, as done in this chapter, is also a contribution to the debate about politicization of European integration. In sum, from both a theoretical and an empirical perspective, European integration is important to study in detail. However, before the empirical analysis, some further reflections on the issue of European integration are needed.

EUROPEAN INTEGRATION AS A POLICY ISSUE

One important aspect of European integration as a policy issue is multidimensionality. Any policy issue is to some extent multidimensional. However, European integration is special because it is a 'compound issue' (Hutter et al. 2016a). It contains a 'polity' or 'constitutive' aspect, i.e. how many members the EU should have, what the role of the Commission is, etc. It also has a policy aspect. The European Union as an institution is involved in many policy areas where its role as an institution may be discussed, but where the main focus is on the content of the policy itself (Senninger 2016). The issue of European integration may thus be either *about* European integration or about policies *through* the European Union (Hertner 2015). In practice, a debate on European integration may relate to anything from whether Turkey should join the European Union to the content of European banking regulation. The following focuses on the polity or constitutive aspect of European integration, but the question will be addressed further below. Hoeglinger (2016) also stresses how the multidimensional character of European integration makes it an ideologically challenging issue for political parties. European integration relates to both the left–right conflict and the new, second conflict. From an ideological perspective, most political parties will therefore be uncertain about European integration. This ideological multidimensionality may easily generate internal party disagreement.

PARTY INCENTIVES AND ATTENTION TO EUROPEAN INTEGRATION

With the multidimensional character of European integration in mind, one can apply the issue incentive model to European integration. The first aspect is issue characteristics consisting of both problem information and problem characteristics. In terms of problem information, European integration has no problem indicators and no continuous flow of information to shape political attention. As an issue, it does not generate information flows parallel to unemployment figures or crime statistics. Nor is it related to policy events like environmental disasters, although there are examples such as the resignation of the European Commission in 1999 and Brexit in 2016. 'Attention windows' are therefore often politically generated events like meetings of the European Council, treaty negotiations, or enlargements (see Hutter et al. 2016b; Senninger 2016). Because they attract media attention, such events might function as 'windows of attention' for parties that want to draw attention to European integration (Boomgaarden et al. 2010). Still, a meeting of the European Council, for instance, does not necessarily provide an attractive opportunity to focus on European integration. This will depend on its actual content. This does not mean that there are no occasions for parties to pay attention to European integration, but the issue provides fewer opportunities than other issues.

In terms of problem characteristics, European integration is a specific type of policy issue in two ways. First, its multidimensionality generates a fundamental uncertainty for political parties about how a political debate over European integration will develop. This is also reflected in public opinion on European integration which is characterized by multidimensionality and complexity (Hobolt and de Vries 2016: 426). Framing is therefore even more relevant to European integration than to any other policy issue (Hooghe and Marks 2009: 13). It plays a key role in explaining the outcome of referendums on European integration (de Vreese and Semetko 2004; Hobolt 2009). This uncertainty about how the issue can be framed ceteris paribus makes it unattractive to large, mainstream parties.

Second, from the perspective of national politics, European integration is a foreign policy issue in the sense that any government needs to protect the interests of its country and influence policymaking in the European Union. Therefore, it is especially risky for large, mainstream parties that want to form the next government to take a very negative position towards the European Union. It will be difficult to implement as influencing the European Union requires compromising. This means that large, mainstream parties will be reluctant to promise the electorate very much in terms of European integration simply because it is much harder to deliver on such a promise than it is on other policy promises. Thus, from an issue competition perspective, European integration appears to be a much more attractive issue for parties that do not aspire to government power and therefore do not expect to have to deal directly with the European Union (cf. Hobolt and de Vries 2015; Sitter 2001).

To sum up, the issue characteristics of European integration do not make it an attractive issue for large, mainstream parties to focus on. There is no stream of problem information to be used as a justification for attention, the actual framing of a debate about European integration is uncertain, and any promise to the electorate is hard to implement once in government.

In terms of issue ownership, Seeberg (2016) shows that European integration is characterized by a stable—but not very strong—issue ownership by the mainstream right. Ceteris paribus, this indicates that the mainstream right-wing parties should be most interested in drawing attention to European integration. However, due to the uncertainty and multidimensionality of voter attitudes towards European integration discussed above, the mainstream right cannot be certain that it will benefit electorally from European integration becoming an important issue on the party system agenda compared to immigration, for instance.

Coalition considerations for European integration appear to be relatively similar across Western Europe due to what is known as the 'inverted U-shaped' pattern of party positions on European integration (Hooghe et al. 2002; Prosser 2016). Parties in the centre, including the large, mainstream parties, are EU positive, whereas the EU-sceptic parties are found on the extreme right and left. This inverted U-shape of course varies somewhat cross-nationally. EU scepticism on the extreme left is typically found in Northern

Europe, and the traditional 2½ party system of the UK has a different structure. However, the large, mainstream parties are generally pro-EU, which is known as the 'permissive consensus' (Hooghe and Marks 2009), and to different degrees they face the EU-sceptical parties at the extremes. This means that the issue differs from most other issues in which the difference between the mainstream left and the mainstream right is the central positional conflict (van der Brug and van Spanje 2009). In terms of coalition incentives, this implies that the EU is often an unattractive issue for large, mainstream parties because they may disagree with the smaller extreme parties, whose support they might need to win government power. Moreover, the issue does not offer them the possibility of differentiating themselves from their traditional opponents.

To sum up, from the perspective of the issue incentive model, focusing on European integration is not necessarily attractive for large, mainstream parties. Beginning with the EU-positive 'permissive consensus', the uncertainty of voters' attitudes towards European integration means that it is unclear whether the issue would be electorally beneficial to focus on. This even applies for large, mainstream right-wing parties that traditionally hold issue ownership. Furthermore, the information stream on European integration rarely contains the positive stories that an EU-friendly party would need in order to draw more attention to the issue. Finally, the EU is not necessarily an attractive issue for a large, mainstream party because the permissive consensus makes it difficult for the party to differentiate itself from other large, mainstream parties.

One possible strategy for especially the large, mainstream right-wing parties would be to break the permissive consensus and apply a more EU-sceptic focus on the issue. However, based on the issue incentive model, one would not expect large, mainstream parties to do so. First of all, parties are basically reluctant to change position, and this is potentially costly for them (see also Janda et al. 1995: 174). They risk internal disagreement, which any party leader wants to avoid (Panebianco 1988), and they risk being accused of pandering (Somer-Topcu 2009). Second, due to the uncertainty of voters' attitudes towards the European Union, a mainstream party cannot be sure whether a more EU-sceptic position will in fact capture the electoral majority. That depends on the framing of the issue. Third, coalition incentives potentially make it attractive for especially large, mainstream right-wing parties to break the permissive consensus in order to strengthen coalition possibilities with extreme (right-wing) parties. However, in countries with EU-sceptic parties at both extremes, a mainstream party moving in an EU-sceptic direction will face a 'strange bed-fellow problem' (Pedersen 1996). It will now position itself with an extreme party from the other side of the political spectrum. Fourth and not least, the government aspirations of large, mainstream parties imply that the difficulties of implementing an EU-sceptic position once in government make such a change of position unattractive. Thus, based on the issue incentive model, large, mainstream parties are not expected to break the permissive consensus in order to make European integration a central issue in party competition. Altogether, one should expect large, mainstream parties to pay as little attention to European integration as possible.

The extreme EU-sceptic parties have strong incentives to focus on the issue. For a number of reasons, they are highly likely to act as 'issue entrepreneurs' (Hobolt and de Vries 2015), parallel to niche parties like green parties on the environment. Even if the framing of an issue determines whether the electoral majority swings towards the EU positive or the EU-sceptic side, all countries have large groups of EU-sceptic voters. This means that the issue has considerable electoral potential for such a party. Furthermore, many large, mainstream parties have witnessed internal dissent with regard to the European Union, which implies that the issue can be used as a wedge issue against them (van de Wardt et al. 2014). Finally, the extreme EU-sceptic parties can largely neglect the difficulties of having to implement an EU-sceptic position in government as they typically do not take part in government coalitions. One would thus expect extreme EU-sceptic parties to pay considerable attention to the issue.

However, for two reasons, these parties are not expected to be able to turn it into a significant issue on the party system agenda, and one therefore expects large, mainstream parties to largely ignore the issue. First, the issue does not offer the attractive 'window of attention' that allows extreme parties to draw attention to it. Events like the 1999 resignation of the Commission do happen, but they are rare. Second, and more importantly, as argued in Chapter 3, large, mainstream parties are the crucial actors in terms of setting the party system agenda. Their competition for office is what structures party politics, and therefore they are expected to be capable of ignoring an issue like European integration if they agree on it.

Thus, applying the issue incentive model to the issue of European integration leads one to expect that it plays a limited role on the party system agenda because large, mainstream parties do not have incentives to focus on it. EU-sceptic parties have incentives and are expected to pay attention to the issue, but they are not expected to be able to make it a central issue on the party system agenda.

POLITICIZATION OF EUROPEAN INTEGRATION

Before turning to the empirical analysis of party attention to European integration, the central conclusions from the literature on politicization of European integration are worth highlighting. The debate about politicization was initiated by Hooghe and Marks (2009) and their argument that European integration had become politicized. Before, the debate was dominated by the idea of European integration as a 'sleeping giant' launched by van der Eijk and Franklin (2007). They argued that European integration had an unexploited potential to become a central issue in European party politics mainly due to widespread Euro-scepticism. Hooghe and Marks (2009, cf. also 2018) argued that the giant had indeed woken up. In the wake of Hooghe and Marks' (2009) claim, an extensive literature evaluating it has emerged (e.g. de Wilde 2011; de Wilde et al. 2016; Green-Pedersen 2012; Hoeglinger 2016; Hutter and Grande 2014; Hutter et al. 2016b; Kriesi 2016). The debate is centred on two questions, namely whether European integration has in fact become politicized, and what the political dynamics behind this alleged politicization are.

From the outset, it is important to be aware that the idea of politicization is broader than issue saliency on the party system agenda, which is in focus here (cf. de Wilde 2011). Hooghe and Marks (2009: 3) focus on whether public and party preferences matter for European integration, i.e. whether it is a matter of controversial mass politics. Hutter and Grande (2014) and Grande and Hutter (2016a) define politicization as having three components, namely issue saliency, actor expansion, and actor polarization. However, issue saliency for political parties plays a key role in the empirical assessment of polarization by both Hooghe and Marks (2009: 7–8) and Hutter and Grande (2014: 1004). In the latter case, issue saliency is even considered a necessary condition for politicization (see also Grande and Hutter 2016a: 10). Thus, even though the focus here is on issue saliency only, the findings still have crucial implications for the debate about politicization of European integration.

In terms of the first question about politicization, the different studies have reached somewhat different conclusions. Hutter and Grande (2014) and Hooghe and Marks (2018) argue that polarization has indeed taken place, whereas Hoeglinger (2016: 144–8), Kriesi (2016), and Grande and Kriesi (2016) all see politicization as more limited and focus more on the variation in politicization. Grande and Kriesi (2016: 283) point to a 'punctuated politicisation' implying that politicization of European integration happens in shorter periods driven by specific events like discussions of entering or leaving the European Union. In terms of the second question, Grande and Kriesi (2016) discuss a number of factors that may lead to politicization. Most importantly, they discuss the role of internal conflict in mainstream parties as well as the role of radical right-wing parties. Furthermore, they highlight how politicization is mostly related to 'constitutive questions', i.e. questions about the development of European integration as such, as discussed above. Thus, unlike the issue incentive model that focused on explaining why large, mainstream parties do not find the issue attractive, the politicization literature has focused on exploring the political dynamics behind the cases of politicization that have indeed been identified.

WHO DOES ACTUALLY PAY ATTENTION TO EUROPEAN INTEGRATION?

With the theoretical expectations developed above and the literature on politicization as a guideline, the attention dynamics with regard to European integration can be analysed empirically. The compound character of European integration as a policy issue of course also raises questions with regard to measuring attention to European integration. Especially the existence of both a polity/constitutive and a policy aspect raises the question about how European integration can be measured. The CAP codebook discussed in Chapter 4 has a category, 1910, that captures attention to European integration related to the polity aspect. However, if for instance a party presents its view on the EU's environmental policy, this is coded as an environmental policy. This, of course, raises the question of whether the CAP data systematically underestimate attention to European integration.

Green-Pedersen (2019) compares attention to European integration in the CAP data with the CMP data. The CMP data contain two categories, per 108 and per 110, that capture positive and negative mentioning of European integration. The two CMP categories are not based on the polity/policy distinction, but based on the CMP codebook, both aspects seem to be included in the coding. Based on this, one would expect that attention to European integration is higher in the CMP data. This is also the finding in Green-Pedersen (2019), but the differences are typically small. Thus, including the policy aspect does not seem to make a substantial difference. The explanation is probably that party manifestos are typically relatively general in nature, and therefore they do not contain a great number of references to very specific EU policies.[1] This will be much more frequent in for instance parliamentary questions (see Senninger 2016).

Turning to the empirical analysis, Figure 8.1 and Table 5.1 (see Chapter 5) show that attention to European integration on the party system agenda has remained limited in all countries, and that it has only once made it into the top three on the party system agenda. Using the two definitions discussed in Chapter 6 does not change this result. Attention to European integration in

---

[1] The Danish and Swedish CAP data sets contain a dummy variable that captures whether or not there is any mentioning of European integration in the sentences. This will always be the case if the sentence is coded as referring to an EU-polity issue, i.e. 1910 in the CAP coding scheme, but it will also be the case for EU policy-related sentences that are coded under for instance the environment or the economy. In Denmark, the latter group of EU policy-related sentences constitutes 0.8% of the total number of sentences, and in Sweden it constitutes 2.3%. The same variable has also been coded for the UK 2015 election, and 5.4% of the total number of sentences coded are EU-policy related.

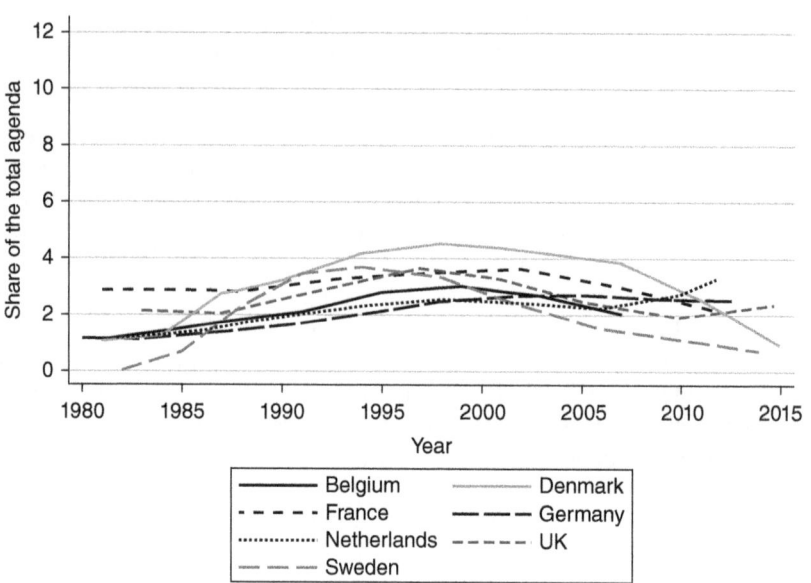

FIGURE 8.1 Party system attention to European integration in seven countries from 1980 and onwards

the Danish 1990 election[2] is the only example of the EU being a top five issue or receiving more attention than one standard deviation above the mean. This is very much in line with what one would expect based on the theoretical consideration presented above. The large, mainstream parties, which were argued to be the crucial actors when it comes to determining the party system agenda, only have limited incentives to pay attention to the issue.

To some extent, this is in disagreement with the idea of politicization found in the literature following Hooghe and Marks (2009); a disagreement which partly relates to the question of how much attention on the party system agenda is required for an issue to be considered important or be politicized. This question was debated in Chapters 5 and 6 in which the argument was to focus on a not too broad definition of top issues on the party system agenda. A broad definition would be to focus on whether the issue receives above the mean attention (Hutter 2016: 306).[3] This also depends on the analytical

---

[2] Actually, the Danish 1990 election is one of the few cases in which an extreme value drives the average across all parties. The Liberals spent 58% of their election programme on European integration. If one takes out the Liberals from the calculation of the party system agenda, attention to European integration drops from 10.1% to 3.3%. There is no indication from other data on the Danish 1990 election that European integration was a specific topic for the Liberals (Green-Pedersen 2012: 124). The most likely interpretation therefore is that the high value for the Liberals is a result of the particular document chosen (see Chapter 4).

[3] Such a definition does still not show much politicization of European integration. European integration has only received above the mean attention (4.35%) in five elections, namely the

perspective. This book focuses on the party system agenda in general and thus on issues that have become prominent on the agenda. The question of why large, mainstream parties are reluctant to focus on European integration should be seen in the light of how they have taken up other issues. The literature on European integration focuses on the issue itself, and when parties pay attention to it.

The theoretical discussion above leads to an expectation of limited party system attention, but also to an expectation that issue entrepreneurs would try to generate attention to European integration on the party system agenda, and that these entrepreneurs are EU-sceptic parties on the extreme left and right, i.e. hard-core EU-sceptic parties. Appendix 1 describes how these parties have been identified. This leads to the question of which parties actually pay attention to European integration. This can be studied by setting up a model predicting how much attention individual parties pay to European integration. Table 8.1 reports the outcome from a linear regression model with robust standard errors and country-fixed effects. The latter has been chosen in order to focus on within country variation.

Across the models, there is a stable and substantial effect of a party being hard-core EU-sceptic.[4] The status as a hard-core EU-sceptic party increases attention to European integration by about 2.0 percentage points. Compared to Grande and Kriesi's (2016: 284–7) conclusions on politicization of European integration, the analysis above thus points to the importance of parties being EU-sceptic rather than just being radical right.[5] The sole focus

TABLE 8.1 *Regression estimates of party attention to European integration*

	Model 1	Model 2	Model 3
Hard-core EU-sceptic party (=1)	1.88* (0.83)*	2.02 (0.83)*	2.16 (0.85)*
EU attention t−1	0.13 (0.1)	0.13 (0.11)	0.13 (0.11)
Mainstream right-wing party (l=1)		0.75 (0.82)	0.76 (0.83)
Vote share of hard EU-sceptic parties (t−1)			−0.05 (0.04)
Government (=1)	0.75 (0.49)	0.67 (0.42)	0.65 (0.40)
Post 1989	1.68 (0.42)***	1.68 (0.42)***	1.93 (0.60)**
Constant	0.29 (0.44)	0.18 (0.53)	0.26 (0.48)
N	398	398	398
Adj. R^2	0.08	0.08	0.08

Note: robust standard errors in parentheses. * p < 0.05, ** p < 0.01, *** p < 0.001. Estimated with country-fixed effects (country dummies not shown).

Danish 1990, 2001, and 2007 elections, and the Swedish elections in 1991 and 1994. The latter two were at the same time that Sweden debated its entrance to the European Union.

[4] All results are substantially the same when excluding the two cases in which parties spent more than 25% of their manifesto on European integration. Besides the Danish Liberals in 1990, as discussed in footnote 2, the other case is the Danish People's Party in 2001.

[5] A dummy variable for a party being radical right, as defined in footnote 5, chapter 7, is significant when entered instead of the hard-core EU-sceptic variable in Model 3, Table 8.1. However, if both variables are included, only the hard-core EU-sceptic variable is significant.

on the radical right neglects that many left-wing parties like the Dutch Socialists and the Danish Red–Green Alliance are EU-sceptic and also focus on the issue (cf. also Meijers 2017).[6] At the same time, the status as a large, mainstream right-wing party is not statistically significant.[7] Hence, the tendency to hold issue ownership does not lead the large, mainstream right parties to try to push the issue on the party system agenda.

Table 8.1 also shows several other interesting aspects of party attention to European integration. Studies of party attention to issues typically find a lagged dependent variable to be significant (e.g. Green-Pedersen and Mortensen 2015; Liu et al. 2011). This was also the findings with regard to immigration in Chapter 7. This is not, however, the case with European integration.[8] This indicates that party attention to European integration is not a stable part of the parties' issue focus.[9] The low adjusted R^2 scores also indicate that party attention to European integration is only explained to a limited extent by the variables included in the models. This conclusion actually fits well with the idea of punctuated politicization, i.e. politicization driven by events drawn by Grande and Kriesi (2016). European integration is not established as an important issue in party competition. Model 3 includes the lagged vote share of the hard-core EU-sceptic parties as Meijers (2017) finds a contagious effect of the electoral strength of EU-sceptic parties on the EU positions of mainstream parties.[10] However, Model 3 finds no such effect on party attention to European integration.[11,12]

---

[6] If a dummy variable for a party being soft EU-sceptic, as defined in Appendix 1, is added to Model 3, Table 8.1 (excluding the large, mainstream right dummy), it is insignificant. This shows that soft EU-sceptic parties do not focus more on European integration than EU-positive parties do.

[7] The analysis does not include large, mainstream Christian Democratic parties, but including them all, or only the German CDU/CSU, does not have any substantial effect on the results.

[8] To avoid losing too many cases when including the lagged dependent variable, data on the last election before 1980 have been included when available. This is the case for Denmark, Sweden, Germany, and the Flemish parties in Belgium (see Chapter 4).

[9] If Model 3 is run as a Tobit model that takes censoring of the dependent variable—attention can only vary between 0 and 100%—into account, all results are the same except that the lagged dependent variable now becomes significant. However, the effect is weaker than found for the other issues (see Chapters 7, 9, 10, and 11).

[10] Meijers (2017) has a broader definition of EU-sceptic parties that also includes 'soft' EU-sceptic parties (cf. Appendix 1). Focus here is on the hard-core EU-sceptic parties only because the soft EU-sceptic parties were not found to pay more attention to European integration (see footnote 6).

[11] The results are substantially the same if one excludes the hard-core EU-sceptic parties themselves.

[12] The same effect is found when running a model with party-fixed effects. The lagged vote share of hard-core EU-sceptic parties continues to be insignificant.

Finally, there is a clear time effect in the sense that attention was significantly higher after 1989. The effect of the election being held after 1989 is a 1.93 percentage point increase in attention to European integration. A parallel dynamic has been identified in the politicization literature (e.g. Grande and Kriesi 2016; Hoeglinger 2016; Hutter and Grande 2014). As studies of politicization also argue (e.g. Hooghe and Marks 2009), this can be explained by the development of European integration itself. The debate leading to the Maastricht Treaty initiated a new process of expanding European integration that caused parties in general to pay somewhat more attention to European integration.

The same development can be seen in the percentage of parties that did not mention European integration in a manifesto as depicted in Table 8.2: 33 per cent in the 1980s, 14 per cent in the 1990s, and 13 per cent in the 2000s. It is, however, also worth noticing that a significant number of parties still completely ignored the issue in the 2000s.

In conclusion, the analysis of European integration on the party system agenda reveals that attention did increase after the 1980s (see also Figure 5.11). However, as argued in Chapter 5, the further deepening of European integration and the expansion of the European Union since then have still not made the issue central on the party system agendas. Even the European debt crisis in the late 2000s did not seem to push politicization to a new level (Grande and Kriesi 2016).[13] The analysis above revealed that EU-sceptic parties try to push the issue on the party system agenda by paying attention to the issue. However, large, mainstream parties, and even the large, mainstream right-wing parties that may hold issue ownership, most often ignore the issue. As the theoretical discussion above concludes, the large, mainstream parties have few incentives to focus on it. This is furthermore a finding that holds across the seven countries studied. This means that there is little cross-national variation to study.

TABLE 8.2 *Percentage of parties mentioning European integration in their election programme across decades*

Decade	Percentage	N
1980s	67%	141
1990s	86%	131
2000s	87%	183

---

[13] This conclusion might be quite different for the countries affected by the sovereign debt crisis and where the crisis was closely linked to European integration (cf. Otjes and Katsanidou 2017).

IS EUROPEAN INTEGRATION POLITICIZED?

The aim of this chapter is to analyse party system attention to European integration from both a theoretical and an empirical perspective. The expectation based on the issue incentive model was that large, mainstream parties were not interested in but largely able to avoid the issue becoming an important issue on the party system agenda despite pressure from EU-sceptic issue entrepreneurs. This expectation was, by and large, confirmed. European integration continues to play a rather limited role on the party system agenda. Even events like the European debt crisis that may be used by issue entrepreneurs, do not push the issue on the party system agenda. They may generate punctuations, as suggested by Grande and Kriesi (2016), but not a stable position of the issue as important on the party system agenda. In the light of the politicization literature, it is important not to misunderstand the precise meaning of these conclusions. Two points are worth stressing in particular:

First, the focus of this book on the party system agenda implies a focus on the issues that have become central to party competition on a stable basis. As argued in Chapter 3, the party system agenda understood in this way is important to study because the issues become important for electoral politics once they establish themselves on the party system agenda, and because the policymaking dynamics change if this happens. However, this also means that a certain issue which plays an important role in a particular election is not the main focus. The argument above does not rule out the possibility of punctuated politicization of European integration as suggested by Grande and Kriesi (2016: 288). One of the clearest examples of this, as provided by Hutter and Grande (2014), is Switzerland during the 1990s when entering the European Union was debated. Figure 5.11 also shows that in Sweden the issue reached the highest level of attention on the party system agenda in 1994 in connection with a referendum on entering the Union. This indicates that the issue can play a more central role on the party system agenda, but that this is not likely to happen very often if it requires a debate about entering the EU. Grande and Kriesi (2016) also point to internal disagreement within mainstream parties as an important dynamic that may generate punctuated politicization. The idea of a wedge issue within political parties typically also refers to European integration (van de Wardt et al. 2014). One such case often mentioned is the UK 1997 election (Evans 1998; Grande and Hutter 2016b: 98–9). However, mainstream parties have strong incentives to try to avoid internal disagreement and will therefore try to keep internal party disagreement from affecting party system attention.[14]

---

[14] In the data set here, the 1997 British election does not stand out in terms of party attention with only 3.7% of the party system agenda (the score based on the CMP data set is 5.3%). Hutter

Second, if politicization refers to the impact of 'mass public and politics' on European integration, this is clearly broader than simply party attention, and it is most clearly something that also happens through the referendums held within the last decades, e.g. in France and the Netherlands in 2005 and most recently in the UK. As Brexit demonstrates, the impact of such referendums can be dramatic. However, in most cases, referendums are under the control of the executive and in this way isolated from party competition more broadly. In the Danish case, four referendums from 1992 to 2000 did not make the issue a central one on the party system agenda. The run-up to the British Brexit referendum is in many ways also illustrative. Looking at Figure 5.11, this did not indicate an increasing role of the issue in British party competition. More precisely, in 2010, the Conservatives dedicated 2.3 per cent of its manifesto to the issue, Labour 1.2 per cent, and the Liberal Democrats 1.7 per cent.[15] Rather, David Cameron called the referendum a response to internal disagreement within the party (Evans and Menon 2017: 6–10).

Of the seven countries analysed in the book, only Germany and Belgium have not had a referendum on European integration in the period analysed. This raises the question of how the existence of such an alternative political venue (cf. Baumgartner and Jones 1993: 31–8) influences party attention to European integration and thus electoral politics. One answer is that a referendum serves exactly as an alternative venue, and the limited role of European integration on the party system agenda can be explained by the existence of this alternative venue. The other answer is a spillover argument (Hooghe and Marks 2009) that referendums generate more party attention. Neither answer finds clear empirical support. A comparison of Germany with no referendums and Denmark with eight altogether shows that there is hardly any difference in attention on the party system agenda. Thus, from the perspective of party competition and electoral politics, referendums are

---

(2016: 311) reports a much higher score, 23.2%, based on media data. This marked difference is likely to be explained by the data sources. Any party has strong incentives to avoid drawing unnecessary attention to issues like European integration in which they are strongly internally divided (Steenbergen and Scott 2004). Therefore, it is not surprising that European integration does not feature prominently in the 1997 manifesto of the British Conservatives (2.5% according to the data used here). However, for modern mass media, internal disagreement in a large, mainstream party easily fulfils the news criteria as a conflict. Therefore, it is not surprising that European integration in the UK in 1997 scores so high on saliency measured through media attention, especially because the Conservative electorate was also divided (Hellström and Blomgren 2016).

[15] The data on the 2015 election do not indicate that the issue has become central in British party competition. The three dominant parties dedicated 1.64% (Labour), 1.18% (Liberal Democrats), and 2.97% (Conservatives) to the issue. However, including sentences relating to EU policy does point to more attention to European integration (see footnote 1).

not alternative venues to party competition. However, if one focuses on the development of the European Union and public influence on it, then referendums are an alternative venue with potentially huge consequences as Brexit has shown.

When the consequences of a referendum are as dramatic as Brexit, this is of course likely to impact electoral politics afterwards. The policy problem emerging from Brexit is of a gigantic nature that will also affect electoral politics significantly. In this sense, referendums may have an indirect effect on electoral politics. However, the Brexit referendum is also unusual in terms of the policy problems it has generated afterwards. In other words, it takes a referendum with an extreme outcome for referendums to be an alternative venue for bringing European integration into electoral politics. Thus, the giant may be awakening in terms of public attitudes to have more impact on the development, but the giant is awakening to a life that remains mostly separate from mainstream electoral politics.

APPENDIX 1
Identification of Eurosceptic parties

The coding of political parties as Eurosceptic is based on Szczerbiak and Taggart (2008); see also Taggart and Szczerbiak (2002). They distinguish between hard-core and soft Euroscepticism, and only the parties classified as hard-core Eurosceptics are considered as such in the following (see Table 8A). The category of hard-core Eurosceptics refers to parties that are fundamentally opposed to European integration and always recommend NO at

TABLE 8A *Overview of Eurosceptic parties*

	Hard-core Eurosceptic parties	Soft Eurosceptic parties
Denmark	Danish People's Party, Red–Green Alliance, Left-Socialists, Common Course, Justice Party	Socialist People's Party, Progress Party, Christian Democrats, Liberal Alliance
Belgium	Vlaams Belang	NVA, FN, CDH
Netherlands	Party of Freedom (PVV), Centre Democrats, Centre Party, Socialist Party, Communist Party, PSP	Green Party, Christian Union, GPV, SGP, RPF, Liste Pim Fortujn
France	Front National	Communist Party
UK	UKIP	Conservatives
Germany		Die Linke
Sweden	Left Party, Green Party, Sweden Democrats	Centre Party

referendums concerning European integration. Soft Eurosceptic parties are against certain aspects of European integration like the euro, and their position in connection with referendums varies.

The classifications largely follow Szczerbiak and Taggart (2008) and are updated by various online sources on the parties including new parties. The only differences are with regard to the Dutch Socialist Party and its predecessors, which are classified as hard-core Eurosceptics, and the Danish Progress Party, which is classified as soft Eurosceptics.

9

Up and Down with the Environment

From the perspective of the issue incentive model, the environment is a mirror image of immigration. Because of left-wing issue ownership, studying the environment puts focus on the coalition considerations of the large, mainstream left-wing parties rather than the large, mainstream right-wing parties. The environment has also attracted attention as a case that allows one to study the impact of niche parties on the party system agenda (e.g. Abou-Chadi 2016; Spoon et al. 2014). This is due to the growth of Green parties with the environment as their *raison d'être*. Environmental problems are also one of the major challenges facing West European societies. This makes it an important issue to study on its own right. A rich literature on environmental politics has also emerged. However, as in most single-issue literature, the drawback is that the political dynamics revolving around the environment are rarely compared to other issues.

THE ENVIRONMENT AS A POLICY AREA

As a first step, it is worth defining what is meant by the environment as a policy area. The question of defining and delimiting the environment as a policy area rarely gets much attention in the literature on the politics of the environment (e.g. Jahn 2016; Repetto 2006). In practice, when the environment is studied as a policy area, focus is on policy measures aimed at the reduction of pollution and the degradation of the environment, often including broader issues such as planning the use of nature. Classic policy questions related to the environment are: air pollution, water pollution from groundwater to oceans, soil pollution, regulation of hazardous substances, regulation of waste, noise pollution, biodiversity and the protection of endangered species, and the protection of unique landscapes and natural reserves (cf. Carter 2007: 1–11). This study follows this often implicit definition of environmental policy. The environment as a policy area is thus broad in the sense that it contains a wide number of policy questions relating to the many ways in which human behaviour influences and potentially degrades the environment.

It is important to note that focus is on the measures to protect the environment. Environmental policy is entangled in many other policy areas such as energy policy, business regulation, and agricultural policy. These are, however, distinct policy areas as they have many aspects not related to the environment, and they should therefore not be included in environmental policy. For instance, the question of whether to introduce or abolish nuclear power is a policy question related to energy policy, and subsidies to introduce ecological farming is a policy question related to agricultural policy. However, environmental consequences of agricultural production or a nuclear breakdown are all part of environmental policy.

THE ISSUE INCENTIVES OF THE ENVIRONMENT

The analysis of the environment first requires an application of the issue incentive model to the issue, i.e. which incentives issue characteristics, issue ownership, and coalition incentives offer large, mainstream parties in terms of attention to the environment.

In terms of issue characteristics, three points are worth highlighting. The first one is that the environment is a valence issue, i.e. everyone agrees that pollution is a problem. This is an important problem characteristic from an agenda-setting perspective (cf. Baumgartner and Jones 1993: 150–2). Hence, it is difficult for an opponent to fight attention to the issue. It also means that in most cases environmental attention will be pro-environmental. Political actors are unlikely to advocate for more pollution.

The second point relates to the interplay between problem information and problem characteristics. Environmental problems are generally measurable and to some extent solvable. This does not imply that measuring environmental performance is simple, or that environmental problems are easy to solve. However, compared to integration for instance, the causal processes of air pollution or hazardous substances are better understood, and it is generally clearer how such problems can be measured and solved. The OECD, for instance, regularly publishes measures of environmental performance (see Jahn 2016: 97–128).

The third point also relates to problem information, namely the occurrence of focusing events. Even if everyone agrees in principle that environmental problems should be addressed, and even if they can often be measured, political attention is not guaranteed. The environment is an unobtrusive issue, which implies that citizens in general do not face environmental problems on a personal level. Media coverage plays a key role (Soroka 2002), and this is most likely generated by focusing events as discussed in Chapter 2.

Among the many examples with regard to the environment, one can mention the Exxon Valdez oil spill in 1989, the Bhopal disaster at the Union Carbide plant in December 1984, and the environmental impact of the Chernobyl disaster in 1986. Such events often play a key role in attention dynamics regarding the environment. They bring political attention to policy questions that are rarely new but have simply not received much political attention before. Once such events happen, all political parties are likely to pay some attention to the related environmental problems. Furthermore, the existence of a broad range of environmental indicators implies that political attention will be sustained after a focusing event, of course depending on what these indicators say about the development of the environment. If information about environmental problems is positive—for instance that regulation is reducing air pollution—it is hard to sustain political attention to that issue.

These issue characteristics do not imply that environmental policy questions are not political—questions about how much pollution is acceptable and who should share the burden of environmental protection are highly political. However, compared to many other policy areas, the political debates are much less about what the problem is as solutions are often available, and their effects can be measured in a relatively simple way.

In terms of the second factor affecting large, mainstream parties' incentives to focus on an issue, namely issue ownership, Seeberg (2017: 482–7) shows that the environment is the issue with the strongest left-wing ownership across time and countries. Thus, the large, mainstream left-wing parties, i.e. Social Democratic parties, have an electoral incentive to draw attention to the environment.

The third and final factor in the issue incentive model relates to coalition considerations, which, as argued in Chapter 3, depend on how an issue fits the left–right structure. From an ideological perspective, the environmental issue can be interpreted in different ways connecting it more or less clearly with the left–right dimension (Andersen 1990; Talshir 2002). One interpretation is an anti-growth, post-materialist interpretation which puts environmentalism beyond left–right. Some thus see the environment as a 'new politics' issue, i.e. not left–right (see Chapter 2). In the other, and prevailing, interpretation, environmentalism is a criticism of modern forms of capitalism and thus a 'left-wing issue'. Green parties have generally positioned themselves as left-wing parties, and the environment has been integrated into the left–right conflict (Carter 2013; Rohrschneider 1993). Left-wing parties generally support regulations on the environment and businesses, and right-wing parties are sceptical of environmental regulations and favour pro-business regulations. Voters also perceive the left as being better at handling environmental problems (i.e. left-wing issue ownership).

Like other issues, this does not imply that party positions on the environment are identical to the general left–right scale. Social Liberal parties like the Dutch D66 or the Danish Social Liberals have often taken relatively pro-environmental positions (Carter 2013: 85–6). On the environment, as on immigration, these parties are typically closer to the mainstream left-wing parties than on other issues—especially regarding macroeconomics, on which they traditionally align with the mainstream right.

Based on this, coalition incentives in many cases reinforce the interests of Social Democratic parties in drawing attention to the environment. Social Democratic parties can often win power by strengthening the left–right bloc. Approaching a Green party by focusing on the environment is an obvious strategy (Mair 2001). It may generate more additional support for Green parties than for Social Democratic parties, but it will strengthen the left-wing bloc in any case. Thus, the entrance of a Green party in a party system with bloc competition for office is likely to make the environment a more attractive issue to focus on for the large, mainstream left, i.e. Social Democratic parties.

Furthermore, in countries like Denmark and Germany, Social Democratic parties have often built coalitions with Social Liberal parties. The pro-environmental orientation of these parties implies that the environment is also attractive for Social Democratic parties that want to rely on these parties to win office. Even in the cases in which Social Liberal parties have decided to support the right-wing bloc, it may still be attractive for Social Democratic parties to focus on the environment to drive a wedge into the unity of the right. When large, mainstream left-wing parties have to cooperate with Christian Democratic parties to win government power, they have fewer incentives to focus on the environment. The environment is not necessarily a problematic issue in terms of internal disagreement between Social Democratic and Christian Democratic parties, but it is less attractive than in coalitions with Green or Social Liberal parties.

The application of the issue incentive model to the environment can be summarized into a number of expectations that guide the empirical analysis. First, one should expect environmental performance to affect attention to the environment. Environmental degradation is relatively easy to measure and is often made visible through media coverage of focusing events. The fact that there are measurable solutions to environmental problems can further make it difficult to sustain attention to specific issues. Second, one should expect that attempts to push the environment towards the top of the party system agenda are most likely to come from the large, mainstream left-wing parties rather than from the large, mainstream right-wing parties. The reason is that the environmental issue is typically owned by the left-wing parties and can be interpreted as part of the left-wing attempt to regulate capitalism. However, whether or not the large, mainstream left-wing parties do in fact try to push the issue to the top of the party system agenda depends on their coalition incentives. The environment is an attractive issue for them if they try to win office with a left-wing coalition including Green parties and/or Social Liberal parties, but much less if they have to cooperate with Christian Democratic parties to win office.

THE PARTISAN POLITICS OF THE ENVIRONMENT

Before the empirical analysis, a review of the main findings from the existing literature on the party politics of the environment is in order. A central theme is the parties' influence on environmental policies or environmental outcomes (Jahn 2016; Knill et al. 2010; Leinaweaver and Thomson 2016). The general findings are that, though conditional on institutional factors, it matters which parties are in government. Party competition for the environment has, however, never been a central theme in the literature on the politics of the environment (see Cao et al. 2014).

The studies of party competition for the environment that do exist mainly focus on Green parties. They have received broad attention in terms of ideology (Talshir 2002), organizational structure (Richardson and Rootes 1995), and more recently performance, including government participation (Müller-Rommel and Poguntke 2002; van Haute 2016). Studies of party competition most often focus on how other parties react to the emergence and growing strength of Green parties (i.e. Abou-Chadi 2016; Meguid 2008; Spoon et al. 2014). Studies with a broader perspective on party competition, like Carter (2013), are rare, and only a few studies include countries where Green parties are weak or absent (though see Andersen 1990; Carter 2006). The literature thus shows that Green parties play a crucial role, but it remains unclear whether and to what extent party system attention to the environment depends on the emergence of a Green party. Finally, most studies typically fail to compare the environmental issue to other issues and to address the comparative differences in the saliency of the environment.

WHICH PARTIES PAY ATTENTION TO THE ENVIRONMENT?

Before one takes a detailed look at what drives party attention to the environment following the analytical strategy in Chapter 6, comments on the operational definition of the comparative agenda project are needed. The above definition of the issue of the environment includes policy questions relating to: air pollution, water pollution from groundwater to oceans, soil pollution, regulation of hazardous substances, regulation of waste, noise pollution, biodiversity and the protection of endangered species, and the protection of unique landscapes and natural reserves. Other issues with a major impact on the environment as well as many non-environmental policy questions were not included, e.g. agriculture and food production, energy policy, and general business regulations. In terms of the policy agenda codebook, this means all sub-issues in the main topic 700, the environment, are included. The same is the case for the subtopics 2100, 2101, and 2103 from the main topic 2100 (public lands and water management) concerning questions related to national parks, nature reserves of specific interest, and the use of natural resources. Subtopic 1902 concerning international agreements on resources and pollution, e.g. the Kyoto Protocol and the Paris Agreement on global warming, is also included. Finally, all countries except Sweden and the UK have a specific subtopic (407) under agriculture (400) concerning the environmental effects of agricultural production.[1] This subtopic is also included.[2]

Figure 9.1 illustrates general tendencies in attention to the environment.[3] In the early 1980s, the environment already received significant attention in Germany, Sweden, and the Netherlands, some attention in Belgium, and limited attention in Denmark, France, and the UK. From the mid-1980s, attention began to rise in all countries. Attention typically peaked in the early to mid-1990s and then declined somewhat. In Denmark, the rise continued until the 2000s, and then attention declined. However, the environment is still a significant issue on the party system agenda in all countries, and in particularly Sweden, environmental attention has also increased somewhat after the millennium.

That the environment is still important on the party system agenda is also illustrated in Table 9.1, which shows the percentage of parties that mention the environment in their manifestos across decades. In the 1980s, some parties—primarily in Denmark and France—did not pay attention to the environment. After that, almost all parties pay attention to it and still do, although attention has generally declined after the early 1990s.

In all seven countries, the environment has been a top issue in an election, also when one uses the more narrow definition of an issue receiving more

---

[1] See, https://www.comparativeagendas.net/pages/master-codebook.

[2] The CMP data set, which is mostly used to study party competition for the environment (e.g. Abou-Chadi 2016; Carter 2013; Spoon et al. 2014) typically records higher levels of party attention to the environment. A likely explanation is that the CMP scheme does not have specific categories for e.g. energy policy or agricultural policy. Therefore, statements related to these policy areas, for instance policy questions about animal rights or nuclear power (Green-Pedersen 2019) are coded as environmental because this is the best coding within the CMP coding scheme.

[3] The figure is identical to Figure 5.9.

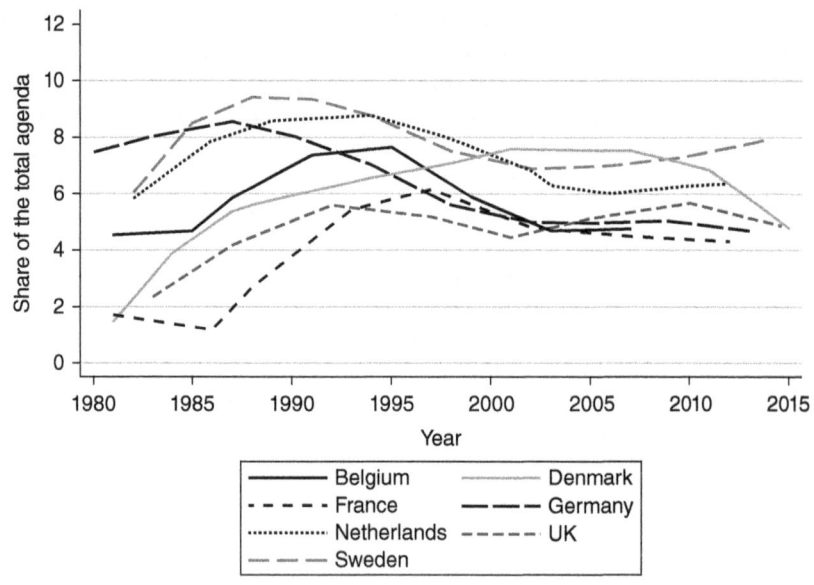

FIGURE 9.1 Party system attention to the environment in seven countries from 1980 and onwards

TABLE 9.1 *Percentage of parties mentioning the environment in their election programme across decades*

Decade	Percentage	N
1980s	88%	141
1990s	97%	131
2000s	95%	183

attention than the average plus one standard deviation. Based especially on the more restrictive criteria, most of these elections took place in the second half of the 1980s and first half of the 1990s or more recently in the Danish 2007 election and the Swedish 2010 election. In terms of cross-national differences, examples of the environment as a top issue are more numerous in Germany, Sweden, and the Netherlands (see Table 9.2).

Based on the above analysis, the general picture is that attention to the environment increased throughout the 1980s, peaked in the early 1990s, and then declined. The issue never disappeared, however, and in some countries, it rose again. The highest levels of attention to the environment were found in Germany, Sweden, and the Netherlands in the second half of the 1980s and early 1990s as well as in Denmark in the mid-2000s.

As stated in Chapter 6, the first step towards explaining these trends is a number of OLS models explaining party attention to the environment. Like

Up and Down with the Environment

TABLE 9.2 *The environment as a top issue*

Elections with the environment as a top five issue (place in brackets)	Party system attention	4.35+1sd	Party system attention > 4.35+1sd
Belgium 1991 (1)	9.1%	6.7%	X
Belgium 1995 (3)	7.5%	7.0%	X
Belgium 1999 (4)	6.5%	6.8%	
Denmark 1987 (4)	8.5%	9.9%	
Denmark 1994 (4)	7.5%	8.4%	
Denmark 2007 (2)	13.2%	9.2%	X
France 1993 (3)	8.6%	7.8%	X
Germany 1980 (5)	7.3%	8.1%	
Germany 1987 (5)	8.2%	7.7%	X
Germany 1990 (1)	10.5%	7.1%	X
Germany 1994 (5)	6.5%	6.8%	
The Netherlands 1986 (1)	7.7%	6.5%	X
The Netherlands 1989 (1)	10.2%	6.9%	X
The Netherlands 1994 (1)	9.5%	6.8%	X
The Netherlands 1998 (2)	8.4%	6.7%	X
The Netherlands 2002 (4)	6.8%	6.6%	X
The Netherlands 2010 (5)	6.5%	6.6%	
The Netherlands 2012 (4)	6.2%	6.5%	
The UK 1992 (3)	7.2%	6.8%	X
The UK 2010 (5)	6.5%	7.1%	
Sweden 1982 (5)	6.8%	10.0%	
Sweden 1985 (4)	6.8%	9.0%	
Sweden 1988 (1)	13.0%	7.7%	X
Sweden 1991 (3)	10.6%	7.8%	X
Sweden 1994 (5)	7.2%	9.2%	
Sweden 2010 (5)	8.0%	7.7%	X
Sweden 2014 (4)	7.7%	7.8%	

the models for the other issues, these models are country-fixed effects models (country dummies) that will focus the first part of the analysis on within country variation. The models are further estimated with robust standard errors and a lagged dependent variable. The lagged dependent is included in continuation of Chapter 3.[4] Parties are generally expected to show stability in their issue focus as it is partly driven by their expectations about other parties' issue focus. One therefore expects a positive impact of the lagged dependent variable. This is also a consistent finding in all the models in Table 9.3, which also show that Green parties pay substantially more attention

---

[4] To avoid losing too many cases when including the lagged dependent variable, data for the last election before 1980 are included when available. This is the case for Denmark, Sweden, Germany, and the Flemish parties in Belgium (see Chapter 4).

TABLE 9.3 *Regression estimates of party attention to the environment*

	Model 1	Model 2	Model 3
Attention to the environment t−1	0.35(0.06)***	0.33 (0.06)***	0.33(0.07)***
Green Party (l=1)	4.52(1.02)***	4.70(1.02)***	4.85(1.00)***
Social Liberal Party (=1)	1.93(0.95)*	1.86(0.93)*	1.88(0.92)*
Large, mainstream left-wing (=1)	0.47(0.45)	0.44(0.45)	0.42(0.45)
Environmental performance		0.12(0.04)**	0.10(0.04)**
Chernobyl disaster		1.61(0.61)**	2.41(0.62)***
Economic growth t−1		0.23(0.11)*	0.15(0.11)
Electoral strength of Green Party (t−1)			−0.30(0.08)***
Government (=1)	−0.36(0.40)	−0.36(0.39)	−0.31(0.38)
Constant	2.95(0.49)***	−7.37(3.14)*	−4.20(3.33)
N	398	398	398
Adj. R^2	0.34	0.37	0.38

Note: robust standard errors in parentheses. * $p < 0.05$, ** $p < 0.01$, *** $p < 0.001$. Estimated with country-fixed effects (country dummies not shown).

to the environment than other parties do (close to five percentage points).[5] As expected based on the discussion above, Social Liberal parties also pay considerably more attention to the environment (close to two percentage points).[6] Finally, the effect of a party being a large, mainstream left-wing party is not statistically significant.

To test the impact of problem information on party attention to the environment, the general environmental performance indicator developed by Jahn (2016: 132–9) is included.[7] It captures 'the state of the environment' based on a series of indicators relating to many aspects of the environment such as atmospheric emissions, waste, and water abstraction. It does not capture all aspects of the environment; for instance issues concerning recycling and pollution of rivers and lakes are measured separately. However, according

---

[5] Green party status is a dummy variable including the following parties: the German Greens (Die Grünen), the French Greens (Les Verts), the Dutch GreenLeft (GroenLinks), the Swedish Green Party (Miljøpartiet), and the Belgian Green Parties (Flemish Agalev and French Ecolo).

[6] These parties are the Dutch D66, the British Liberal Democrats, the German FDP, the Belgian Spirit Party (running in 2003), the Danish Social Liberals, and the Swedish People's Party. Having the Green variable dummy in the model implies that attention from Social Liberal parties is not compared to Green parties. If the Green party dummy is left out, the Social Liberal dummy is insignificant. This shows that Social Liberals pay more attention than all other parties but the Green parties.

[7] The measure is only available until 2012 (see <http://comparativepolitics.uni-greifswald.de/environment.html>). As for the countries where elections after 2012 are included (Germany 2013, Sweden 2014, Denmark 2015, and the UK 2015), values have been generated based on linear extrapolation.

Up and Down with the Environment 123

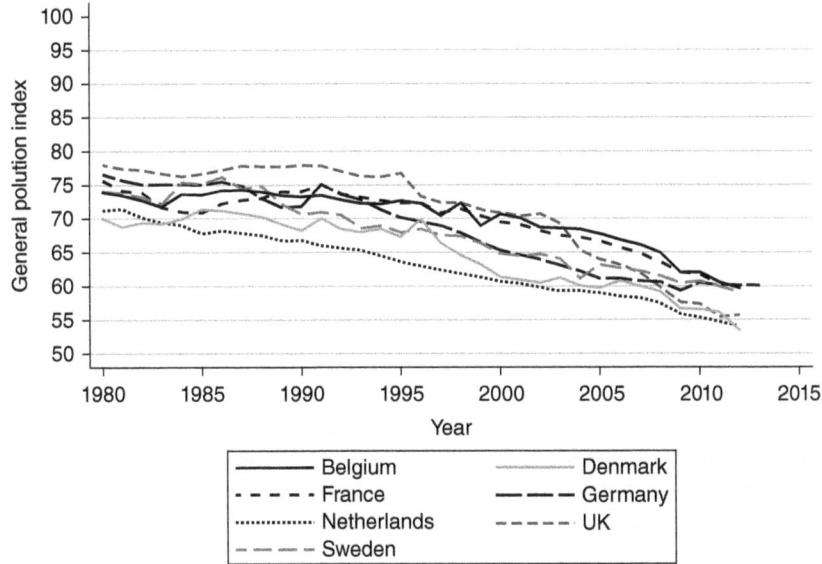

FIGURE 9.2 The development of the general environmental index (Jahn 2016)

to Jahn (2016: 135–6), the measure captures broad aspects of the environment and the majority of the most politically contested aspects. As further discussed by Jahn (2016: 136–56), the state of the environment has improved in most countries after 1980. Figure 9.2 also shows that the index has decreased substantially in all seven countries included in this book, which means that the general environmental performance has improved. However, except for Sweden and the Netherlands, this development began in the 1990s. In Sweden, the environmental improvement began in the late 1980s, and in the Netherlands, it has been continuous over the period. When environmental performance is included in Model 2, Table 9.3, it shows a positive and substantial effect. Thus, a higher score on the index, i.e. worse environmental performance, leads to more party attention to the environment. For instance, in Germany the index improved from 76.6 in 1980 to 60.1 in 2012, which equals a 1.65 percentage point reduction in party system attention based on Model 3.

As discussed above, focusing events are also expected to influence attention to the environment. The focusing event most often discussed with regard to environmental attention is the Chernobyl disaster in April 1986 because of its widespread environmental impact. Like models in other studies (e.g. Abou-Chadi 2016: 12), this book's models therefore include a dummy variable for whether the election was before or after the disaster. As in Abou-Chadi's study (2016), the results above also show that this event generated a substantial increase in party attention to the environment; 2.4 percentage points based on Model 3. Moreover, a measure of economic growth is included to capture the idea that an improving economy means more attention to non-economic issues (see also Spoon et al. 2014, 370–1).[8] This variable is not significant in the final model (Model 3).

Finally, Model 3 includes the lagged (i.e. the election before) electoral support for Green parties.[9] Based on the theoretical discussion above, one would expect the other parties to react to the growing strength of the Green parties. Model 3 shows that they do so negatively. When Green parties become stronger, party attention to the environment decreases.[10] A five percentage point increase in electoral support for Green parties decreases attention to the environment by 1.5 percentage points.[11] Thus, in line with Abou-Chadi (2016), the other parties decrease attention to the environment when Green parties increase their support. The entrance of a Green party into a party system thus has a contradictory effect on the party system agenda. When Green parties become part of the party system agenda, it has a 'mechanical' effect because Green parties focus much more on the environment than other parties do. The environment thus gets a strong voice, but once Green parties grow stronger, the other parties react with less attention to the environment.[12]

To sum up, the statistical analysis tests some of the theoretical expectations derived from the issue incentive model at the beginning of the chapter.[13] The relatively poor environmental performances of all the countries in the 1980s

---

[8] The measure of economic growth is taken from the OECD (2017b) and is lagged by one year.

[9] Besides the Green parties included in this data set, also the Danish Green Party running for election in 1987, 1988, and 1990 is included as well as the various Green parties in the UK.

[10] A variable that simply measures whether a Green party has gained representation in the election before is not significant when entered in Model 3 instead of lagged Green party support.

[11] Excluding Green parties from Model 3 yields substantially the same results. Such an analysis would be similar to the one by Spoon et al. (2014) which focuses on non-Green parties based on the CMP data set, but with a model without a lagged dependent variable and country dummies. Spoon et al. (2014) find a positive effect of increasing support for Green support on attention by other parties. Abou-Chadi (2016), however, based on the CMP data and a statistical model with a lagged dependent variable and party-fixed effects, also finds a negative effect of increasing electoral support for Green parties, but he only focuses on mainstream parties. If Model 3 is run with party-fixed effects, the effects of lagged electoral support for Green parties and for environmental performance, the Chernobyl disaster and the lagged economic growth are generally the same as in table 9.3.

[12] If Model 3 is run excluding the three cases in which a party spends more than 25% of its manifesto on the environment, the effects of Social Liberal parties become insignificant. One of the three cases is the Danish Social Liberals in 2007 spending 27.8% of its manifesto on the environment. The other two cases are the Swedish Greens in 1988, and the Flemish Greens (Agalev) in 1991.

[13] The results from a Tobit model, which takes the censuring of the dependent variable between 0 and 100 into account, are similar to the ones presented in Table 9.3.

coupled with focusing events like the Chernobyl disaster generated rising attention to the environment throughout the 1980s and into the 1990s. In some countries like Germany, Sweden, and the Netherlands, the environment was already a top issue in the early 1980s. The rest of the countries followed suit to various extents and with different timing until party system attention to the environment generally declined again in the 1990s. The statistical analysis suggests that this development is driven by clear improvements in environmental performance in all countries shown in Figure 9.2 (see also Jahn 2016). However, it is also clear that problem information does not account for the cross-national difference in attention to the environment. As can be seen from Figure 9.2, countries like Germany and Sweden with high levels of party system attention to the environment in the late 1980s and early 1990s did not stand out negatively in terms of overall environmental performs.

COALITION CONSIDERATIONS AND THE ENVIRONMENT

As argued in Chapter 6, the expectations of the role of coalition considerations are difficult to explore in a regression framework, and the remainder of the chapter will therefore focus on individual country cases like the previous chapters. This also makes it possible to account for some of the variation over time in party system attention to the environment that cannot be accounted for by problem information. The expectation is that coalition considerations can make the environment attractive to the large, mainstream left, i.e. Social Democratic parties, in two ways. First, the entrance of a Green party in parliament could make a left-wing bloc majority possible. Second, the environment would be an issue that would draw Social Liberal parties towards a left-wing rather than a right-wing government. Both dynamics can be found in the German case and thus offers an explanation for how the environment became a top issue in Germany in the late 1980s/early 1990s.

Before the 1980s, party competition and government formation in West Germany was centripetal. Until 1966, with the exception of 1957–61, the Christian Democrats cooperated with the Social Liberal FDP to win office. In 1966, the Social Democrats first entered government in a grand coalition with the Christian Democrats, and from 1969, they were in coalition with the FDP.

The SPD had issue ownership of the environment compared to a CDU-led government (Seeberg 2017), which has made the environment attractive to focus on for the SPD. In the late 1970s and early 1980s, the environment was also an attractive issue for the SPD from a coalition perspective. From that perspective, the key challenge for the SPD was to avoid that the FDP would defect to the Christian Democrats. Whereas macroeconomic policies were a

TABLE 9.4 *Party attention to the environment in Germany, 1980–2013*

	Greens	SPD	FDP	CDU/CSU	Party system agenda
1980		6.1%	11.2%	4.4%	7.3%
1983	6.3%	10.3%	14.7%	2.5%	8.5%
1987	10.5%	7.2%	6.6%	8.4%	8.2%
1990	21.5%	8.7%	8.9%	8.9%	10.5%
1994	10.5%	6.5%	9.1%	4.3%	6.5%
1998	7.9%	3.5%	6.3%	3.1%	4.8%
2002	12.1%	2.5%	2.9%	3.7%	4.3%
2005	8.5%	2.8%	4.1%	2.6%	4.5%
2009	9.0%	5.2%	6.7%	7.1%	6.3%
2013	5.8%	3.3%	4.6%	4.6%	4.3%

source of disagreement between the SPD and the FDP, the FDP itself, like other Social Liberal parties, also paid considerable attention to the environment as visible from Table 9.4. The environment was an issue that the FDP had been focused on since the 1970s (Malunat 1987: 35–7). A focus on the environment would thus unite the SPD/FDP coalition.

Eventually, the SPD/FDP coalition broke down in 1982 mainly due to disagreement over the macroeconomic policies (Lohneis 1983; Poguntke 1999). After this, winning back the FDP was not likely to be a successful strategy for the SPD. The environment was then a potential wedge issue for the SPD that could be used to generate internal disagreement in the CDU/CSU/FDP coalition, though the FDP began to focus less on the environment (see Table 9.4). From this perspective, it is not surprising that the SPD increased attention to the environment from 6.1 per cent in 1980 to 10.3 per cent in 1983 (see Table 9.4).

The German Greens began to emerge as a political party oriented towards parliamentary influence in the early 1980s (Jahn 1993: 183–4). Right after the FDP's change of side, the Greens made their breakthrough in the 1983 federal election. Potentially, this opened up the chance of bipolar competition (Mair 2001). However, to begin with, the Greens were not accepted as a coalition partner. The Green Party was divided between 'Fundis' and 'Realos', which made the Green Party a difficult coalition partner at the federal level (Bukow 2016: 114–16). However, at the Länder level, the Green Party entered the first coalition with the Social Democrats in Hesse in 1985 (Bukow 2016: 114–16). Thus, a left-wing coalition between the Social Democrats and the Greens at the federal level became increasingly realistic in the late 1980s, and a continued focus on the environment was important to pave the way for such a coalition.

The German reunification and the 1990s election was a setback for the Greens because of their approach to the reunification. However, the Green Party that emerged from the merger with the East German Greens made a left-wing coalition realistic (Bukow 2016: 116–24). From the early 1990s, German party politics became bipolar (Mair 2001). The broader Social Democratic strategy of building a left-wing majority finally paid off when the Red–Green coalition took office in 1998 (Rüdig 2002). Once government power had been achieved, the issue seemed less important to the Social Democrats.

The German 2005 election, in which the Red–Green coalition lost power, also changed the SPD's coalition incentives. The majority together with the Greens not only disappeared, it also seemed out of reach. The SPD was left with two options: to aim for a left-wing coalition that would include the Left Party or to enter a grand coalition with the Christian Democrats. Even in the two instances when the first option was feasible in terms of seats (2005 and 2013), the SPD opted for a grand coalition with the Christian Democrats. However, regardless of which option the SPD chose, the environment would not be a central issue as it was when the party was building a coalition with the Greens. With the more limited focus from the SPD, the issue has lost attention on the party system agenda, but it has clearly not disappeared as shown in Figure 9.1 and Table 9.4. In sum, the SPD's coalition incentives appear to have given the environment a prominent position on the German party system agenda in the 1980s and early 1990s.

The German case raises the question of whether the SPD's focus on the environment was in fact driven by coalition incentives or was part of an 'accommodative strategy' when the Greens entered the German parliament. From such a perspective, Social Democratic parties focus on the environmental issue to prevent the Greens from stealing left-wing voters (Meguid 2008: 22–40). To shed light on this question, one compares the German case with Belgium, which is the only other case with a Green party establishing itself in parliament in the early 1980s. In the Belgian case, the Green parties Ecolo from Wallonia and Agalev from Flanders entered parliament in the 1981 election (Bulens and Deschouwer 2002). However, coalition formation gave the large, mainstream left-wing parties, SPA in Flanders and PS in Wallonia, little hope of a left-wing majority including the Greens. Government participation required cooperation with the Christian Democratic parties, which had dominated Belgian governments since the Second World War as well as holding the position of Prime Minister in most periods. Thus, the large, mainstream left-wing parties in Belgium did not pay much attention to the issue in the 1980s.[14] As Figure 9.1 and Table 9.2 show, the environment did not become a top issue in Belgium as it did in Germany. In other words, when facing different

---

[14] The share of their manifestos spent on the environment in the 1980s is: SPA 3.8% (1981), 5.9% (1985), 2.1% (1987). PS 1.6% (1981), 3.4% (1985), 2.7% (1987). With the exception of SPA in 1985, these figures are below the average for all parties, i.e. the party system agenda.

coalition incentives, the Belgian Socialist parties reacted differently than their German counterpart to the Greens' entrance in parliament.[15] After the 1987 election in Belgium, the Socialist parties joined a Christian Democratic coalition.

As also visible in the German case, Social Democratic parties' coalition incentives in terms of the environment cannot be reduced to a question of the effects of Green parties on coalition patterns. The Swedish case is a clear example of this. In terms of coalition incentives, the Swedish Social Democrats governed uninterruptedly from the Second World War to 1976, based either on its own majority or with tacit support from the Communists. The only exception was the period from 1951 to 1957 when the Centre Party was included in the government. The period from 1976 to 1982 when the Swedish right governed and was able to gain power for more than one election term despite huge internal disagreement was thus a big change for the Swedish Social Democrats and made them search for new issues to focus on.

The environmental issue was obvious from a vote-seeking perspective,[16] and it could be used for 'wedge issue competition' against the right-wing bloc (see Table 9.5). The related issue of nuclear energy had already caused great internal disagreement within the Swedish centre-right governments from 1976 to 1982. It was central to the resignation of the centre-right government in

TABLE 9.5 *Party attention to the environment in Sweden, 1982–2014*

	Greens	SD	Centre Party	Conservatives	People's Party	Party system agenda
1982		11.8%	9.0%	3.0%	2.4%	6.8%
1985		11.5%	9.8%	3.4%	3.9%	6.8%
1988	25.8%	10.9%	15.9%	8.0%	11.6%	13.0%
1991	24.4%	18.1%	13.6%	3.0%	4.7%	10.6%
1994	15.2%	3.2%	11.8%	3.1%	3.4%	7.2%
1998	16.3%	2.3%	6.6%	4.6%	5.4%	7.4%
2002	13.3%	5.2%	6.1%	2.7%	7.6%	6.6%
2006	8.3%	4.0%	6.2%	6.2%	6.2%	6.1%
2010	12.5%	12.5%	7.8%	7.8%	7.8%	8.0%
2014	13.0%	4.2%	7.9%	7.9%	7.9%	7.7%

Note: Identical figures for parties in the 2006, 2010, and 2014 elections are due to common manifestos.

---

[15] The two countries are also similar in terms of Green support: 4.5% in Belgium in 1981 and 5.6% in Germany in 1983, and they faced similar levels of environmental problems in the early 1980s. In 1980, Belgium scored 74.0 on the general environmental performance index; Germany scored 76.6 (Jahn 2016: 137).

[16] In the 1979 election, the Swedish Social Democrats dedicated 9.8% of its party manifesto to the environment compared to 2.6% in 1976. The only other party to pay considerable attention to the issue in 1979 was the Centre Party with 7.6%.

1978 when the Centre Party ended up leaving the cabinet. The party had opted for a much Greener profile than the other non-socialist parties. More focus on the environment was thus a way for the Swedish Social Democrats to challenge the internal cohesion of the Swedish right (Vedung 1988: 94–101). The focus on the environment continued after the Social Democrats had regained power, especially in the period surrounding the 1988 election. The Green Party had been quite far from gaining parliamentary representation in the 1982 and 1985 elections but had done well in opinion polls before the election. The Chernobyl disaster, among other things, had drawn attention to the environment (Bennulf and Holmberg 1990). After the 1994 election, the Greens established themselves permanently in the Swedish parliament (Bennulf 1994). As for the Swedish Social Democrats, sustaining the environment as an important issue on the party system agenda thus became important to ensure that the Greens would become an integrated part of the left-wing bloc that would secure Social Democratic government power (cf. Bolin 2016).

Denmark is another case where coalition incentives made the environment an attractive issue for the large, mainstream left-wing party, but without a Green party in parliament. The environment received very little party attention in the early 1980s, but the issue grew on the party system agenda in the mid-1980s. This development was part of the Danish Social Democrats' opposition strategy after they lost government power in 1982. The centre-right government that took office in 1982 was based on the support of all non-socialist parties, including the Social Liberals and the Christian Democrats which both had a pronounced pro-environmental profile. As for the Social Democrats in opposition, the environment was a perfect wedge issue in order to challenge the internal cohesion of the right-wing bloc. The Social Democrats even managed to persuade the Social Liberals to support environmental policy measures in parliament against the will of the minority government (Andersen 1990; Green-Pedersen 2012: 92–101).

When the Social Democrats regained power in 1993 with the Social Liberals, the Social Democrats were able to build a strong Green profile, not least by holding the Ministry of Environmental Policy (Green-Pedersen 2012: 92–101). Thus, when the party found itself back in opposition after the 2001 election, the environment was one of the most attractive issues for the Social Democrats and their support parties, the Socialist People's Party and the Social Liberals, in terms of challenging the right-wing government. This was especially clear in the 2007 election when the environment was a top issue (see Table 9.2). This strong focus on the environment came after a period when the Social Liberals had threatened to leave the left-wing bloc (Bille 2007). The Social Democrats' opposition strategy put pressure on the government not only to address the environmental issue but also to pass a series of pro-environmental policy measures (Seeberg 2016).

Germany, Sweden, and Denmark are all cases where Social Democratic parties have driven the environment to the top of the party system agenda. Coalition incentives have played a crucial role in making the issue attractive for Social Democratic parties in all three countries. In Germany, the environment was first attractive in terms of keeping the FDP on the Social Democratic side, and later on, it became attractive to build a coalition with the Greens. In Denmark and Sweden, the environment was attractive as a wedge issue to challenge environmentally friendly Social Liberal/Centre parties' support for the right-wing bloc. Furthermore, in Sweden, focusing on the environment was attractive as a strategy to keep the Green Party as part of the left-wing bloc after the party had established itself in parliament.

As argued above, in the cases in which winning government power requires cooperation with less pro-environmental Christian Democratic or right-wing parties, large, mainstream left-wing parties, i.e. the Social Democrats, will not find the environment particularly attractive to focus on. The Belgian case is discussed above, and another example is the Netherlands. As discussed in Chapter 7, Dutch coalition building takes place around the centre. Either coalitions have been with the Christian Democrats, the CDA, cooperating to the right with the VVD or to the left with the PvdA, or the PvdA has cooperated across the centre with the VVD. From that perspective, it is not surprising that the PvdA has not been central in pushing the environment towards the top of the party system agenda unlike its sister parties in Sweden and Germany (see Table 9.6).

The PvdA was, however, active on the environment in the early 1970s, especially in its joint electoral programme in 1972 with the D66 and the PPR (van der Brug 2000: 188–90).[17] This was part of a 'polarization strategy

TABLE 9.6 *Party attention to the environment in the Netherlands, 1982–2012*

	GreenLeft	PvdA	D66	CDA	VVD	Party system agenda
1982		2.7%	6.8%	8.4%	3.4%	6.0%
1986		3.7%	10.1%	9.1%	8.6%	7.7%
1989	11.2%	7.9%	17.3%	12.4%	12.6%	10.2%
1994	15.3%	8.6%	12.4%	13.4%	6.7%	9.5%
1998	13.0%	9.3%	7.1%	8.7%	4.8%	8.5%
2002	8.7%	8.2%	7.9%	4.7%	8.6%	6.8%
2003	7.1%	4.9%	6.8%	0.0%	5.8%	4.7%
2006	6.0%	2.8%	6.2%	4.4%	2.8%	6.0%
2010	8.0%	3.9%	5.2%	3.6%	4.3%	6.5%
2012	9.1%	3.8%	7.6%	2.6%	3.4%	6.2%

[17] The PPR was a Christian left-wing party with a strong focus on the environment, and the party merged into the GreenLeft in 1989.

of the Dutch Social Democrats in the early 1970s with the aim of building a left-wing majority in Dutch politics' (Tromp 1989). However, the strategy failed, and during the 1980s, the PvdA focused on making itself an attractive coalition partner for the Christian Democrats. In this strategy, the environment was not particularly attractive. The strategy succeeded when the PvdA re-entered government with the CDA in 1989 (Green-Pedersen and van Kersbergen 2002). Even after the establishment of the GreenLeft in the Dutch parliament in 1989, seeking a left-wing majority has remained an unrealistic strategy for winning government power, and the PvdA has not focused particularly on the environment.

Despite the PvdA's strategy in the 1980s, the environment made it to the top of the party system agenda in the Netherlands. As Tables 9.2 and 9.6 show, it was a top issue on the Dutch party system agenda from the mid-1980s to the end of the 1990s and has remained an important issue ever since. Table 9.6 clearly shows that the parties driving this development were the Social Liberal D66 and the two parties governing the Netherlands from 1982 to 1989, the CDA and the VVD. As discussed above, Social Liberal parties like the D66 have an electoral interest in the environment, but what is more surprising is the strong focus on the issue in the CDA and the VVD.

In France and the UK, the two final cases, the large, mainstream left-wing party has rarely had coalition incentives to focus on the environment due to the electoral systems. In France, the French Greens have found it difficult to establish themselves in the parliament and to play a role as a coalition partner. The party's government participation from 1997 to 2002 was exceptional from this perspective (Boy 2002). Not until 1993 did the French Socialist Party pay any attention to the issue (5.5 per cent) but has otherwise not focused much on it (Boy 2002: 64–5). Finally, in the UK, the electoral system has also largely prohibited a Green party from entering parliament and playing a role as coalition partner for the Labour Party, and Labour has not shown great interest in the issue (Carter 2006). The Liberal Democrats have had some focus on the issue, and in some cases, they were even joined by the Conservatives (Carter 2009).

The role of coalition considerations for large, mainstream left-wing parties, i.e. Social Democratic parties, is clear across all cases. In most cases in which the environment becomes a top issue, it has been attractive for Social Democratic parties from a coalition perspective. There are typically two situations when coalition incentives make the environment attractive. One is if when a Social Democratic party is seeking to win government power with Green parties. This has been the case in Germany as well as in Sweden once the Green Party had established itself in the party system in the 1990s. The other is when Social Democratic parties are trying to draw environmentally friendly Social Liberal/Centre parties away from the right-wing bloc. Here the environment is an attractive wedge issue. Sweden and Denmark in the 1980s are the clearest examples of this.

The fact that Social Democratic parties have rarely tried to push the issue towards the top of the party system agenda without coalition considerations pointing in that direction also shows how important these considerations are. In France and the UK where the electoral systems limit the importance of coalition considerations, the large, mainstream left-wing parties have not focused particularly on the environment, and it has rarely made it to the top of the party system agenda. From this perspective, the findings in Table 9.3 that large, mainstream left-wing parties do not in general pay significantly more attention to the environment are not surprising. They only do so when coalition considerations point in that direction.

One explanation why Social Democratic parties do not automatically rush towards the issue is ideological. Andersen (1990) and Talshir (2002) show that a 'Greening' of the Social Democratic parties is not unproblematic for them. While they have no problem with focusing on regulating capitalism, a more radical Green agenda of anti-growth measures is not necessarily in line with a Social Democratic focus on job creation, for instance. While the environment is probably attractive from an electoral perspective, there are limits to how much Social Democratic parties will focus on the issue based on electoral incentives. Other electorally attractive issues like social policies include less ideological tension for Social Democratic parties.

WHAT DRIVES ATTENTION TO THE ENVIRONMENT?

The analyses presented above give rise to a number of conclusions on the drivers of party attention to the environment. In terms of the issue incentive model, the importance of issue characteristics and especially problem information is clear when one looks at the over-time pattern of attention to the environment. During the 1980s, all countries struggled with environmental performance, and focusing events like the Chernobyl disaster drew attention to the issue. The conditions were perfect for parties that wanted to draw attention to the environment, and in the second half of the 1980s and the beginning of the 1990s, party system attention to the environment peaked in almost all countries. The improvement of the state of the environment in all countries from the 1990s has generated less attractive conditions for parties wanting to draw attention to the environment, and party system attention has declined, but far from disappeared.

The importance of studying the incentives of the large, mainstream left-wing parties is also clear. These parties do not automatically focus on the issue, but coalition considerations can make it attractive, and then they are able to push it towards the top of the party system agenda. Thus, the analysis of the environment highlighted the central role of coalition considerations. Furthermore, it seems to matter whether these parties find themselves in opposition or in government. Losing power made Social Democratic parties consider which issues to focus on in order to win back government power. In Germany and Denmark after 1982 and in Sweden from 1976 to 1982, the environment was an attractive issue to choose from both a coalition and an electoral perspective.

In terms of the role of Green parties, Table 9.3 shows that the effect of increasing Green party strength is actually negative. Other parties seem to leave the issue to Green parties when it becomes strong. This is in line with Abou-Chadi's (2016) findings, whereas Spoon et al. (2014) found the opposite effect. Still, the discussion of the individual countries indicated that one should be cautious about very general conclusions on how the existing party system and especially large, mainstream parties respond to the growth of Green parties for two reasons. First, Green parties established themselves in very different contexts in terms of party system attention to the environment. In the Netherlands and Sweden, Green parties established themselves at a time when the environment had already been a top issue on the party system agenda for years, and their entrance did not change the coalition incentives towards the environment for the large, mainstream left-wing parties. Second, the coalition incentives that their entrance generated for large, mainstream left-wing parties vary. In Germany and Belgium, Green parties established themselves when the environment was new on the party system agenda, but generated varying coalition incentives.

In line with this, the emergence of a strong Green party does not seem a necessary condition for the environment to move to the top of the party system agenda. The issue was already a top issue in Sweden and the Netherlands before Green parties were represented in parliament, and the issue has reached the top of the party system agenda in Denmark without a Green party. However, the German case shows how the emergence of a strong Green party was sufficient for the issue to move to the top of the party system agenda because it made the environment a highly attractive issue for Social Democrats from a coalition perspective. Moreover, other parties, especially Social Liberal parties, have also acted as issue entrepreneurs before Green parties established themselves, e.g. in Sweden and Denmark.

In sum, the issue incentive model is able to explain many of the patterns of attention to the environment identified above like the overall time pattern and the breakthrough of attention in Germany and Sweden in the 1980s. However, the Dutch case is puzzling. The environment was a top issue in Dutch politics from the mid-1980s and until the end of the 1990s. In this period, the coalition considerations of the Dutch Labour Party did not point in the direction of focusing on the environment, and the party did not focus on the issue. In addition, the state of the Dutch environment was not bad from a comparative perspective, and the Greens were not able to establish themselves in parliament until 1989. What is puzzling is the extent to which the governing parties, the CDA and the VVD, embraced the issue and turned it into a top issue. Likewise, the peak of environmental attention in Belgium in the 1990s is clearly not the result of a push from the large, mainstream left but rather that of a number of parties taking up the issue. The valence of the environmental issue might play a role here (cf. Abou-Chadi 2016). Thus, in the cases in which the large, mainstream left-wing parties have not really taken up the issue or left it again, like in the Netherlands, large, mainstream right-wing parties might, to some extent, try to take advantage of the issue.

10
Attention to Education in the Post-Industrial Society

As with the other issues chosen for detailed analysis, there are both theoretical and empirical reasons for analysing education. In terms of the issue incentive model, education is attractive because of its issue characteristics that are distinct from the three issues analysed so far. The fact that a large part of the population is in close contact with the educational system implies that it is an obtrusive issue with a broad scope. It is also a valence issue. Nobody is against education. Furthermore, decentralization of the provision of educational services means that national policymakers control the actual provision of educational policy to varying degrees. Education also differs from the three other policy issues studied so far because niche parties with regard to education do not exist. Though some parties might focus more on education than others do, no party has education as its *raison d'être*.

From an empirical perspective, educational policies have gained increased political and scholarly interest. Politically, the idea of a 'knowledge society' has generated increased attention to education (see Figure 5.15), and the increased political attention has generated increased scholarly attention (cf. Busemeyer and Trampusch 2011; Jakobi 2011; Moe and Wiborg 2017).

EDUCATION AS A POLICY AREA

Studies of education (e.g. Ansell 2010; Busemeyer 2015) rarely devote much space to defining education, most likely because education is relatively straightforward to define. Education primarily includes all policy questions relating to primary and secondary education as well as higher education and vocational training. The major question of delimitation is with regard to the active labour market policy, which also often has a large element of education. Here, the major line of delimitation is whether a programme is set up specifically to train either unemployed or people already employed or as an educational offer to typically younger people. The former cases belong to the labour market policy; the latter are part of the policy area of education. Questions about research are sometimes, but not always, closely related to higher education and are therefore not included in education. However, universities are typically viewed as an educational policy rather than research institutions, and therefore they are typically included in education policy.

THE ISSUE INCENTIVES OF EDUCATION

The first step in the analysis is to apply the issue incentive model to education, i.e. a discussion of how the three factors that shape the incentives of large, mainstream parties, namely issue characteristics, issue ownership, and coalition incentives, apply to education.

In terms of issue characteristics, four aspects relating to the interplay between problem information and problem characteristics are worth highlighting. The first one is the broad scope of people for whom education is relevant. Primary education is or has been relevant to everyone in society, either in the form of government funded schools or regulation of privately funded schools. The majority of citizens also enter either higher education or vocational training. Education is not only relevant to almost everyone, it is also crucial for people's job opportunities. Thus, education is not only broad in scope, it is also 'obtrusive', i.e. an issue with which ordinary citizens have regular and important experience (Soroka 2002). This implies that people have relevant problem information about education on a personal level.

The second aspect is that education is a 'valence' issue. No one is really against education, and for large, mainstream parties that want to appeal broadly to the electorate, education is an attractive policy issue. In Ansell's words (2010: 136): 'Promising to support education is an archetypical crowd-pleaser'.

The third relevant problem characteristic is that education to some extent is a 'wicked' problem. Everyone agrees that students should learn as much as possible, but it is often debated what is most important for students to learn, i.e. how should the acquisition of social skills be valued in comparison with mathematical and reading skills? Furthermore, education is an area with relatively limited understanding of the causal processes involved. Research on education and teaching is of course abundant and offers numerous insights into learning and teaching dynamics. However, new solutions and technological advances are rare compared to new wastewater cleaning methods or new medication. This implies that there are few generally accepted indicators of educational quality. Hence, it is much less obvious what relevant problem information is with regard to education than with regard to unemployment or environmental performance. Additionally, education being an obtrusive issue also means that personal experience with the system has a major effect on problem perceptions.

The fourth problem characteristic of education is that education is labour intensive. Therefore, the provision of educational services is typically decentralized to municipalities, regions, or federal states. Depending on how the education system is decentralized, national politicians only partially have responsibility or control over educational provision. This is, ceteris paribus, likely to imply less attention to education from large, mainstream parties.

To sum up, education has a number of problem characteristics that generally make it attractive for large, mainstream parties to focus on. It is both an obtrusive and a valence issue that affects a large part of the population in a significant way. Furthermore, education as a policy problem is never solved, and indicators of educational performance are likely to be contested to the extent that they exist. Attention to education is therefore not closely linked to 'objective indicators'. Finally, actual provision of education is often decentralized, which is likely to reduce attention from national political parties, depending on the exact structure of decentralization.

The second factor that Chapter 2 argues will shape the vote and office incentives of large, mainstream parties is issue ownership. Seeberg (2017: 482–7) reports a tendency towards left-wing issue ownership, but it is not very pronounced, and it has declined over time. As far as cross-national variation goes, right-wing issue ownership is the general tendency in France, and one cannot formulate a cross-national expectation about whether large, mainstream parties from the left or the right are most likely to focus on education. Issue ownership has to be discussed at the level of individual countries.

The third factor, coalition considerations, is determined by how education fits the left–right dimension. Even though education is argued to be a valence issue in the sense that all political parties support education, political parties do not have similar positions on education. For instance, financial support for private schools is likely to divide political parties on the traditional left–right conflict dimension (Gingrich 2011: 131–74). Furthermore, there are no niche parties on education, i.e. parties whose *raison d'être* is education. Coalition considerations for large, mainstream parties thus generally follow the left–right divide, and focusing on education does not offer them any particular incentives to use education as a wedge issue against competitors or as a means to build a coalition with niche parties.

To sum up, in terms of the issue incentive model, issue characteristics are the most decisive factor in terms of shaping the incentives of large, mainstream parties with regard to education. The fact that the issue is an obtrusive valence issue provides strong incentives for large, mainstream parties on both sides to focus on education. In some cases, issue ownership may make education more attractive for the large, mainstream left-wing parties, but this is not expected to be the case for all countries. Coalition considerations are not expected to be central to party attention to education as party positions will generally follow the left–right scale. Though problem indicators also exist with regard to education, they are expected to be much more politically contested. This implies that attention to education is not expected to be closely linked to any specific indicator. This does not mean that problem indicators cannot play an important role, but they are not automatically accepted as important problem indicators in the same way as for instance unemployment figures.

THE PARTISAN POLITICS OF EDUCATION

In terms of the scholarly literature on the party politics of education, this literature has primarily developed from the large body of literature on welfare state development and has taken over the 'does politics matter?' question that has been central to welfare state research. A dominant question in studies of the party politics of education has thus been whether left-wing governments spend more on education than right-wing governments (Busemeyer and Trampusch 2011: 416–18). The findings are mixed. Some studies point in this direction (Busemeyer 2007, 2009; Iversen and Stephens 2008), some find no partisan effects (Garritzmann and Seng 2016; Jensen 2011c), and some find the opposite effect (Ansell 2010; Rauh et al. 2011).

The mixed findings on partisan effects on spending have more recently generated a number of studies on the party politics of education (Ansell 2010: 136–43; Busemeyer et al. 2013; Jakobi 2011; Kraft 2017).[1] This literature provides four central findings. First, Ansell (2010: 138–9) and Busemeyer et al. (2013: 538) find that mainstream parties pay more attention to education than non-mainstream parties do. Second, Jakobi (2011: 198–202) finds an increase in party attention to education over time (cf. also Busemeyer et al.

---

[1] All these studies are based on the CMP data set and item 506 in the coding system which captures mention of education expansion, and sometimes item 507 which captures mention of education limitation. However, as Busemeyer et al. (2013: 532–3) point out, item 507 is hardly ever used, i.e. parties hardly ever mention education limitation. This is what one should expect given that education is a valence issue. Consequently, studies of party preferences for education measured via the CMP coding scheme are in reality studies of party attention to education. This is not to say that there are no party conflicts on education, as for instance with regard to government funded vs. privately funded schools (Gingrich 2011: 131–74). However, the CMP categories of positive and negative mention of education are much too broad to capture the ideological differences.

2013) in response to the emergence of the 'knowledge society' where education becomes increasingly important for career opportunities and many other outcomes in life (cf. also Moe and Wiborg 2017). Third, Busemeyer et al. (2013: 536–9) point to cases in which the mainstream left focuses more on education than the mainstream right as well as cases in which Social Liberal parties have more focus on education than other parties. Fourth, Kraft (2017; see also Busemeyer 2009) finds that education as an investment in the future is an important issue characteristic in terms of how parties approach the issue. According to Kraft (2017), 'core parties', i.e. parties that have typically dominated government formation, focus on education—and other investment policies that provide long-term benefits for the economy—because they expect to govern in the future.

This recent literature on the partisan politics of education complements the expectation derived from the issue incentive model in many ways. The problem characteristics of education make it an attractive issue to focus on for large, mainstream parties. Furthermore, in some cases, Social Democratic parties have issue ownership of the issue, but not in all cases. Finally, Social Liberal parties generally focus more on education than other parties do.

WHICH PARTIES PAY ATTENTION TO EDUCATION?

Before one takes a detailed look at what drives party attention to education, a few words about the operational definition in the CAP project are needed. The above definition of the issue of education includes policy questions relating to primary and secondary education as well as higher education and vocational training. What is not included are policy measures directly related to active labour market policy and research policy.

The CAP coding system has a major topic 6 concerning education, including the subcategories 601 (higher education), 602 (primary and secondary education), 603 (education of underprivileged students), 604 (vocational training), 606 (special education for youth with learning disabilities and the handicapped), 607 (libraries and improvement of the level of education), 698 (educational research), 600 (general), and 699 (others).[2] There are few

---

[2] Compared to the CMP data set, which has typically been used to study party competition for education, as discussed in footnote 1, Green-Pedersen (2019) shows how the CAP data typically report higher levels of attention to education. The most likely explanation is that the CMP coding scheme is developed to capture party ideology and therefore has categories related to for instance underprivileged groups like students or equality in which statements about educational policy will sometimes be coded.

cross-national differences in the coding scheme. France and Belgium have generated a special subcategory 608 for private schools, which is also included in the following.[3]

Figure 10.1 illustrates a number of general tendencies with regard to party system attention to education.[4] As noticed in Chapter 5, and in line with Jakobi's (2011) findings based on the CMP data set, party system attention to education has generally increased cross-nationally. Table 10.1 points in the same direction. Even though most parties already mentioned education in the 1980s, the number has increased even further.

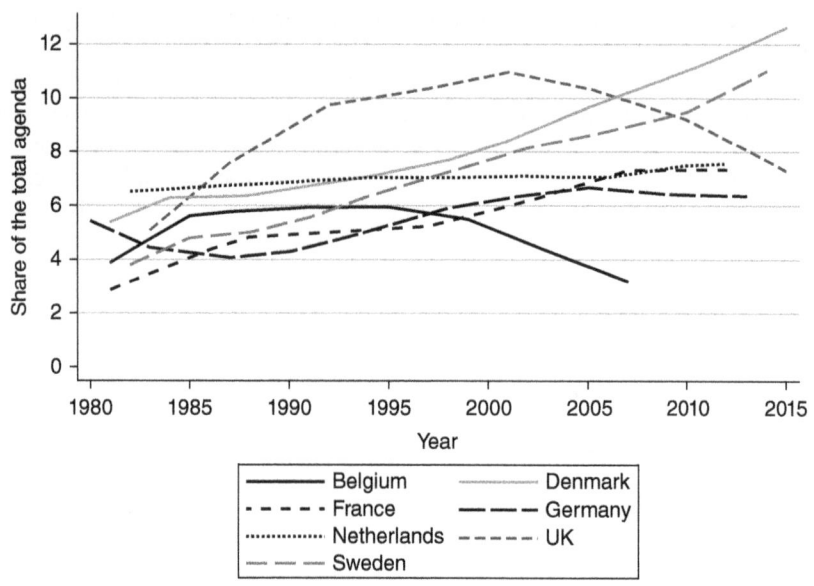

FIGURE 10.1 Party system attention to education in seven countries from 1980 and onwards

TABLE 10.1 *Percentage of parties mentioning education in their election programme across decades*

Decade	Percentage	N
1980s	91%	141
1990s	95%	131
2000s	95%	183

[3] Some countries (the Netherlands, the UK, and Germany) originally had subcategories related to culture and sports within the 600 main-topic. These are not included in education in the following.
[4] The figure is identical to Figure 5.15.

Figure 10.1 also shows that a considerable cross-national variation has emerged over time. In Denmark, Sweden, and the UK, increasing party system attention to education has been most pronounced, though declining again in the UK. France has seen the same tendency, but less pronounced. The Netherlands has the highest level of party system attention to education in the beginning of the period, but this has only increased marginally. Germany has also seen a stable level of party system attention to education, but generally at a lower level than in the Netherlands. Finally, party system attention to education in Belgium has declined since the late 1980s.

Table 10.2 shows when education became a top issue, and the picture is similar to Figure 10.1. In Denmark, Sweden, the Netherlands and the UK, education has been a top issue on a stable basis. In France and Germany, education has been a top issue in some of the more recent elections; in Belgium only in the 1987 election. The general increase in attention to education on the party system agenda over time is also visible from Table 10.2. Of the 37 examples with education as a top five issue, 21 are from the 2000s, and only 16 from the first two decades included in the analysis.

As laid out in Chapter 6, the first step towards explaining the trends in party system attention to individual issues is a number of OLS models explaining party attention to education. As with the other issues, these models are country-fixed effects models (country dummies) in order to focus the first part of the analysis on within country dynamics. The models are further estimated with robust standard errors and a lagged dependent variable. As with the models for the other issues, the lagged dependent is included in continuation of Chapter 3. Parties are generally expected to show stability in their issue focus as it is partly driven by their expectations of which issue other parties will pay attention to. One therefore expects a positive impact of the lagged dependent variable, which is also a clear result from both models in Table 10.3.[5]

The discussion above indicates that large, mainstream parties would pay more attention to the issue than other parties do.[6] Both models also find a positive effect of a party being a large, mainstream party, and in Model 2, the effect borders statistical significance. Furthermore, if Model 2 is run excluding the three cases when a party spends more than 25 per cent of its manifesto on education, the effect of large, mainstream party status is statistically

---

[5] To avoid losing too many cases when including the lagged dependent variable, data on the last election before 1980 are included when available. This is the case for Denmark, Sweden, Germany, and the Flemish parties in Belgium (see Chapter 4).

[6] The common programmes of the Swedish right (the Alliance) in 2006, 2010, and 2014, and the Swedish left (the Left Alliance) in 2010 are a mixture of large, mainstream parties and other parties and are therefore excluded from the analysis. Therefore, N in Table 10.3 is smaller than in the similar tables in the other issue chapters.

TABLE 10.2 *Education as a top issue*

Elections with education as a top five issue (place in brackets)	Party system attention	4.35+1sd	Party system attention > 4.35+1sd
Belgium 1987 (5)	6.6%	7.7%	
Denmark 1981 (5)	5.4%	10.3%	
Denmark 1987 (5)	6.8%	9.9%	
Denmark 1988 (5)	9.0%	9.9%	
Denmark 1994 (5)	6.1%	8.4%	
Denmark 1998 (4)	8.7%	8.2%	X
Denmark 2001 (4)	7.8%	8.2%	
Denmark 2005 (3)	11.4%	9.0%	X
Denmark 2007 (5)	6.9%	9.2%	
Denmark 2011 (2)	13.6%	8.9%	X
Denmark 2015 (2)	11.7%	8.6%	X
France 2007 (2)	8.0%	6.8%	X
France 2012 (3)	7.4%	7.7%	
Germany 2002 (3)	8.3%	7.0%	X
Germany 2009 (4)	6.8%	7.5%	
The Netherlands 1982 (5)	6.5%	7.2%	
The Netherlands 1986 (4)	6.9%	6.5%	X
The Netherlands 1989 (4)	6.8%	6.9%	
The Netherlands 1994 (4)	6.6%	6.8%	
The Netherlands 1998 (3)	7.9%	6.8%	
The Netherlands 2002 (1)	8.0%	6.6%	X
The Netherlands 2006 (3)	7.6%	6.7%	X
The Netherlands 2010 (2)	7.3%	6.6%	X
The Netherlands 2012 (2)	7.7%	6.5%	X
The UK 1987 (3)	8.4%	7.2%	X
The UK 1992 (2)	9.4%	6.8%	X
The UK 1997 (1)	11.7%	7.2%	X
The UK 2001 (3)	9.2%	7.2%	X
The UK 2005 (1)	12.6%	7.6%	X
The UK 2010 (2)	8.4%	7.1%	X
The UK 2015 (3)	7.3%	6.5%	X
Sweden 1985 (5)	6.4%	9.0%	
Sweden 1998(2)	9.3%	8.7%	X
Sweden 2002 (4)	8.3%	7.7%	X
Sweden 2006 (5)	7.8%	7.7%	X
Sweden 2010 (3)	9.2%	7.7%	X
Sweden 2014 (3)	11.1%	7.8%	X

significant.[7] Thus, the analysis of party attention provides some support for the expectation that large, mainstream parties pay more attention to education than other parties do.

[7] If Model 2 is run as a Tobit model to take the censoring of the dependent variable between 0 and 100% into account, the effect of large, mainstream party status is also statistically significant. All other results stay the same.

TABLE 10.3 *Regression estimates of party attention to education from 1980 and onwards*

	Model 1	Model 2
Attention to education t−1	0.36 (0.1)**	0.33(0.09)***
Social liberal party (=1)	2.80 (1.21)*	3.15(1.17)**
Large, mainstream party (=1)	0.91(0.56)	1.03(0.55)
Deindustrialization		0.40(0.12)**
Economic growth (lagged)		0.27(0.11)*
Government (=1)	−0.45(0.51)	−0.30(0.49)
Constant	2.87(0.59)***	−30.6(9.99)**
N	396	396
Adj. R^2	0.20	0.24

Note: robust standard errors in parentheses. * $p < 0.05$, ** $p < 0.01$, *** $p < 0.001$. Estimated with country-fixed effects (country dummies not shown). The observations of both the right-wing and the left-wing alliances in Sweden are not included as they contain other parties than large, mainstream parties.

Furthermore, the suggestion that Social Liberal parties are particularly focused on education (Busemeyer et al. 2013: 536) clearly finds support in Table 10.3. Based on Model 2, the effect of a party being social liberal is an increase in attention to education of about three percentage points, i.e. a much stronger effect than that of being a large, mainstream party.[8] Finally, like with the other issues, there is no effect of a party being in government.

Jakobi (2011) pointed to the increased importance of the 'knowledge economy' as an explanation for the general increase in party attention to education. The idea of a knowledge economy is not easy to measure by a single variable, and Jakobi does not provide a simple operationalization. However, studies like Iversen and Stephens (2008) and Jensen (2011b) focus on the increased importance of education or human capital for labour market outcomes and empirically use a measure of 'deindustrialization' to capture this. Jensen (2011b) shows how deindustrialization leads to more educational spending.[9] As Table 10.3 shows, deindustrialization has a positive impact on party attention to education (see also Green-Pedersen and Jensen 2019).[10]

---

[8] If the large, mainstream party dummy variable is replaced in Model 2 with either a dummy variable for a party being large, mainstream left or a dummy variable for a party being large, mainstream right (both with and without Christian Democratic parties), both are clearly insignificant. A dummy variable for Green party status added to Model 2 is also insignificant.

[9] More precisely, deindustrialization is measured by an index calculated as 100 minus the sum of manufacturing and agricultural employment as a percentage of the working-age population (Jensen 2011c: 419). Data come from OECD (2017c). Data are not available after 2013. Values for the election years after 2013 (Sweden 2014, Denmark 2015, the UK 2015) are generated by linear extrapolation.

[10] An interaction effect between deindustrialization and a party being a large, mainstream party was tested to see whether large, mainstream parties react more strongly to the growth of the 'knowledge society' than other parties. This effect was not statistically significant.

Finally, economic growth, lagged one year, has a positive impact on attention to education. When the economy is doing well, parties focus more on education.[11]

However, this analysis still leaves aside the questions about comparative variation in party system attention to education. As discussed above, the most pronounced cross-national differences are the substantial increase in party system attention to education in the UK, Sweden, and Denmark as well as the declining level of attention in Belgium since the late 1980s. A closer look at these cases will also allow one to go into the behaviour of large, mainstream parties with regard to education, including whether the large, mainstream left-wing parties in some cases can take advantage of issue ownership. Furthermore, even though there are no generally accepted statistics on 'problem development' on education, problem information might still play an important role in certain cases, and this can also be investigated through the case studies.

THE POLITICS OF PRIMARY SCHOOLS

Beginning with the Danish case, data on issue ownership of education are available from 1998 and onwards (Stubager et al. 2016: 17).[12] Generally, it is a close race with the right-wing bloc having issue ownership until 2005 when the left-wing bloc took over. In other words, neither side has a greater incentive to focus on education based on issue ownership. Furthermore, educational policy, especially with regard to primary schools, is traditionally decided in broad agreements including the large, mainstream parties on both sides (Christensen 2000).

As Tables 10.4 and 10.2 show, education has always been a central issue on the party system agenda in Denmark. The Social Liberals have focused most on the issue, and the party is known to have had close contact with the Danish Union of Teachers (Jensen 2011b: 150). However, from the 1998 election and onwards, the large, mainstream parties on the left, the Social Democrats, and the right, the Liberals, both began to focus more on the issue. This has pushed education higher on the party system agenda, most clearly in the 2011 and 2015 elections when the issue was second on the party system agenda, and in the 2005 election when the issue was number three (cf. Table 10.2).

---

[11] If Model 2 is run with party-fixed effects instead, the effects of deindustrialization and lagged economic growth remain the same.

[12] The question concerns competence in delivering quality teaching in primary schools. The Danish survey question asks whether the left-wing or the right-wing bloc is best at this (Stubager et al. 2016: 17).

Attention to Education in Post-Industrial Society 145

TABLE 10.4 *Party attention to education in Denmark, 1981–2015*

	Liberals	Social Democrats	Social Liberals	Party system agenda
1981	8.7%	6.4%	6.4%	5.4%
1984	9.4%	2.7%	11.7%	6.4%
1987	4.7%	7.2%	23.1%	6.8%
1988	4.0%	6.0%	20.1%	9.0%
1990	0.4%	6.3%	4.0%	3.7%
1994	1.3%	15.0%	12.5%	6.1%
1998	10.2%	13.2%	12.9%	8.7%
2001	14.1%	12.9%	8.9%	7.8%
2005	13.1	16.8%	10.9%	11.4%
2007	0.9%	1.2%	2.8%	6.9%
2011	12.1%	13.9%	37.0%	13.6%
2015	0.0%	10.1%	Missing	11.7%

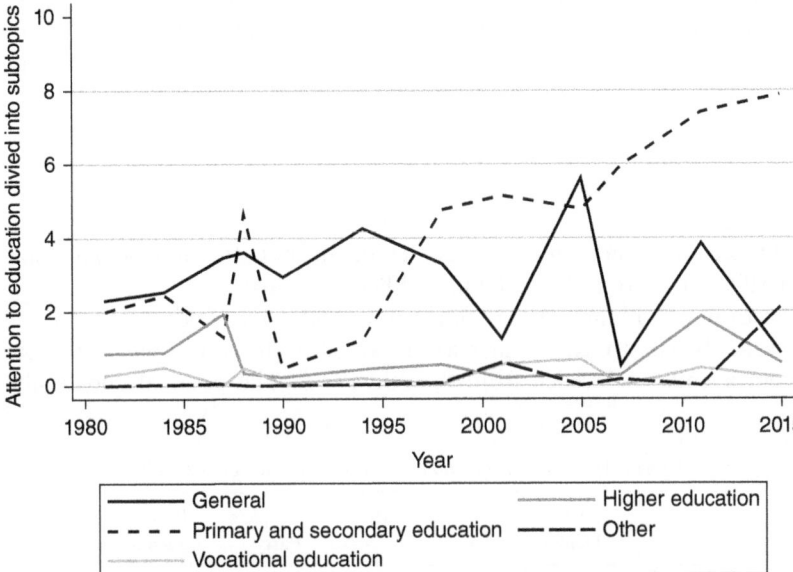

FIGURE 10.2 Party system attention to education divided into subcategories in Denmark, 1981–2015

Figure 10.2 breaks down attention to education in Denmark on the different subcategories of education in the CAP coding scheme described above.[13] The increase in attention to education over the period is largely the result of

---

[13] The category 'other' contains the subcategories 603 (education of underprivileged students), 606 (special education for youth with learning disabilities and the handicapped), 607 (libraries and improvement of the level of education), 698 (educational research), and 699 (others).

increasing attention to primary and secondary education. The attention to primary and secondary education is driven by a political debate about Danish pupils' scores in different international tests of school performance, especially the PISA tests (Gustafsson 2012: 159–84; Jensen 2011b).

A liberal minister of education had enrolled Denmark in an international investigation of reading abilities in the 1980s, and Denmark performed at the same level as countries like Venezuela and Trinidad and Tobago. When the result gained public awareness in 1994, political attention to primary schools increased substantially (Gustafsson 2012: 180; Jensen 2011b: 150–1). Since then, the publications of PISA reports in 2001, 2004, 2007, 2010, and 2013 have served as focusing events that have kept the political debate about primary schools alive. Especially Danish pupils' reading abilities have been central to the debate. Although Denmark has often performed at the OECD average, this has been interpreted as a failure because the scores have not improved. Major reforms of the Danish primary schools were passed in 2003 and 2013 by the large, mainstream parties with a clear focus on strengthening reading abilities. This has been done by introducing mandatory tests, longer school days, etc. (Gustafsson 2012: 185–213; Jensen 2011b: 152–3).

Turning to Sweden, Christensen et al. (2015: 147) show that there is no clear issue ownership of education. In terms of party attention, Table 10.5 shows that the two large, mainstream parties, the Social Democrats and the Conservatives, have always paid attention to education. The Conservatives have paid more attention than the Social Democrats, but attention increased in the mid-1990s; also from the social liberal People's Party.

According to Figure 10.3, attention to the category of primary and secondary schools has driven the increase in attention to education on the party system agenda in Sweden from the mid-1990s. The political debate about

TABLE 10.5 *Party attention to education in Sweden, 1981–2014*

	Social Democrats	Conservatives	People's Party	Party system agenda
1982	0.0%	6.1%	1.2%	3.2%
1985	4.4%	8.5%	6.3%	6.4%
1988	4.3%	4.0%	7.2%	5.0%
1991	2.2%	7.6%	5.2%	4.5%
1994	5.8%	9.7%	9.6%	5.0%
1998	10.3%	9.1%	14.1%	9.3%
2002	10.4%	7.7%	12.9%	8.3%
2006	10.1%	12.4%	12.4%	7.8%
2010	9.7%	9.6%	9.6%	9.2%
2014	18.9%	10.7%	10.7%	11.1%

Note: Identical figures for parties in the 2006, 2010, and 2014 elections are due to common manifestos.

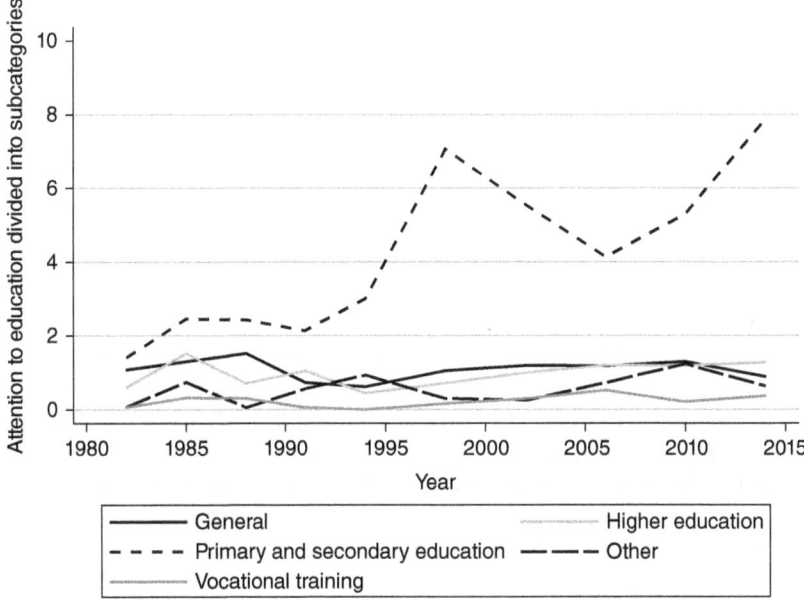

FIGURE 10.3 Party systems attention to education divided into subcategories in Sweden, 1982–2014

primary schools took off in the 1990s following a wave of decentralization reforms including the primary school sector (Premfors 1998). The decentralization reforms had broad political support, including from the Social Democrats, but then it led to a political debate about quality control from the central government (Gustafsson 2012: 107–30; Wiborg 2015). The debate was not a response to a perception of a crisis in the Swedish school system. Such a perception developed throughout the 2000s caused by, among other things, disappointing Swedish performance in the PISA tests in the early 2000s (Ringarp and Rothland 2010). The social liberal People's Party was very entrepreneurial in portraying Swedish primary schools as an educational failure (Gustafsson 2012: 132–6). Once the perception of the crisis had been widely accepted, a number of policy measures introducing tests and a new grading system were passed. With some hesitation from the Social Democrats, these policy measures had broad support in parliament (Gustafsson 2012: 132–6).

Denmark and Sweden are thus quite parallel cases. A perceived failure of the primary school sector is a policy question that no large, mainstream party can ignore, and the large, mainstream parties in Denmark and Sweden did not do that. The large, mainstream parties in the two countries did not necessarily agree from the outset on the policy reforms to be implemented. In both countries, the large, mainstream right-wing parties were from the outset focused on delegitimizing existing ideas of 'progressive education' and pushed policy in the direction of more assessment of the pupils. The large, mainstream left-wing parties went in the same direction with some hesitation (Gustafsson 2012). However, in terms of attention, both sides focused strongly on the issue once the idea of a policy failure of primary schooling began to prevail.

In the British case, the large, mainstream left-wing party, i.e. Labour, holds stable issue ownership of education (Seeberg 2013b: 67). Furthermore, considering that essentially only two parties compete for the majority in parliament to secure government power (Webb 2000), Labour should find education an attractive issue to focus on when in opposition after the 1979 election.

However, as Table 10.6 shows, it was not until the 1990s that Labour began to focus strongly on education. Actually, the Conservatives paid more attention to the issue in the 1987 election and followed up with the Great Education Reform Bill in 1988 (Lawton 2005: 103–4). But from the 1992 election and onwards, education has been central to the electoral strategy of the Labour Party. In 1996, Labour leader Tony Blair declared that the three highest priorities in government were 'education, education, education' (Kavanagh et al. 2006: 572–4). The strong Labour focus on education pushed the issue to the top of the party system agenda in 1997, and the focus continued when Labour was back in power from 1997 to 2011. The issue has stayed among the top three issues of the party system agenda ever since (see Table 10.2).

Figure 10.4 also reveals that, as in Denmark and Sweden, attention to primary and secondary education generated the increase in attention on the party system agenda. The Great Education Reform Bill already focused on primary and secondary schools, and this was also the focus of the Labour Party in the 1990s; both before and after they regained government power in 1997 (Lawton 2005: 108–22). Furthermore, with a focus on tests, league tables, and a national curriculum, the content of these policy initiatives was not far away from the initiatives of the previous Conservative

TABLE 10.6 *Party attention to education in the UK, 1983–2015*

	Labour	Conservatives	Party system agenda
1983	5.7%	5.1%	5.1%
1987	7.2%	9.3%	8.4%
1992	10.7%	6.3%	9.4%
1997	12.9%	10.6%	11.6%
2001	11.6%	7.0%	9.2%
2005	13.1%	16.9%	12.6%
2010	9.5%	6.7%	8.4%
2015	8.2%	7.3%	7.3%

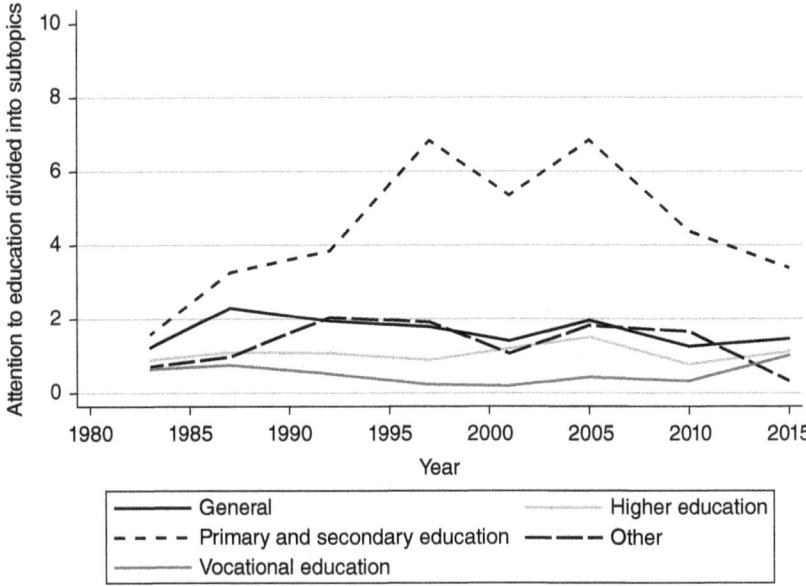

FIGURE 10.4 Party system attention to education divided into subcategories in the UK, 1983–2015

government, and they were also close to the content of the policies enacted in Denmark and Sweden.[14]

The four other countries have not seen the same significant growth in attention to education. In the Netherlands, the issue was relatively important on the party system agenda to begin with, and attention has only increased slightly (cf. Figure 10.1). The Netherlands have not seen the same boom in attention to primary and secondary education as Denmark, Sweden, and the UK. France has also seen a slight increase in attention to education, but it has not seen the boom in attention to primary schools.[15] France did not do very well in the PISA tests, but this generated relatively little media attention (Dixon et al. 2013), and the French policymakers reacted by questioning the whole PISA approach (Dobbins and Martens 2012). The large, mainstream

---

[14] Unlike in Denmark and Sweden, the PISA scores played a limited role in the UK debate: partly because the UK did relatively well when the first PISA results were released in 2001, and partly because the UK had already implemented policy initiatives to improve basic reading and mathematical skills (Grek 2009; Knodel and Walkenhorst 2010).

[15] If one produces a similar figure to Figures 10.2–10.4 for the Netherlands and France, they reveal no similar increase in attention to primary and secondary education.

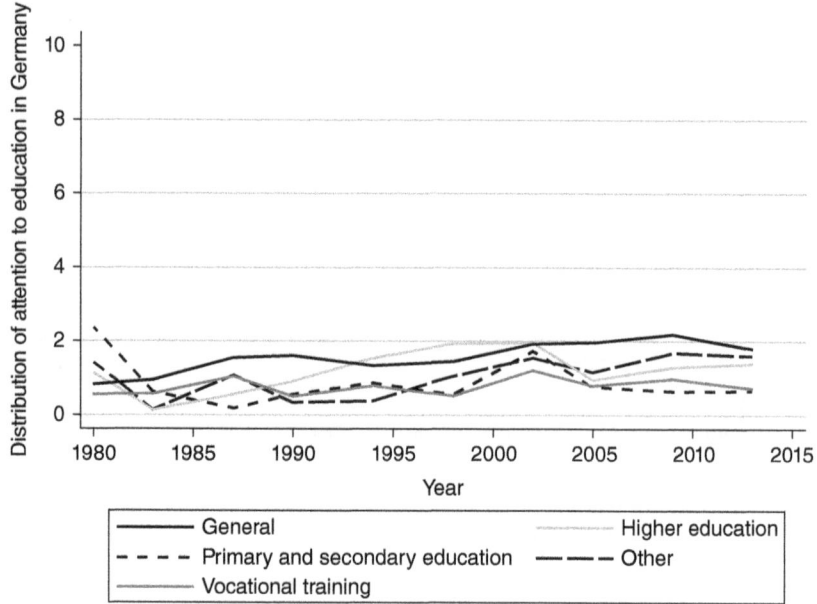

FIGURE 10.5 Party system attention to education divided into subcategories in Germany, 1981–2013

right-wing parties have typically had issue ownership of education (Seeberg 2017: 484), but they have not used the PISA scores to increase attention to education.

In Germany, the PISA scores did lead to an extensive public debate about the failure of the German primary and secondary educational systems (Grek 2009; Ringarp and Rothland 2010). Niemann (2010: 84) even talks about a 'PISA shock'. However, as Figure 10.5 shows, German national politicians did not pick up primary and secondary education like their counterparts in Denmark, the UK, and Sweden. The most likely explanation is that policy responsibility for education is decentralized to the Länder, which is where most of the political reactions to the PISA scores came from (Dixon et al. 2013). Large, mainstream parties therefore did not pick up the issue to the same extent as they did in Denmark and Sweden.

Finally, in Belgium, attention to education on the party system agenda has declined since the late 1980s. The reason probably is that the 1988 constitutional reform in Belgium transferred educational policy to the new regions established in the new federal state. As shown by de Rynck (2005), this implied the end of an all-Belgian educational policy. Like in Germany, education has become a less relevant policy issue to include in party competition.

WHY ALL THIS ATTENTION TO EDUCATION?

Summarizing the analysis in the light of the issue incentive model, the analysis shows that large, mainstream parties' incentives are the key factor in explaining the dynamics of party system attention to education. However, compared to the three issues analysed before, problem characteristics rather than coalition considerations and issue ownership shape the incentives of large, mainstream parties. The fact that education is an obtrusive valence issue relevant to more or less the whole population implies that it is an issue which large, mainstream parties cannot ignore if public debates about policy problems emerge. The increased focus on education and human capital in the knowledge society has thus led to an increased focus on education.

However, this focus has clearly been most pronounced in countries where it has materialized itself in a debate about the quality of primary schools. In Denmark, and later on also in Sweden, this debate came as a reaction to what were seen as disappointing PISA scores. In the UK, the PISA scores played a limited role in the debate about primary schools. In France, PISA scores that could also have been seen as disappointing did not generate any wider debate about primary schools (Dixon et al. 2013). Thus, the question of problem definition of education and primary schools in particular deserves further attention. The PISA scores may play an important role, but not necessarily. For instance, the German case shows that the public debate about PISA scores had limited impact on the party system agenda at the national level because policy responsibility for education belongs to the Länder. In terms of party differences, education is not an issue like the environment or immigration where one side of the political spectrum has clear issue ownership across countries. However, in the British case, Labour's stable issue ownership (Seeberg 2013b: 67) made the issue attractive for Labour when Tony Blair took over the party leadership and focused on winning back government power.

Finally, the role of Social Liberal parties in party competition for education deserves some discussion. A potential alternative explanation to the focus on large, mainstream parties would be that the increase in party system attention to education is the result of Social Liberal parties acting as issue entrepreneurs on the issue. As pointed out by Green-Pedersen and Jensen (2019), Social Liberal parties' strong focus on education can be seen as a confirmation of Beramendi et al.'s (2015) argument that education has become part of the new, second conflict with Social Liberal parties representing the libertarian pole by expressing the interest of socio-cultural professionals. However, in terms of explaining the attention dynamics of education, especially the rise in party system attention to education, pointing to Social Liberal parties as issue entrepreneurs is a questionable explanation. These parties and their attention to education are far from new, and they were already present when education played a more limited role on the party system agenda. Furthermore, unlike issues such as immigration or the environment, which have clearly been driven by one of the large, mainstream parties, both the mainstream left and right have paid increasing attention to the issue. Thus, the conflict over education between the large, mainstream parties is quite different from other issues belonging to the new, second conflict such as immigration and the environment. Finally, if the rising attention to education should be seen as the result of Social Liberal parties pushing the interest of socio-cultural professionals, it is hard to explain why focus in most of the countries has been so strong on primary schools. From the perspective of the interest of socio-cultural professionals, a focus on higher education would seem more logical.

A different interpretation would follow the argument of Kraft (2017) who argues that a key characteristic of education is the fact that it is an investment in the future. This makes 'core parties', i.e. the parties focused on government power, interested in the issue as they want to present themselves as investing in the future when they (re)gain governmental power. The concept of core parties is close to the idea of large, mainstream parties which appear to focus more on education. Furthermore, Social Liberal parties typically belong to the group of small, mainstream parties as discussed in Chapter 3.[16] Social Liberal parties like the German FDP or the Danish Social Liberals have a long tradition for being in government, which gives the same 'core party' interest in education as an investment as the large, mainstream parties have. They also expect to govern in the future. Following Kraft (2017), it seems that the parties oriented towards future government participation are the ones most focused on education.

---

[16] The difference in size between small and large, mainstream parties makes them prioritize between vote and office differently. Small, mainstream parties have to prioritize votes higher because significant electoral losses can mean losing parliamentary representation.

11

Everyone Really Loves Health Care

Health care has many similarities with education in terms of the incentives that the issue offers to large, mainstream parties: It is both a valence and an obtrusive issue with a broad scope. Furthermore, niche parties that focus intensively on health care do not exist. However, there are important differences between education and health care in terms of problem characteristics. Most importantly, technological progress has a central impact on the politics of health care, but it plays a more limited role with regard to education. This frequently makes health-care politics an exercise in blame avoidance as will be described below. Thus, from the perspective of the issue incentive model, analysing health care provides the opportunity for further analysis of the importance of issue characteristics.

Empirically, health care is interesting because it has gained increasing importance on the party system agendas as shown in Figure 5.14. Health care is not a new issue, but it is certainly an issue that has become much more important for politics in industrialized countries. There is also an immense literature on health-care policy, but there are surprisingly few studies of party competition on health care. This, in itself, is an important reason for studying the issue.

HEALTH CARE AS A POLICY AREA

Studies of health-care policy (see Blank and Burau 2014: 1–6) typically distinguish between health policy (all government actions with health implications for citizens) and health-care policy (the policies governments enact to provide health services to citizens). Questions relating to health-care policies are naturally a central part of the policy issue of health care. With regard to health policy, many policy areas have health implications, i.e. environmental policy, social policy, and labour market policy. In addition to health implications, such policy areas have many other important implications not related to health care and are therefore not included in the following. However, questions related to 'public health' are included, i.e. various measures that governments take to influence citizens' daily lives directly in a healthy direction, for instance campaigns against smoking or guidelines for breastfeeding babies. Additionally, health-care policy is closely linked to the immense research efforts by the pharmaceutical industry to develop new medication. This type of research is therefore also considered part of the policy area of health care. What is not part of health care are policy questions related to the care of elderly people when the purpose is not directly medical, but about more support for everyday activities like shopping, cooking, or cleaning.

THE ISSUE INCENTIVES OF HEALTH CARE

Having delimited the policy issue of health care, the analysis of party system attention requires the application of the issue incentive model to the issue, i.e. a discussion of how issue characteristics, issue ownership, and coalition considerations shape the vote and office incentives of large, mainstream parties.

In terms of issue characteristics, i.e. the interaction between problem characteristics and problem information, four aspects of health care are worth highlighting from the perspective of large, mainstream parties. First, health care is an issue with a very broad scope—health care is relevant to everyone; even people with private health care are dependent on public regulation. It is also an obtrusive issue—most people have either recent personal experience with the health-care system or have relatives or friends who have. Second, it is a valence issue. No one is against health care, and sick people are generally seen as highly deserving of public help (Jensen and Petersen 2017). Combined, these two aspects shape the relevant political question about health care. This is not about whether it should be provided, but how.

The third important aspect of the issue is technological progress. Immense technological progress has already happened within health care, and there is no reason to expect less of it in the future. However, technological progress has not implied that health-care problems are 'solved' from a political perspective, on the contrary. Health care is unique in the sense that unlike most other areas, technological progress does not lead to cheaper services (Cutler and McClellan 2001). In fact, technological progress is seen as the best explanation of rising health-care costs (Okunade and Murthy 2002). For political parties, this implies that meeting public expectations of health-care services while at the same time controlling costs becomes increasingly difficult. Thus, the politics of health care will often be what Weaver (1986) described as 'an exercise in blame avoidance' (Mortensen 2013). Despite rising health-care costs in all countries, public demand for health care is likely to remain unsatisfied (Green-Pedersen and Jensen 2019). This will lead the public to blame politicians—especially those in government—for not managing the health-care system well. Thus, from a vote-seeking perspective, health care presents political parties with a dilemma. On the one hand, they will find it an attractive issue to pay attention to because of its universal importance. On the other hand, blame avoidance is likely to be just as important in the politics of health care as credit claiming.

The fourth aspect of health care that is important for large, mainstream parties is that health-care provision can differ significantly in terms of organization, funding, and actual service provision. This generates different health-care systems, not least concerning the role of the central government and the extent to which other societal actors are involved in health-care provision (Böhm et al. 2013). This affects the extent to which political blame for problems within the health-care sector falls solely on the central political level, including political parties, or whether it is partly 'defused' to other societal actors as well. Thus, health-care systems in which societal actors are strongly involved will open opportunities for blame avoidance strategies (cf. Pierson 1994). In such systems, parties do not have to focus as much on health care as in countries where the state dominates health care. Here, any health-care problem easily becomes the problem of the central government and thus of the political parties at the national level.

To sum up, health care has a number of problem characteristics that make the issue difficult for large, mainstream parties to ignore. It is a valence issue that affects large parts of the population in a significant way. Hence, everyone cares about health care. At the same time, technological change increasingly opens up new possibilities of detecting and treating all kinds of illnesses. As for political parties, this often makes health care an exercise in blame avoidance. The need to keep costs at bay implies that all health-care systems will produce cases in which health-care services could be better or treatments are rationed in one way or another. The obtrusive character of the issue means that such cases are likely to shape the public image of the health-care system because people experience them personally or hear about them from relatives or friends. Furthermore, such cases are quite likely to be picked up by the media. Politicians might refer to statistics showing that more public money is being spent, more patients are being treated, and life expectancy is rising. However, public perception of the health-care system is more likely to be shaped by the frequent cases of unmet expectations. Thus, health care is an issue that no political party can avoid, even though blame avoidance is often an important aspect of the politics of health care. However, the organization of the health-care system might make it possible to share some of the blame with other societal actors.

The second factor that Chapter 2 argues will shape the vote and office incentives of large, mainstream parties is issue ownership. Seeberg (2017: 482–7) reports left-wing issue ownership in most cases, but not as strong as on the environment or social security, and it has declined over time.[1] As with education, rather than assuming general left-wing issue ownership, one has to look at the specific countries.

The third factor is coalition considerations. These are determined by how health care fits the left–right dimension. Even though the issue is argued to be a valence issue in the sense that all political parties want to secure health-care services for citizens, political parties do not have similar positions on health care. Especially the role of private actors in the health-care sector and the use of market-based principles in the funding and provision of health care are likely to divide the left and the right (Gingrich 2011: 79–130). Coalition considerations for the large, mainstream parties therefore follow the general left–right dimension, and a focus on health care does not provide any particular incentives to use health care as a wedge issue against competitors or as the means to build a coalition with niche parties. The latter do not exist within health care.

To sum up, in terms of the issue incentive model, issue characteristics are the most decisive factor in terms of shaping the incentives of large, mainstream parties with regard to health care. Given the importance everyone attaches to health care, all political parties need to signal to the electorate that the issue is of importance to them. In some cases, issue ownership may make health care more attractive to the large, mainstream left-wing parties, but not in all countries. In terms of coalition considerations, party positions on health care follow the general left–right dimension. This implies that there are no coalition incentives to focus on health care rather than on other issues. Across time, new technology and medication are likely to be important for party attention to health care. Technological changes make it increasingly difficult for political actors at the central level, including political parties, to satisfy public demands for health care although parties are likely to pretend that they can. In many ways, health care is thus the prime example of what Green and Jennings (2017) call the 'politics of competence'. Cross-national differences in health-care systems are finally likely to generate cross-national difference in the growth of party attention to health care. The reason is that they, to varying degrees, concentrate blame for unmet expectations with the central government and thus the political parties.

---

[1] For several countries, data on issue ownership are not available or only available on time. Looking at the countries studied here, only Sweden, Denmark, and the UK have more than one measurement of issue ownership of health care reported by Seeberg (2017).

THE PARTISAN POLITICS OF HEALTH CARE

A scholarly literature on the 'party politics of health care' is surprisingly absent. The large, body of literature on health-care policy also deals with 'the politics of health care' (e.g. Blank and Burau 2014: 37–76), but political parties are largely ignored. There are plenty of studies on health-care politics (cf. Marmor and Wendt 2012), especially with focus on health-care reforms (cf. Hacker 2004), but political parties are again almost absent. The large comparative literature on the welfare state is much more focused on political parties, but as argued by Jensen (2011a), it rarely deals with health care. Furthermore, when the literature on the welfare state deals with health care, it focuses on political parties' policy strategies and their attempts to reform the health-care system in different directions (Gingrich 2011; Hacker 2004; Jensen 2011a; Jordan 2011). Health care as an issue of party competition is rarely in focus. Finally, the literature on party competition and issue politics, which, as argued in Chapter 2, has boomed in recent years, also rarely studies health care.[2] Thus, the increasing importance of health care in party competition has hardly been captured in the issue competition literature.

The party politics on health care has received surprisingly little attention. The literature primarily offers two insights. First, in a broad sense, health-care politics is shaped by the dilemma of technological advancement and public expectations on the one side, and the need to control costs on the other side (Blank and Burau 2014: 24–37; Green-Pedersen and Jensen 2019; Green-Pedersen and Wilkerson 2006). Second, the left and the right have different views on how health care should be supplied. This is—at least to some extent—visible from the reform strategies they have pursued in relation to the health-care sector (Hacker 2004; Jensen 2011a).

WHICH PARTIES PAY ATTENTION TO HEALTH CARE?

Before one takes a detailed look at what drives party attention to health care following the analytical strategy setup in Chapter 6, a few words on the operational definition in the comparative agendas project are in order. The above definition of the issue of health care includes policy questions relating to

---

[2] One explanation is the absence of categories for health care in the CMP coding scheme, which has been the most common data source for the study of issue competition. Measures of saliency and the position of parties on health care are also absent from the Chapel Hill Expert Survey, which is the other major data source.

all aspects of health-care systems, elements of public health as well as research targeted specifically at developing new medication and improving health-care technology. Policy measures on elderly care are not included.

Major topic 3 in the CAP coding system concerns health care. It includes the subcategory 300 for general questions, 301 for comprehensive health-care reforms, 302 for issues about coverage, 321 for regulations of treatments and medication, 322 for health-care facilities, 323 for payment of health care, 324 for medical liability, and 325 for medical professions. Finally, 331 deals with disease prevention, 333 mental health, 341 tobacco abuse, 342 alcohol and drug abuse, and 398 medical research. Some countries have introduced additional subcategories by dividing existing subcategories, but these have then been merged back into the relevant subcategories.[3]

Figure 11.1 shows a general increase in party system attention to health care over the decades.[4] At the beginning of the period, health care took up between 2 per cent and 4 per cent of the party system agenda, and at the end of the period this had grown to somewhere between 5 per cent and 10 per cent.

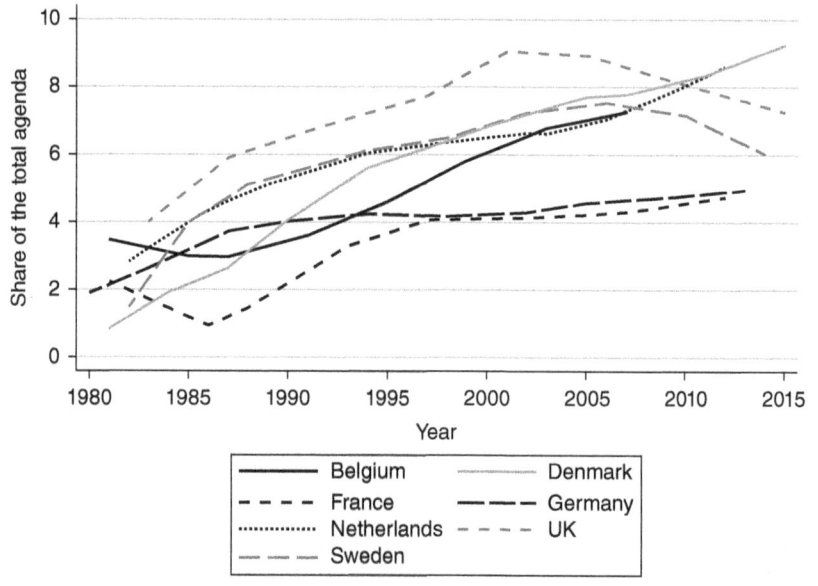

FIGURE 11.1 Party system attention to health care in the seven countries from 1980 and onwards

---

[3] The Netherlands, Belgium, and France have a special subcategory 320 for medical-ethical questions like abortion and euthanasia. This subcategory is included in the main category 2 relating to personal rights.

[4] The figure is identical to Figure 5.14.

Table 11.1 shows that while about 20 per cent of the parties did not mention health care in the 1980s, this had dropped to 2 per cent in the 2000s. Further, Table 11.2 shows eighteen examples of health care being a top issue as defined in Chapter 6. Twelve of these examples are after the year 2000, and only six are from the two preceding decades.

As with the other issues, there are important cross-national differences. Table 11.2 shows that health care as a top issue is most pronounced in the UK. It has been a top issue in all elections since 1987 when focus is on the top five issues. When a top issue is defined as an issue that receives more attention than the mean plus one standard deviation, health care has been a top issue in all elections since 1987, except in 1992. Health care has also been a top issue in Denmark, Sweden, the Netherlands, and Belgium, but less persistently than

TABLE 11.1 *Percentage of parties mentioning education in their election programme across decades*

Decade	Percentage	N
1980s	79%	141
1990s	96%	131
2000s	98%	183

TABLE 11.2 *Health care as a top issue*

Elections with health care as a top five issue (place in brackets)	Party system attention	4.35+1sd	Party system attention > 4.35+1sd
Belgium 2003 (3)	7.4%	7.1%	X
Belgium 2007 (3)	7.3%	6.9%	X
Denmark 1998 (3)	9.2%	8.2%	X
Denmark 2001 (3)	7.8%	8.2%	
Denmark 2011 (3)	11.6%	8.9%	X
The Netherlands 2003 (5)	6.3%	7.7%	
The Netherlands 2006 (5)	7.0%	6.7%	X
The Netherlands 2010 (1)	7.9%	6.6%	X
The Netherlands 2012 (1)	8.7%	6.5%	X
The UK 1987 (5)	7.5%	7.2%	X
The UK 1992 (4)	5.9%	6.8%	
The UK 1997 (3)	8.0%	7.2%	X
The UK 2001 (5)	8.9%	7.2%	X
The UK 2005 (3)	10.3%	7.6%	X
The UK 2010 (3)	7.2%	7.1%	X
The UK 2015 (5)	7.3%	6.5%	X
Sweden 1988 (5)	7.3%	7.7%	
Sweden 1991 (5)	6.9%	7.8%	
Sweden 2006 (4)	8.5%	7.7%	X

in the UK. Finally, even though attention to health care has increased in both Germany and France, it has not been a top issue.

As laid out in Chapter 6, the first step towards explaining the trends in party system attention to the individual issues is a number of OLS models explaining party attention to health care. As with the other issues, these models are country-fixed effects models (country dummies) in order to focus the first part of the analysis on the within country variation. The models are estimated further with robust standard errors and a lagged dependent variable. As with the other issue models, the lagged dependent is included in continuation of Chapter 3.[5] Parties' issue focus is generally expected to be stable as it is partly driven by their expectations of which issue other parties will pay attention to. One therefore expects a positive impact of the lagged dependent variable, which is also a consistent finding in all the models in Table 11.3.

In terms of party difference, Model 1 includes a dummy for the large, mainstream left-wing parties (Social Democratic parties) in order to test whether they focus more on health care than other parties. This is not the case.[6] A test of large, mainstream parties in general, not just left-wing, yields similar negative results. The coefficient is positive, which indicates more attention from large, mainstream parties, but it does not meet the standard criteria for statistical significance.[7]

TABLE 11.3 *Regression estimates of party attention to health care*

	Model 1	Model 2	Model 3
Attention to health care t−1	0.35(0.07)***	0.35(0.07)***	0.22(0.08)**
Large, mainstream party (=1)		0.58(0.41)	0.60(0.38)
Large, mainstream left-wing (=1)	0.30(0.39)		
Economic growth (lagged)			0.35(0.09)***
Number of health related patents			0.01(0.003)***
Share of the population above 65			0.20(0.19)
Government (=1)	0.29(0.40)	0.09(0.44)	0.24(0.39)
Constant	3.18(0.46)***	3.00(0.48)***	−5.19(2.40)*
N	398	396	396
Adj. R^2	0.16	0.16	0.26

Note: robust standard errors in parentheses. * p < 0.05, ** p < 0.01, *** p < 0.001. Estimated with country-fixed effects (country dummies not shown). The drop in N from Model 1 to Model 2 is due to the inclusion of the 'Alliance' in Sweden that contains both large and small, mainstream parties.

---

[5] To avoid losing too many cases when including the lagged dependent variable, data on the last election before 1980 have been included when available. This is the case for Denmark, Sweden, Germany, and the Flemish parties in Belgium (see Chapter 4).

[6] Other party type dummies were tested without any being significant.

[7] If Model 3 is run excluding the one case of more than 25% party attention to health care (the Danish Socialist People's Party in 2011), the effect of large, mainstream party status borders statistical significance. Other results remain the same.

To capture the influence of technological development, a variable measuring the number of health-care patents is included (cf. Green-Pedersen and Wilkerson 2006). For each country, an index is constructed with the number of health-care patents in 1980 as baseline (100), and the index value for the following years is calculated using a two-year average to smooth out fluctuation in individual years (Green-Pedersen and Jensen 2019). The growth in the index varies somewhat by country. In Belgium, the index has grown to 620 in 2003, and in Germany, it has grown to 370 in 2005.[8] In Model 3, there is a clear effect on party attention from the rise in the number of health-care patents. An increase like the one in Belgium, for instance, would lead to a 5.2 percentage point increase in party attention. Thus, the findings clearly show that the pressure on the health-care system from technological developments generates party attention to health care.[9] Economic growth lagged by one year also seems to drive attention to health care. Higher economic growth generates more attention to health care as well. In times of high economic growth, political parties are more able to satisfy the demands for better health-care services, and this makes the issue more attractive to focus on.

Beyond the technological development, another societal development that puts the health-care system under pressure is the increasing elderly share of the population. The elderly, i.e. the share of the population above 65, is therefore also included as a control variable. This demographic development can also turn into a political development in which the increased elderly share of the electorate generates a pressure on political parties to focus more on the demands of the elderly such as health care. However, in Model 3, Table 11.3, the share of the population above 65 is not significant.[10] One possible explanation is that pensioner parties representing this segment rarely gain representation (cf. Vanhuysse and Goerres 2012).[11] Thus, the rising elderly

---

[8] The data on health-related patents come from the 'Patents by main technology and by International Patent Classification (IPC)' data series, accessed via OECD Statistics (OECD 2017d). The series on pharmaceuticals and medical technology were combined to form the health-related patent index. Values do not exist after 2013, and the values for the years with elections after 2013 (Sweden 2014, Denmark 2015, the UK 2015) were generated using linear extrapolation.

[9] An interaction model was also tested to see whether mainstream parties responded more to the rise in health-care patents than other parties did. The results pointed in this direction but did not meet conventional levels of statistical significance.

[10] Data are taken from the OECD databank (<https://data.oecd.org/pop/elderly-population.htm>). Data on the elections after 2013 (Sweden 2014, Denmark 2015, the UK 2015) are derived from linear extrapolation.

[11] The Netherlands is the only country studied here where pensioner parties have gained some electoral success including parliamentary representation. This includes the AOV and the U55+ in the 1994 election, and the 50Plus in the 2012 election. These parties pay more attention to health care than the average (party system agenda), but only somewhat more: the AOV 8.4% (6.0), the U55+ 8.1% (6.0), and the 50Plus 9.6% (8.7).

share of the population does not generate a distinct political pressure beyond the one emerging from technological development.[12]

To sum up, the results from the regression approach show that the rapid technological development generates more party-political attention to health care. This is in line with the literature on health-care policy which emphasizes the political challenge of satisfying the growing expectations of health-care services while controlling costs (Green-Pedersen and Jensen 2019). The results above also show that parties across the board are responding with more attention to health care.[13]

THE POLITICS OF HEALTH-CARE SYSTEMS

However, the descriptive analysis pointed to important cross-national differences in the growth of party system attention to health care, which, as argued above, may be due to different ways of organizing health-care systems. The three countries, the UK, Denmark, and Sweden, which have what Böhm et al. (2013) describe as a 'national health care system' where societal actors play a limited role, have all seen a significant increase in party system attention to health care. In the countries with different versions of 'social health insurance systems', the growth in party system attention to health care is less pronounced; especially in France and Germany.[14] The structure of the health-care system is likely to condition the extent to which the technological development leads to increased party attention to health care. This claim can be investigated by comparing the UK and Germany as they represent two quite different types of health-care systems.

Beginning with the UK, health-care politics in Britain is about the NHS system established in 1948; a standard example of the 'national health-care system' with the state in charge of organizing, funding, and providing health care (Böhm et al. 2013: 265). The UK health-care system has been under pressure due to the technological progress, but in this regard, the UK is no

---

[12] If Model 3 is run without the patents index, the elderly share of the population has a positive and significant impact on party attention to health care, but as can be seen from Model 3, Table 11.3, this effect disappears when the patents index is included.

[13] Similar findings as in Model 3 concerning patents, lagged growth, and elderly share are obtained from a model with party-fixed effects. Running Model 3 as a Tobit model considering the censuring of the data—they can only vary between 0 and 100—yields similar results.

[14] Böhm et al. (2013) differentiate between social health insurance systems as found in Germany and étatist social health insurance systems as found in France, Belgium, and the Netherlands. The difference has to do with a stronger state involvement in the latter cases.

different from the other countries.[15] Nevertheless, based on Table 11.2 and Figure 11.1, the UK is a pronounced case of growth in party system attention to health care. In terms of issue ownership, health care in the UK has been rather clearly owned by Labour (Seeberg 2013b: 67).

In the decades following the establishment of the NHS, party politics on the system was characterized by a consensus and a view of the NHS as a success (Klein 2013: 96–101). The Conservative Thatcher government that came into power in 1979 had a clear overall agenda of more market and less state (Pierson 1994). This agenda was not absent from the health-care policy in the 1980s, yet the NHS was not the main ideological battleground. Thatcher declared that 'the NHS is safe with us' (Klein 2013: 112), and the Conservative government mainly focused on 'value for money' to be achieved through managerial reforms (Klein 2013: 105–34). However, these reforms were not successful in the sense that the NHS continued to be a political liability to the government. It was under strong pressure to spend more on the NHS to deal with a common perception of inadequate service (Klein 2013: 140–1). Especially burgeoning waiting lists were seen as a clear indication of this (Giaimo 2002: 44–8).

The response from the government was the 'Working for Patients' manifesto published in 1989, and it was generally seen as an ideological attack on the NHS. The response from Labour and other societal actors was fierce opposition. In the end, the policies implemented were not that market oriented, and the Conservative government's policy legacy was not one of privatization, but a series of more or less successful managerial reforms aimed at gaining more value for money (Giaimo 2002: 48–64; Klein 2013: 152–8; Pierson 1994: 132–6).

At the same time, party system attention to health care increased substantially (see Table 11.4). The Labour opposition focused on health care and education to win back government power in 1997 (Kavanagh 1997: 31). As for the Conservative government, substantial attention to health care was necessary to reassure the electorate that the NHS was safe with the Conservatives.

The New Labour government announced its willingness to spend more on the NHS, which it also did to a substantial degree. An important part of this was a strong focus on reducing waiting lists (Klein 2013: 199–204). However, Labour was generally not rewarded for this in the sense that the negative perception of the NHS lingered (Klein 2007). For instance, a large outbreak of influenza in 2000 flooded hospitals with patients, and again the media painted the NHS as being unable to deliver adequate service (Klein

---

[15] The index of new health-care patents has also grown in the UK from 100 in 1980 to 420 in 2001 and has then declined slightly to 372 in 2012.

2013: 203). In the 2001 and 2005 elections, the Conservatives could thus attack Labour on this despite continuing but declining Labour issue ownership of health care (Seeberg 2013b: 67). Even though the Conservatives emphasized market solutions to some extent, the core of the attacks concerned the NHS' underperformance (Klein 2013: 212). The same pattern repeated itself when Gordon Brown had replaced Tony Blair. Despite increased spending on health care and visible results like falling waiting lists, Labour could still not fully convince the electorate that they were clearly 'the party of the NHS', and health care continued to be a contest for the best managerial competences rather than ideology (Klein 2013: 268–73). When the Conservative/Liberal coalition took over in 2010 it launched further reforms of the NHS systems. These reforms simply changed the NHS to the 'politics of blame avoidance' for the coalition and strengthened Labour's role as 'the party of the NHS' (Klein 2013: 279–99).

The content of party competition for health care in the UK can be further described by looking at the subcategories (see Figure 11.2). Two aspects have dominated party attention to health care. One is 'general aspects' which refers to general statements about the NHS and its future.[16] The other is coverage

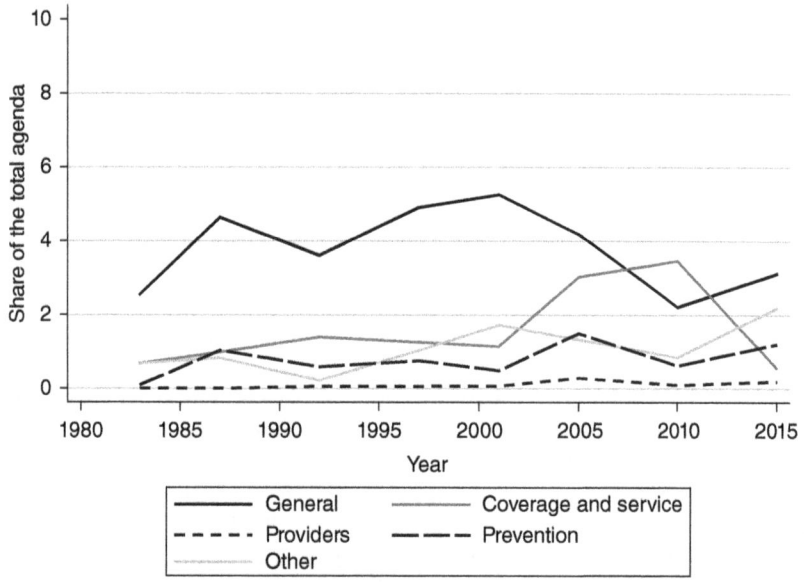

FIGURE 11.2 Party system attention to health care divided into subtopics in the UK, 1983–2015

[16] This refers to subcategories 300 and 301 in the coding system.

and service aspects which typically include statements about patients' rights to treatment, plans to reduce waiting lists, and improvement of hospital services.[17] The latter group, however, declined again at the end of the period.

In sum, despite clear ideological differences between Labour and the Conservatives, especially concerning the role of private actors, the core of party competition has been about the party in government trying to deliver the top quality services promised without costs exploding. However, as discussed above, this has been a very difficult task. Table 11.4 suggests that the party in opposition has the greatest focus on the issue (cf. Seeberg 2013a, 2013b). This is the case for Labour in 1992, 1997, and 2015 and for the Conservatives in 2001 and 2005. Even without issue ownership, focusing on the issue has also seemed attractive for the Conservatives once in opposition.

The German system is an example of a 'social health insurance system' (Böhm et al. 2013) in which societal actors in the form of health insurance funds typically organized along occupational lines play an important role together with the central state and the German Länder. Unlike education, health care is not an issue that is constitutionally delegated to the German Länder. The German health-care system implies a diffusion of responsibility that a national health-care system like the British one does not. It also implies that the exact service provided can vary significantly between sickness funds (Giaimo 2002: 86–94; Pfaff 2009). German health-care reforms, e.g. the 1993 and 2007 reforms, have focused on cost control and prevented that sickness funds constantly raise contributions (Gerlinger 2010; Pfaff 2009: 92–9).

Left–right differences across the large, mainstream parties can be found with regard to the introduction of market-based elements in the system (Gerlinger 2010: 130–4), but otherwise party politics on the major reform is characterized by consensus and broad compromises (Gerlinger 2010: 130–4;

TABLE 11.4 *Party attention to health care in the UK, 1983–2015*

	Labour	Conservatives	Party system agenda
1983	3.2%	4.8%	4.0%
1987	7.4%	8.6%	7.5%
1992	9.1%	3.9%	5.9%
1997	7.0%	6.3%	8.0%
2001	8.3%	10.2%	8.9%
2005	10.8%	13.8%	10.3%
2010	8.9%	6.7%	7.2%
2015	7.8%	7.0%	7.3%

---

[17] This covers the subcategories 302, 322, and 334. Providers cover the subcategories 323 and 336, and prevention covers the subcategories 331 and 341–4. Finally, 'other' includes 321, 324, 325, 332–5, 398, and 399.

TABLE 11.5 *Party attention to health care in Germany, 1980–2013*

	SPD	CDU	Party system agenda
1980	3.4%	0.7%	2.4%
1983	4.4%	0.3%	1.4%
1987	2.7%	4.2%	4.4%
1990	4.4%	6.3%	5.5%
1994	4.0%	1.7%	3.9%
1997	3.1%	1.8%	3.2%
2002	5.0%	4.7%	5.2%
2005	4.6%	4.4%	4.3%
2009	4.1%	6.4%	4.7%
2013	6.7%	3.1%	4.9%

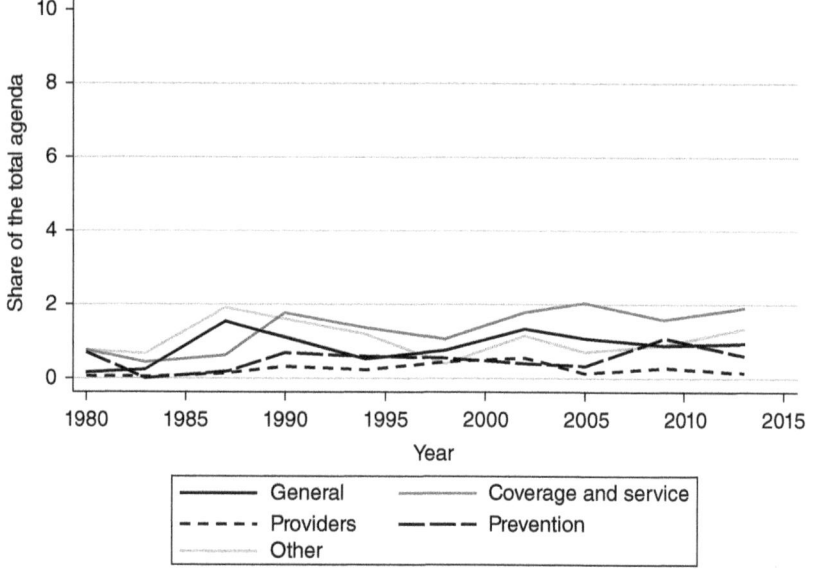

FIGURE 11.3 Party system attention to health care divided into subtopics in Germany, 1980–2013

Pfaff 2009: 109–10). Table 11.5 indicates that neither the SPD nor the CDU has consistently focused more on health care than the other party. The table does also not indicate any government/opposition dynamic in which the large, mainstream party in opposition focuses more on the issue than the one in government. Furthermore, Figure 11.3 shows that attention to coverage and service has not played the same role in Germany as in the UK. In addition, attention to 'general' questions has also been more limited in Germany. This indicates that the German system puts political parties under less pressure to promise certain services than in a national health-care system like the British.

This tendency towards party consensus rather than party competition can be explained by the incentives emerging from the structure of the German health-care system. Not only does the system make service provision less of a national issue, it also means than none of the large, mainstream parties are fully in opposition. They will almost always be in office in one of the several Länder, which are also heavily involved in the provision of health care (Pfaff 2009: 88–91). Compared to a national health-care system, the exact service provided does not become a national policy issue in the same way. The structure of the German health-care system therefore makes it more difficult to blame the problems of the system on the opponent in office. This makes the issue less attractive for party competition.[18] From 2005 to 2009 and from 2013 and onwards, the CDU and the SPD have also governed together in the grand coalitions.

In sum, as demonstrated in Table 11.5, the large, mainstream parties in Germany have increasingly focused on health care. They have had to attend to the challenges of the system in terms of control or contribution when public demands increase due to technological developments. However, compared to the British case, the structure of the German health-care system provides fewer incentives for the large, mainstream parties to focus on the issue. Service standards are less of a national issue, and both large, mainstream parties constantly find themselves involved in the governance of the health-care system due to the role of the Länder and grand coalitions at the national level. Based on this as well as on Figure 11.1 and Table 11.2, it is not surprising that Germany and France, which also does not have a national health-care system, represent the two cases with the least growth in party attention to health care.

IS THERE A PARTY POLITICS ON HEALTH CARE?

Based on the issue incentive model, the importance of issue characteristics for understanding the rising party system attention to health care is clear. Health care is an obtrusive issue of great importance to everyone, so large, mainstream parties have a strong incentive to focus on the issue. However, as it is difficult to satisfy public demands, party attention is often an exercise in blame avoidance. Rapid progress within health-care technology has thus generated more party system attention to the issue because parties are struggling to meet

---

[18] In terms of issue ownership, Seeberg (2017) reports no clear issue ownership for the 2000s (Table A5, online appendix). Data are not available before.

public demands while controlling costs. Comparative differences in how much the attention to health care has increased can be explained to some extent by the comparative differences in health-care systems. The more responsibility for health care is concentrated with the state (see also Jordan 2010), the more party attention because parties have to address all kinds of questions about service provision. When responsibility is defused to societal actors, political parties attend less to the issue.

The analysis reveals no significant party differences in attention to the issue. There are no niche parties on the issue and no strong tendency for the large, mainstream parties to pay more attention to the issue than other parties do. Thus, health care seems to be an issue to which all political parties have to pay attention. There is also no clear evidence that issue ownership is decisive. Even when a large, mainstream party has clear issue ownership as Labour has in the British case, the Conservatives still focus strongly on the issue, especially when in opposition. Hence, a large, mainstream party in opposition will see it highly attractive to add to the criticism of the incumbent party for delivering on health care. For the incumbent party, avoiding this blame avoidance dynamics is highly difficult, even when it is spending more money.

In terms of issue characteristics, education and health care share several characteristics such as being an obtrusive valence issue with a broad scope. For both issues, the organization of service delivery also seems to play an important role for party attention, but in somewhat different ways. Dealing with health care, the exact role of the state in service delivery seems to matter for how much the party system attention has grown across countries. When responsibility for health care is shared in different ways with societal actors for instance, political parties can defuse some of the blame involved in cost containment to these actors and focus less on health care.

With regard to education, the role of the state in the actual provision of services also varies. Some countries have more decentralized primary school systems. This does not seem to affect party attention to education in the same way as within health care. In all five unitary states, party attention to education has increased. The exact structure of provision seems less important. However, when the federal government does not hold authority over education, as in Germany and Belgium, political parties at this level pay less attention. In other words, parties generally like to focus on education, especially those with a focus on government power, if they hold the authority over the issue. With regard to health care, parties are presented with a dilemma. They would like to signal to the electorate that they deliver high quality services, but they would like to pass some of the unavoidable blame on to others. Finally, unlike education, health care does not imply the same long-term perspective on investment that makes parties with a long-term focus on governing interested in the issue (cf. Kraft 2017). Thus, neither large, mainstream parties nor social liberal parties focus specifically on health care.

12

The Issue Content of West European Party Politics

The Central Role of Large, Mainstream Parties, but for How Long?

The aims of this book have been both theoretical and empirical. The theoretical aim has been to explain the development of the issue content of West European party politics. The central theoretical argument of the book, contained in the issue incentive model, is that the incentives that different policy issues offer large, mainstream parties in terms of vote and office-seeking is the key to understanding why the wider party system comes to focus on certain issues. The issue incentive model offers a comprehensive account of the development of the party system agenda in general. The development of the individual issues is thus explained based on an understanding of the general dynamics of party attention to issues, not on a theory of individual issues. The empirical aim has been to describe the development of the issue agenda of West European party politics for the seven countries covered.

This final chapter summarizes the findings of the book in terms of both its theoretical argument and empirical aims. Furthermore, the chapter lays out the implications of these findings for two larger debates within the study of West European party politics. One debate is about the role of niche parties and the consequences of their growth for the West European party system. The second debate is about the linkage between voters and political parties in contemporary Western societies. Discussing these implications also sheds light on more recent developments within West European party systems, especially the declining electoral strength of exactly the parties that this book argues are decisive for the development of the issue content of West European party politics, namely large, mainstream parties. Instead of these parties, niche parties, specifically radical right-wing parties like the German AFD and the Dutch PVV, have gained considerable electoral strength.

WHAT HAS HAPPENED TO THE ISSUE CONTENT OF WEST EUROPEAN PARTY POLITICS?

A starting point for this book has been the transformation of West European party politics away from class-based politics towards issue-based politics. Despite the large body of literature on many aspects of this transformation, surprisingly few studies systematically map the issue content of West European party politics. The booming literature presented in Chapter 2 on the many different aspects of issue politics typically only focuses on a few issues without much attention to the overall party system agenda. The studies that come closest to systematically mapping the issue content of West European party politics are the studies on the new, second dimension of West European party politics (e.g. Hooghe and Marks 2018; Kriesi et al. 2008, 2012).

The first expectation typically drawn from the decline of 'class politics' is the decline of economic or material issues (Green-Pedersen 2007; Norris and Inglehart 2019; Kriesi et al. 2012: 109–13). As shown in Chapter 5, this expectation is confirmed in the sense that compared to the early 1980s, party system attention to economic issues defined as policy questions relating to macroeconomics, the labour market, and business has generally declined. However, the fact that these issues have become less dominant clearly does not mean that they are not important issues on the party system agenda. The financial crisis also increased attention to them in several countries, though not to the same level as in the early 1980s.

Furthermore, as pointed out by Kriesi et al. (2012: 109–13), it is important to be precise when it comes to this claim about the decline of economic issues. It does not mean that material issues have declined in attention. Questions related to the overall welfare state remain central to the party system agenda in all the countries studied. As shown in Chapter 5, party attention to social policy remains stable and high, and attention to education and health care has generally risen. Thus, party system attention to the welfare state has shifted away from labour-market issues towards life-cycle issues (Green-Pedersen and Jensen 2019; see also Kriesi et al. 2012: 111). This development in the party system agenda has received surprisingly little attention. However, it is important from both an empirical and a theoretical perspective. Empirically, political parties have not only increased attention to health care but also spending (Green-Pedersen and Jensen 2019). Party attention has policy consequences and an increasing spending on health care in order to satisfy the unending demand for health care services will, to some extent, crowd out other expenses. Theoretically, this development is important as any theoretical account of the dynamics behind the party system agenda also has to explain the rising attention to issues like health care and education where no niche parties exist.

The second implication typically drawn from the transformation of West European party politics is the growing importance of issues related to the new, second dimension like immigration and European integration (Hooghe and Marks 2018; Kriesi et al. 2012: 109–13). These issues have generally come to play a greater role (see Chapter 5), but in terms of issue content, the notion of the new, second dimension or 'new politics' is typically rather vaguely described. For instance, different studies have different views on whether or not the environment should be seen as such an issue (cf. Kriesi et al. 2012: 109–13; Stubager 2010). More importantly, there is considerable variation both across issues and across countries in terms of which issues have received the most attention. For example, in Denmark and Sweden, attention to new politics issues has grown considerably. In Denmark it applies to immigration, and in Sweden it applies to personal rights and women's rights in particular (cf. Cowell-Meyers 2017).

Chapter 5 also shows how party system attention to defence and foreign policy issues has declined in Germany, the Netherlands, and Denmark, where they were important issues on the party system agenda in the 1980s. These issues can also be seen as belonging to the new, second dimension, especially when understood more narrowly as a transnational cleavage (Hooghe and Marks 2018). The attention to these issues in the 1980s most likely reflects the intense political conflicts related to the Cold War, especially NATO's double decision which implied a deployment of nuclear missiles in Europe (cf. Kriesi et al. 1995). Due to the Cold War context, defence and foreign policy were closely related to the left–right party competition. After the Cold War, problem perception in foreign and security policy changed dramatically. In the period studied in this book, defence and foreign policy became preoccupied with responding to regimes and conflicts in particularly the Middle East by sending troops and accepting the loss of soldiers. However, this new problem perception has been much more decoupled from party conflict, and attention has declined. Attention to these issues thus seems to be driven by quite different dynamics than issues like immigration and European integration.

One limitation to the empirical part of this book is that it only covers seven West European countries and mainly North-West European countries. This, of course, raises a question about generalizability beyond the seven countries, which has both a theoretical and an empirical aspect to it. Theoretically, there is no reason to expect that the theoretical model developed should not be applicable to party systems not analysed in the book, at least as long as they share the same basic characteristics with the countries included in the book. Two such characteristics are worth mentioning. First, political parties are unitary actors dominated by election and office-minded politicians and not just coalitions of interest groups and activists as suggested by Bawn et al. (2012) with reference to the US. Second, it is the party systems, i.e. relatively stable configurations of parties, which are being analysed (Bardi and Mair

2008). In addition to data availability, unstable party systems are the reason for not including Eastern European countries or a country like Italy. This does not imply that the theoretical arguments of this book are irrelevant for Eastern European countries, Italy, or the US for that matter, but just that in these cases, other dynamics not included in this book might have a strong impact on the content of party politics.

In terms of the empirical generalizability, a number of further points are worth spelling out. First, a general finding is a considerable cross-national similarity in terms of the issue content of party politics. Across all five issues, there are clear cross-national similarities like limited attention to European integration, rising—and then declining—attention to the environment, rising attention to health care, etc. These tendencies are found despite the variation in both party systems and political systems across the seven countries and are the results of the similar incentives that these issues offer large, mainstream parties across all the countries. Kriesi et al. (2012: 109–20), who include Austria and Switzerland (not covered in this book), generally also observe quite similar developments in terms of the issue content of party politics. This does not mean that important cross-national variation does not exist. The strong focus on immigration in Denmark starting in the 1990s as well as the strong focus on crime and justice in Belgium in the 1990s are both examples of more country-specific developments. Thus, if moving beyond the countries studied here, a revelation of additional cross-national variation in the content of party politics could be expected. However, the general tendencies found for all issues studied here are also expected to exist in countries not covered. The relatively high degree of similarity in party system attention across countries is worth highlighting because it points towards the importance of more issue-specific factors like issue characteristics.

HOW TO EXPLAIN PARTY SYSTEM ATTENTION: THE ISSUE INCENTIVE MODEL

The theoretical argument of this book presented in the issue incentive model is that the vote and office incentives of large, mainstream parties are the key to explaining how policy issues rise and decline on the party system agenda. Furthermore, the argument is that the vote and office incentives of large, mainstream parties depend on three factors, namely issue characteristics, issue ownership, and coalition considerations. It is now possible to draw a number of conclusions as to the role of these factors and thus evaluate the issue incentive model.

Issue Characteristics

As explained in Chapter 3, the importance of issue characteristics has long been pointed out as a significant driver of political attention in the policy agenda-setting literature. At the same time, this literature has struggled to determine more precisely how issue characteristics matter. A number of issue typologies have been developed, but the classification of issues based on these typologies has typically turned out to be difficult. Inspired by Grossmann (2012), rather than developing a typology, this book has developed a general understanding of which issue characteristics are potentially important. Then each issue is discussed in terms of which issue characteristics are the most important. It is important to stress that these are the issue characteristics which are argued to be the most important with regard to the vote and office incentives of large, mainstream parties. If one moves away from electoral politics and into policy decision-making, other aspects like distribution of interest and formation of interest groups surrounding an issue are likely to be much more important (cf. Hacker and Pierson 2014). Thus, the issue characteristics highlighted here—the interaction between problem information and problem characteristics (i.e. solubility, scope, valence, and policy type)—are not argued to be the most important issue characteristics per se, but they are the most important ones if one wants to understand the vote and office incentives of large, mainstream parties.

The issue chapters clearly show the crucial importance of issue characteristics in terms of both problem information and problem characteristics. Regarding all five issues, problem information in various forms was found to be important for the over-time development of party system attention. Citing just two examples, the development of environmental problems is important for understanding why the environment generally rose on the party system agendas during the 1980s and then declined again after the mid-1990s. The number of health-care patents as a measure of medical technological development is crucial for explaining rising party system attention to health care. This reflects the struggle of political parties to satisfy the voters' expectation that they have unlimited access to the latest technologies and medication. Focusing events like the Chernobyl disaster, the Maastricht Treaty, and the results of the PISA scores also clearly affected party system attention. Another example is the growth in party system attention to crime and justice in Belgium following the Dutroux scandals (Walgrave and Varone 2008). Events can thus be an important driver of party system attention, but their effect depends on the incentives of large, mainstream parties. The Chernobyl disaster increased party system attention to the environment, but it came at a time when large, mainstream parties of especially the left had already begun to focus on the environment. When the Fukushima disaster happened in 2011, the incentives of the large, mainstream parties to focus on the environment were more limited, and there is no sign of a surge in party system attention to the environment in the following elections.

Problem information is one aspect of issue characteristics. The other is problem characteristics which are stable features of policy problems related to policy issues. The old phrase in policy research that 'policy determines politics' (Freeman 1985) is clearly supported in this book. Political attention to policy issues is always about something, and that something is policy 'problems', but policy problems vary hugely in nature. As for the party system dynamics, the question of whether an issue is a valence issue, for instance, seems to matter significantly for the party system dynamics (cf. also Abou-Chadi 2016).[1] Dealing with valence issues like education, health care, and the environment, issue ownership seems less important for whether large, mainstream parties focus on the issue. In the UK, where Labour has typically owned the issue of health care, the Conservatives also focus strongly on health care. When looking at the environment, increases in party system attention are not always driven by the large, mainstream, left-wing parties only, but also by the other large, mainstream parties. Belgium and the Netherlands are clear examples of this. Thus, although there are differences in how much parties focus on valence issues, party attention is less determined by the incentives of the large, mainstream party owning the issue. When it comes to a positional issue like immigration, party system attention seems to depend more critically on the willingness of the large, mainstream party owning the issue to focus on it. In the case of immigration, party system attention is dependent on the large, mainstream right-wing parties focusing on it.[2]

Focusing on the issue characteristics of European integration in comparison to other issues also shows the importance of issue characteristics. The lack of clear problem indicators and the fact European integration is closely related to foreign policy limit the interest of large, mainstream parties. The issue can be difficult to handle for large, mainstream parties once they are in government. Thus, as laid out in Chapter 8, party system attention is 'punctuated' as described by Grande and Kriesi (2016). The investment character of education also partly shapes party interest in the issue (Kraft 2017), and party competition for health care is impossible to understand without taking the blame avoidance perspective into account.

---

[1] Abou-Chadi (2016) highlights how the interaction between the valence nature of the environment and the existence of Green parties shapes the strategies of mainstream parties. The inclusion of valence issues like health care and education with no niche parties and attention from almost all mainstream parties would indicate that the valence character is more important than the existence of niche parties.

[2] It is also worth noticing that social liberal parties and other smaller, mainstream parties like the Swedish Centre Party have focused strongly on the environment as well. Compared to immigration, the valence nature of the environmental issue thus seems to make it attractive for other issue entrepreneurs than Green parties.

The strong findings of the importance of issue characteristics are also a warning against theorizing about party competition dynamics based on single issues like European integration, immigration, or the environment. This has been a very common practice in the literature on issue competition as described in Chapter 2. Of course, there are general lessons to be learnt from single issues, but the dynamics found for a single issue might just as well be the result of the characteristics of that specific issue. A study like Abou-Chadi (2016) that covers only two issues immediately finds significant variation across the two issues.

In many ways, it is surprising how little theoretical focus there has been on the role of both aspects of issue characteristics, i.e. problem information and problem characteristics, in the otherwise booming literature on issue competition. The theoretical challenge is to move beyond the basic findings that issue characteristics matter. The effect on party system attention of factors like environmental problems or health-care patents could be seen as though parties are simply responding to 'objective' problem indicators. However, this would be a much too simplistic interpretation. Especially the role of problem information deserves much more attention. For instance, how do societal conditions come to be seen as specific problems that can be measured in a certain way? And why can political parties sometimes ignore problem information? Problem information is a necessary condition for party attention to a given issue in the sense that it is very hard to draw attention to an issue presenting it as a response to a policy problem. Parties rarely talk about education, health care, or immigration in the abstract. They talk about the policy problems related to these policy issues.

The effect of the PISA scores on party system attention to education (see Chapter 10) points to the complex relationship between problem information and party system attention. In Denmark and Germany, the PISA scores generated a shock that generated party attention, though in Germany not at the national level. In France, similar scores did not generate much party system attention. In the UK and Sweden, party system attention existed before the PISA scores, and the scores were seen as a justification of existing policy measures. It is therefore impossible to understand why certain issues rise and decline on the party system agenda without taking into account the character and the development of the problems related to the relevant policy issues. However, a more precise understanding of how these issue characteristics matter is still a major challenge for the literature on issue competition.

Issue Ownership

The second factor highlighted in the issue incentive model is whether a large, mainstream party has issue ownership of an issue in comparison to other large, mainstream parties. The mainstream left-wing issue ownership of the environment and the mainstream right-wing issue ownership of immigration are argued to make them potentially interested in these issues. However, the findings also indicate that this does not imply that they necessarily focus on these issues. The large, mainstream left was not found to pay more attention in general to the environment than other parties did. However, in more specific cases, issue ownership has played an important role. In the UK, issue ownership played a critical role for Labour's strong focus on health care and education in the 1990s. It was also important for the Danish Liberal Party's focus on immigration from the 1990s and for the German SDP's focus on the environment in the 1980s.

This points towards three conclusions of when issue ownership is important for the strategies of large, mainstream parties. First, following Seeberg (2013a, 2013b), opposition status seems to matter. When large, mainstream parties need a strategy to regain power, issue ownership is an important aspect of their choice as to which issue to focus on. The Danish Liberals' focus on immigration after losing power in 1993 and Labour's focus on education and health care in the 1990s are cases in point. However, once they regain power, they do not simply give up their focus on the issues because they have successfully built coalitions on them and mobilized voters. From that perspective, it is not surprising that the regression analyses in the preceding chapters show no effect of government/opposition status.

Second, when focusing on immigration and the environment, issue ownership mainly seems to play a role when reinforced by coalition incentives. For instance, Labour did not focus specifically on the environment in the 1990s. This would indicate that issue ownership or not, large, mainstream parties find issues more attractive when they are closer to their left–right ideology. Unless other factors like coalition considerations are important, large, mainstream left-wing parties would rather compete on issues related to the welfare state than on the environment.

Third, in several countries, issue ownership of education and health care is unclear. This does not mean that large, mainstream parties stay away from these issues; issue ownership is thus not a necessary condition for the parties to focus on a given issue. As discussed above, issue ownership seems less important for parties when it comes to valence issues. They often focus on such issues without issue ownership.

Coalition Considerations

The third factor in the issue incentive model is coalition considerations. Coalition considerations emerge when party positions on an issue diverge from the overall left–right dimension that typically structures the forming of office coalitions.[3] Focusing on a specific issue is a way for a large, mainstream party to generate coalitional support from a niche party or to conduct 'wedge issue competition' to challenge the office coalition of a competing large, mainstream party (van de Wardt et al. 2014). Such coalition incentives clearly play an important role in explaining party system attention to immigration in Denmark and to the environment in Germany and Sweden as well as the rather limited interest of large, mainstream parties in European integration.

The findings of the importance of coalition considerations for party system attention are worth highlighting for several reasons. First, coalition considerations have received rather limited attention from the issue competition literature. How the emergence of niche parties has affected party competition, and especially how mainstream parties react to niche parties have been investigated intensively as discussed in Chapter 2. However, the impact is almost always understood in terms of vote-seeking. Going back to the pioneering work of Meguid (2005), niche parties have rarely been seen as potential coalition partners for large, mainstream parties. They have mainly been analysed as competitors for votes (Adams et al. 2006; Ezrow 2007). However, the findings in this book clearly show that the growth of niche parties has important coalition effects.

Second, the role of coalition considerations also shows that party positions on issues play a very important role for how much attention large, mainstream parties pay to issues. Where large, mainstream parties are placed with respect to an issue compared to other parties is crucial for their issue strategies. Thus, the focus in this book on issue attention should in no way be interpreted as an argument that party positions do not play a crucial role in party competition. Any general theory of party competition clearly has to incorporate both. The question is how issue attention and party positions are most fruitfully combined. A central question is from which end to begin when explaining competition, attention, or position, respectively. The argument of this book is that attention is often the most fruitful analytical starting point because it is the most dynamic aspect of party behaviour (cf. Abou-Chadi et al. 2019). Though voters also have expectations of which issues parties focus on, i.e. associative issue ownership (Walgrave et al. 2012), especially large, mainstream parties have much more flexibility in terms of issue focus than in terms of party positions. Parties can change positions, but they risk being accused of pandering (Somer-Topcu 2009), they risk internal conflicts (Schumacher et al. 2013), and voters may not even notice it (Adams et al. 2011). From that perspective, it is not so surprising that party positions have typically been found to be rather stable (Dalton and McAllister 2015).

---

[3] These are either coalitions holding office or coalitions between minority governments and support parties.

Third, the role of coalition considerations also points to the role of political systems in shaping the party system agenda. In several cases, coalition considerations have been an important reason why large, mainstream parties have begun to focus on new issues. Clear examples are the German SPD's focus on the environment in the 1980s and the Danish Liberals' focus on immigration from the early 1990s. Coalitions are largely non-existent in France and the UK due to the institutional setup of their political systems. The large, mainstream parties have not ignored issues like immigration and the environment in these two countries, but they have not embraced them as strongly as large, mainstream parties have in the countries where a strong focus on these issues was helpful for coalition building and thus for winning office. As discussed in Chapter 5, party system attention to 'new politics' issues was also generally somewhat lower in France and the UK than in the other countries. Hence, it seems that in political systems in which coalition dynamics play a more limited role, the large, mainstream parties tend to keep the party system agenda more focused on the traditional left–right issues.

One way to summarize the factor shaping the incentives of large, mainstream parties and thus the evaluation of the issue incentive model is in terms of necessary and sufficient conditions. As discussed above, issue characteristics concerning problem information can be seen as a necessary condition. Without problem information, large, mainstream parties have few incentives to focus on an issue. Issue characteristics may also be sufficient when they provide large, mainstream parties with strong incentives to focus on specific issues. Issues being valence issues with a broad scope like education and health care are cases in point. Issue ownership and coalition considerations are not necessary conditions. Large, mainstream parties sometimes focus on issues they do not clearly own. Coalition considerations may be sufficient for large, mainstream parties, but typically only when the large, mainstream party has concurrent issue ownership.

PARTY SYSTEM AGENDA

As the final element, it is worth highlighting the implications of the issue incentive model's focus on explaining the party system agenda. Behind this concept (cf. Green-Pedersen and Mortensen 2010) is the importance of understanding political parties as part of a competitive system (Bardi and Mair 2008). The underlying argument is that one cannot observe and analyse political parties in isolation of their competitive environment. Political parties influence each other and are also influenced by each other. Concepts like issue yield (de Sio and Weber 2014) and issue ownership (Budge 2015) rightly point out that parties have preferred issues. However, political parties do not present themselves to the electorate in isolation of other parties, but as part of a competitive system. This must also be taken into account when analysing which issues political parties focus on in a party manifesto. Focusing on explaining the party system agenda is a conceptual strategy to include this in the analysis. The focus on the party system agenda also helps recognizing the importance of coalition considerations that have largely been overlooked in the issue competition literature.

THE ISSUE INCENTIVE MODEL AND THE ROLE OF THE NEW, SECOND DIMENSION OF PARTY CONFLICT

Before moving to the implications of the issue incentive model and the findings of this book on broader debates about West European party politics, it is worth summarizing the theoretical discussion of the literature on the new, second dimension of West European party politics (Hooghe and Marks 2018; Kriesi et al. 2008, 2012). This has been the most dominant perspective on the issue content of West European party politics and has been discussed throughout the book. It also represents the dominant bottom-up approach to understanding the content of party politics. Contrasting the issue incentive model with the literature on the new, second dimension thus helps clarifying the implications of the top-down nature of the issue incentive model.

The difference between the two perspectives is not so much in empirical terms. The findings of this book are not very different from those of for instance Kriesi et al. (2008, 2012), even though findings like the growth in attention to health care and education receive surprisingly little attention in the literature on the new, second dimension. Thus, the growth of issues related to the new, second dimension is in general a correct description of the development of the issue content of West European party politics, but it is also a rather vague one. Quite diverse issues are characterized as belonging to the second dimension, and there is considerable variation across issues and countries in terms of how much attention the issues actually receive, also when one only focuses on 'transnational issues' (Hooghe and Marks 2018). For instance, European integration remains a relatively minor issue in party competition in all the countries whereas immigration has become a more important issue on the party system agenda in Denmark than in the other countries. Thus, each issue has its own dynamic in terms of party attention. As also indicated by the MDS analysis in Chapter 6, it is difficult to see whether attention to issues related to the new, second dimension is driven by the same underlying dynamic. For instance, the two issues of European integration and immigration have followed different trajectories. It is also important to notice that attention to issues related to the new, second dimension typically declined again after the financial crisis. In a way, this is not surprising, but from a theoretical perspective, it underlines the importance of 'problem developments' for party system attention and the limitation of focusing on changes in societal conflicts.

It is also important to distinguish between a long- and medium-term perspective. For instance, the works of Kriesi et al. (2008, 2012) have a more long-term perspective than this book. The emergence of the new, second conflict line within the electorate based on exposure to globalization or education (see Langsæther and Stubager 2018) and manifesting itself with regard to a range of different policy issues is an important long-term development. How voters' attitudes are distributed on a given issue is clearly important if the issue becomes subject to party competition as vote-seeking is an important motive for political parties. Furthermore, changes within the electorate are crucial for understanding the electoral potential of niche parties. The question, however, here is how much this general, long-term development shapes the content of party politics in the medium term. When one focuses on why certain issues dominate the party system agenda over several elections, i.e. in the medium term, the argument implied in the issue incentive model is that these long-term changes within the electorate say much less than the literature on the second dimension typically recognizes.

When discussing how the literature on the second dimension explains the issue content of West European party politics, it is rather important to be aware that the analytical focus of this literature is only indirectly the issue content of party politics. The direct focus is on the 'format' of party competition, more specifically whether the new, second dimension found within the electorate can also be found at the party level. This is in itself a debated issue (see van der Brug and van Spanje 2009). However, a more general question is why the format of party competition in general should be the main analytical focus. After all, parties do not present themselves to the electorate in terms of their placement in a two-dimensional space, but by outlining their position on specific policy issues. How parties position themselves on such issues compared to the general left–right scale is crucial, as discussed in the preceding chapters, but only to the extent to which parties pay attention to the issues. Thus, the strong focus on the format of party competition is useful in describing long-term developments in party politics, but it is a much less fruitful starting point for actually analysing party competition.

Implicit in this discussion is also a question about the right analytical level from which to analyse the issue content of West European party politics. The literature on the new, second dimension automatically pools a number of issues argued to belong to the second dimension. Studies like Tavits and Potter (2015), Ward et al. (2015), and Norris and Inglehart (2019) also analyse broad groups of issues organized in terms of economic/non-economic, redistributive/value-based, or material/cultural. The usefulness of such a pooling obviously depends on one's research focus. However, if one's research focus is to understand which issues political parties compete on, the findings in this book suggest that pooling different policy issues in such broad categories, though helpful in providing an overview, is problematic. The problem is that the issues which are pooled together in fact vary considerably when analysed from the issue incentive model. Pooling issues together is of course attractive in order to reduce complexity and avoid having to deal with a large number of policy issues like the 23 issues included in the basic issue scheme of this book. However, if the aim is to explain the dynamics of party competition, the argument based on the findings in this book is that a more disaggregated analytical level like policy issues is necessary.

In sum, the literature on the new, second dimension clearly highlights important long-term changes within the electorate. These changes are an important element of the context in which political parties today develop the strategies that shape the party system agenda. In this sense, the bottom-up approach of the studies of the new, second dimension and the top-down approach of the issue incentive model are not in disagreement. The question is how much these changes within the electorate can explain about the actual content of party politics. In other words, to which extent is the strategic room to manoeuvre limited for elite actors like political parties. The issue incentive model implies considerably more room to manoeuvre or compete for political parties than implied in the literature on the new, second dimension.

BOTTOM-UP VS. TOP-DOWN LINKAGE: THE ROLE OF NICHE PARTIES

One of the reasons why studying the issue content of party politics, i.e. explaining the party system agenda, is important is that it sheds light on a broader theoretical debate about the linkage between voters and the political system in contemporary democracies. Following Lawson (1980), political parties provide the most important linkage, and the understanding of what shapes the issue content of party politics is therefore important for understanding how parties link voters to the political systems (cf. Dalton et al. 2011). The top-down and bottom-up approaches offer different perspectives on this linkage. The core theoretical difference is with regard to the mechanism proving the linkage between parties and voters or more precisely: the dynamics of party competition.

From the perspective of the issue incentive model, the changes highlighted in the literature on the new, second dimension affect both the party competition and the party system agenda because they affect the vote and office incentives of large, mainstream parties. How voters, depending on their educational background, place themselves along a new, second dimension on a number of issues with relevance to party competition, affects the vote incentives of large, mainstream parties. Furthermore, when new parties emerge based on issues related to the new, second dimension, it potentially affects the coalition incentives of large, mainstream parties as clearly shown in several case studies in this book. This is a quite different linkage mechanism than the bottom-up perspective of the literature on the new, second dimension. From that perspective, changes in the electorate are the analytical staring point. However, from a top-down perspective, changes are not automatically relevant. They only become so if the issues become politically relevant, and this has to do with the development of the policy problems related to the issues as discussed in the preceding chapters.

In the literature on the new, second dimension, the mechanism linking the electorate with party competition is clearly the emergence of new parties. They mobilize based on the issues related to the new, second dimension, and this is argued to generate party attention to the issues (cf. Kriesi et al. 2008, 2012). Hooghe and Marks (2018) have elaborated the bottom-up perspective further and emphasize, like the previous cleavage literature (cf. Chapter 2), that party conflicts are sticky. New political parties become important at 'critical junctures' like the euro crisis after the financial crisis in 2008 and the recent years' migration crisis. The role of niche parties thus remains central also in this version of a sociological perspective. Therefore, the findings on niche parties in this book are worth summarizing.

The issues studied above are chosen to provide variation on the existence/ absence of niche parties, and a number of conclusions can be drawn from the role of niche parties. First, the issue chapters clearly show that rising party system attention to issues is not dependent on niche parties promoting these issues. Party system attention to education and health care has risen in most countries without the existence of niche parties, and immigration and the environment have also received attention in the UK without the existence of strong niche parties. The chapter on European integration clearly shows that even when niche parties or issue entrepreneurs exist that try to push an issue on the party system agenda, the large, mainstream parties can still largely ignore the issue. However, only if they all do so. In terms of immigration, the statistical analysis indicated a direct, but weak effect on the other parties in the sense that the growing electoral strength of radical right-wing parties led to more party system attention. However, when it comes to the environment, the finding on the direct effect of Green parties was the exact opposite.

The Central Role of Large, Mainstream Parties

This does not imply that niche parties are unimportant for issue competition. On the contrary, they may change the competition dynamics fundamentally when they create new coalition incentives for large, mainstream parties. The growth of the Danish People's Party in Denmark and the Greens in Germany are clear examples. However, as the other cases show, this effect is not automatic. Radical right-wing parties in Belgium and the Netherlands have not yet had the same effect on the party system agenda. The effect depends on how the growth affects the coalition interests of the large, mainstream right-wing parties. Thus, the argument of this book is not that niche parties and their growth are unimportant but rather that one needs to analyse this development within a broader theoretical focus on large, mainstream parties to be able to judge its implications. From a broader theoretical perspective, the book thus argues against a 'mobilization' perspective where the main mechanism generating increasing party system attention to an issue is the mobilization of the issue by niche parties. The argument is not that such mobilization dynamics do not exist, but rather that this is a less important mechanism because the impact of niche parties depends on how they affect coalition dynamics.

Going back to the question about top-down vs. bottom-up and the linkage between political parties and the electorate, the perspective of the issue incentive model can now be specified more precisely. What is offered is clearly a top-down or elitist perspective in the sense that the starting point for explaining the party system agenda is the large, mainstream parties' incentives and not the electorate's. The argument is that the driving mechanism behind changes in the party system agenda is rarely changes in the electorate, but rather changes in policy problems or the information on them. This does not imply that voters and their positions on policy issues are unimportant, on the contrary. They are crucial elements of the opportunity structure of large, mainstream parties. Once issues gain attention on the party system agenda, voter positions become increasingly important for the large, mainstream parties and make them willing to adjust their policy positions.

The issue incentive models share similarities with what Kitschelt and Rehm (2015) label a 'dealignment' perspective on the linkage between voters and parties in post-industrial societies. The saliency of an issue is seen as the key to understanding when parties pay attention to voters' preferences. However, this does not imply that the content of party politics is highly fluid, and that only an analysis with a short-term focus is fruitful (Kitschelt and Rehm 2015: 183). The preceding chapters clearly show that party competition for issues from a medium-term perspective is structured by a number of factors that make it predictable. One such factor is party positions on issues and how they relate to an overall left–right structure that drives coalition incentives. Furthermore, issue ownership is a factor in the way large, mainstream parties evaluate issues with regard to their willingness to pay attention to them.

Factors such as left–right positions and issue ownership are important because they are well-known political benchmarks for voters. They draw on voters' basic perceptions of party ideology, which again have strong societal and historical roots. Thus, the focus on saliency does not imply that party competition is highly fluid and detached from voters' ideological dimensions.

The issue incentive model also differs from the cartel perspective on political parties developed by Katz and Mair (1995, 2018; see also Kitschelt and Rehm 2015: 184–5). From this perspective, parties are able to form a cartel that effectively keeps new issues and parties away from the party system and makes voter positions of limited importance. This perspective underestimates large, mainstream parties' incentives to use issues to gain office at the expense of other large, mainstream parties. Here, voter positions are central. Still, when one looks at European integration, the cartel perspective appears relevant. The 'permissive consensus' has implied limited attention to European integration and limited impact of Euroscepticism. Brexit is obviously clear evidence of the impact of Euroscepticism, but the call of the Brexit referendum was not the result of European integration having reached the top of the party system agenda in the UK before the call.

A further implication of the elite approach implied in the issue incentive model is that the electorate is not the analytical starting point. The underlying idea is that the party level has its own dynamic shaped by the fact that political parties are a small group of strategic actors who compete with each other, and this has been the starting point for understanding their development. This is a fundamentally different point of departure compared to the electorate where voters do not compete with each other. The electorate is not a strategic actor who thinks about how its surroundings (other parties and voters) perceive its actions. The electorate is the sum of many individuals who respond without a particular strategic focus on the information they receive. This does not mean that parties do not care about the electorate. They certainly do. But to political parties, reflecting the dimensions found within the electorate is in itself not important. Votes are.

Summing up, the issue incentive model is top-down in its starting point. Large, mainstream parties' incentives provide the theoretical starting point for understanding the dynamics of the party system agenda. Still, it is worth highlighting that the party system agenda does not find a stable equilibrium isolated from the surrounding society including the electorate. As Baumgartner and Jones (1993: 3–16) point out, politics never finds a stable equilibrium. This is only found at the subsystem level of specific policy issues or policy questions. The primary reason is that the world is not stable. New political problems emerge or existing ones are reinterpreted, and this opens up new opportunities for vote- and office-seeking political parties. Policy problems, a factor that has not received much attention in the issue competition literature, thus constitute a crucial source of political change. This is clear from studying party attention to issues like the environment, health care, and immigration. Moreover, unlike a cartel version of a top-down perspective, this book stresses the importance of competition for vote and office between large, mainstream parties. This competition makes voter positions on issues central, but only once large, mainstream parties compete for them.

THE FUTURE ROLE OF LARGE, MAINSTREAM PARTIES

For any observer of West European party politics after 2010, the theoretical focus of this book on large, mainstream parties may seem odd in the sense that this period has substantially challenged the dominant role of these parties in West European party systems. Hence, these parties have witnessed a period of electoral decline. The other side of this development is the rising electoral strength of niche parties, especially radical right-wing parties. This development has been ongoing for decades, but the growing electoral strength of parties like the German AFD, the Sweden Democrats, the Danish People's Party, the French Front National, and the PVV in the Netherlands implies increasing pressure on the dominant role of large, mainstream parties. To put it differently, Chapter 3 distinguishes between large and small, mainstream parties and niche parties. Maybe one needs to distinguish between large and small, niche parties as well in order to indicate that some niche parties have grown as strong—or even stronger—as large, mainstream parties in electoral terms. Furthermore, the question is what this implies for the dynamics of the party system agenda. Does it imply that the issues that large, niche parties focus on, immigration for instance, gain a more prominent role simply because the electoral size of niche parties forces other parties to adapt to their agenda?

The answer to this is: not automatically. The special role of large, mainstream parties in setting the party system agenda is not simply a matter of size, but also of these parties' long tradition for being in government and having a broad ideological profile including issue focus. As discussed in Chapter 3, being in government means having to address a large number of policy issues. Of course, parties can focus on some issues, but parties in government need to be prepared to deal with all kinds of issues. This has been the reality of large, mainstream parties for decades, and the other parties' as well as the voters' perceptions of them are adjusted to this. They are expected to deliver a broad issue package to the electorate (Bertelli and John 2013). The question of government participation becomes increasingly pressing for niche parties as their electoral strength grows. Government participation puts pressure on the strong focus on one or a few issues. What if a new economic or environmental crisis emerges? It is therefore not surprising that seeking office has not been a strong motive for niche parties. This is, however, also what limits their impact on the party system agenda. A large, radical right-wing party is likely to be crucial during a refugee crisis, but it is silent on many other issues.

This is not to argue that the growing electoral strength of niche parties at the expense of large, mainstream parties is unimportant. On the contrary. But the major effect is more likely to come through its effect on coalition building. As recent government formation efforts in Germany, the Netherlands, and Sweden have shown, large, mainstream parties have often been unwilling to cooperate with strong radial right-wing parties, which have perhaps not been particularly interested in government participation in the first place. However, the problem is that building governing coalitions has become increasingly difficult. The prolonged government formation processes in the Netherlands in 2017 as well as in Germany and Sweden in 2018 are examples of this.

One outcome is increased cooperation among the large, mainstream parties, for example the grand coalition formed in Germany in early 2018. This coalition was perhaps not what any of the two large, mainstream parties preferred, but it allows them to govern together, and it may generate a more stable party system agenda because competition between the large, mainstream parties becomes more limited (cf. Walgrave and Nuytemans 2009)—especially as there is no large, mainstream party in opposition trying to change the party system agenda by generating more attention to its preferred issues.[4] This development may strengthen the cartel tendencies that emerge when large, mainstream parties do not compete for the content of the party system agenda. European integration is a clear example of such cartel dynamics; another is the immigration issue in Sweden. Despite the growing electoral strength of the Sweden Democrats following their entrance into the Swedish parliament in 2010, the Swedish Conservatives still declined to cooperate with the Sweden Democrats. At least until 2014, the large, mainstream parties have managed to keep party system attention to immigration at a relatively low level.

If the electoral strength of niche parties continues to grow or just stabilizes, their role in the party system and their interaction with large, mainstream parties will continue to be the central issue in terms of party system development in Western Europe. Will large, mainstream parties move in the cartel direction where they cooperate and form governments together (cf. Katz and Mair 2018: 134–8), even if reluctantly, as happened in Germany in 2018? Or will especially the large, mainstream parties on the right 'defect' and try to win

---

[4] The French case with the election of Emmanuel Macron as President and the birth of his party La République en Marche is a special case of a new party that appears to behave very much like a large, mainstream party. However, with its centrist orientation, its breakthrough resembles a situation of cooperation between large, mainstream parties.

government power with the radical right? This is what happened in Denmark already in the 1990s. The likelihood of this development of course also depends on the behaviour of the radical right-wing parties. Do they present themselves as reliable coalition partners as they have in Denmark by including an issue profile that is more similar to large, mainstream parties? This will give them more influence on the party system agenda, but of course, they risk losing their distinctiveness in the eyes of the electorate.

References

Abou-Chadi, Tarik. 2016. 'Niche Party Success & Mainstream Party Policy Shifts'. *British Journal of Political Science* 46, no. 2: 417–36.
Abou-Chadi, Tarik, Christoffer Green-Pedersen, and Peter B. Mortensen. 2019. 'Parties' Policy Adjustments in Response to Changes in Issue Saliency'. *West European Politics*. Advance online publication.
Adams, James, Samual Merill III, and Bernhard Grofman. 2005. *A Unified Theory of Party Competition*. Cambridge: Cambridge University Press.
Adams, James, Michael Clark, Lawrence Ezrow, and Garrett Glasgow. 2006. 'Are Niche Parties Fundamentally Different from Mainstream Parties? The Causes and Electoral Consequences of Western European Parties' Policy Shifts'. *American Journal of Political Science* 50, no. 3: 513–29.
Adams, James, Lawrence Ezrow, and Zeynep Somer-Topcu. 2011. 'Is Anybody Listening? Evidence that Voters Do Not Respond to European Parties' Policy Statements during Elections'. *American Journal of Political Science* 55, no. 2: 370–82.
Akkerman, Tjitske. 2012. 'Comparing Radical Right Parties in Government: Immigration and Integration Policies in Nine Countries (1996–2010)'. *West European Politics* 35, no. 3: 511–29.
Albright, Jeremy. 2010. 'The Multidimensional Nature of Party Competition'. *Party Politics* 16, no. 6: 699–719.
Alonso, Sonia and Saro Claro da Fonseca. 2012. 'Immigration, Left and Right'. *Party Politics* 18, no. 6: 865–84.
Andersen, Jørgen Goul. 1990. 'Denmark, Environmental Conflict and the Greening of the Labour Movement'. *Scandinavian Political Studies* 13, no. 2: 185–210.
Andersen, Jørgen Goul. 2003. 'The General Election in Denmark, November 2001'. *Electoral Studies* 22, no. 1: 186–93.
Ansell, Ben W. 2010. *From Ballot to the Blackboard*. Cambridge: Cambridge University Press.
Aragonès, Enriqueta, Micael Castanheira, and Marco Giani. 2015. 'Electoral Competition through Issue Selection'. *American Journal of Political Science* 59, no. 1: 71–90.
Armingeon, Klaus, Virginia Wenger, Fiona Wiedemeier, Christian Isler, Laura Knöpfel, David Weisstanner, and Sarah Engler. 2018. *Comparative Political Data Set 1960–2016*. Bern: Institute of Political Science, University of Bern.
Arndt, Christoph. 2016. 'Issue Evolution and Partisan Polarization in a European Multiparty System: Elite and Mass Repositioning in Denmark 1968–2011'. *European Union Politics* 17, no. 4: 660–82.
Bakker, Ryan, Catherine de Vries, Erica Edwards, Liesbet Hooghe, Seth Jolly, Gary Marks, Jonathan Polk, Jan Rovny, Marco Steenbergen, and Milada Anna Vachudova. 2015. 'Measuring Party Positions in Europe: The Chapel Hill Expert Survey Trend File, 1999–2010'. *Party Politics* 21, no. 1: 143–52.

Bale, Tim. 2003. 'Cinderella and Her Ugly Sisters: The Mainstream and Extreme Right in Europe's Bipolarising Party Systems'. *West European Politics* 26, no. 3: 67–90.

Bale, Tim. 2008. 'Turning Round the Telescope: Centre-Right Parties and Immigration and Integration Policy in Europe'. *Journal of European Public Policy* 15, no. 3: 315–30.

Bale, Tim, Christoffer Green-Pedersen, André Krouwel, Kurt Richard Luther, and Nick Sitter. 2010. 'If You Can't Beat Them, Join Them? Explaining Social Democratic Responses to the Challenge from the Populist Radical Right in Western Europe'. *Political Studies* 58, no. 3: 410–26.

Bardi, Luciano, Stefano Bartolini, and Alexander H. Trechsel. 2014. 'Responsive and Responsible? The Role of Parties in Twenty-First Century Politics'. *West European Politics* 37, no. 2: 235–52.

Bardi, Luciano and Peter Mair. 2008. 'The Parameters of Party Systems'. *Party Politics* 14, no. 2: 146–66.

Bartolini, Stefano and Peter Mair. 1990. *Identity, Competition and Electoral Availability*. Cambridge: Cambridge University Press.

Baumgartner, Frank R., Christian Breunig, and Emiliano Grossman, eds. 2019. *Comparative Policy Agendas: Theory, Tools, Data*. Oxford: Oxford University Press.

Baumgartner, Frank R. and Bryan D. Jones. 1993. *Agendas and Instability in American Politics*. Chicago: University of Chicago Press.

Baumgartner, Frank R. and Bryan D. Jones. 2009. *Agendas and Instability in American Politics*, 2nd ed. Chicago: University of Chicago Press.

Baumgartner, Frank R. and Bryan D. Jones. 2015. *The Politics of Information: Problem Definition and the Course of Public Policy in America*. Chicago: University of Chicago Press.

Baumgartner, Frank R., Bryan D. Jones, and Michael McLeod. 2000. 'The Evolution of Legislative Jurisdictions'. *Journal of Politics* 62, no. 2: 321–49.

Baumgartner, Frank R., Bryan D. Jones, and Peter Bjerre Mortensen. 2017. 'Punctuated Equilibrium Theory: Explaining Stability and Change in Policy Making'. In *Theories of the Policy Process*, 4th ed., edited by Christopher Weible and Paul A. Sabatier, 55–102. Boulder, CO: Westview Press.

Baumgartner, Frank R., Bryan D. Jones, and John D. Wilkerson. 2002. 'Studying Policy Dynamics'. In *Policy Dynamics*, edited by Frank R. Baumgartner and Bryan D. Jones, 29–46. Chicago: University of Chicago Press.

Bawn, Kathleen, Martin Cohen, David Karol, and Seth Masket. 2012. 'A Theory of Political Parties: Groups, Policy Demands and Nominations in American Politics'. *Perspectives on Politics* 10, no. 3: 571–97.

Bélanger, Eric and Bonnie M. Meguid. 2008. 'Issue Salience, Issue Ownership, and Issue-Based Vote Choice'. *Electoral Studies* 27, no. 3: 477–91.

Bennulf, Martin. 1994. 'The Rise and Fall of Miljöpartiet de Gröna'. In *The Green Challenge: The Development of Green Parties in Europe*, edited by Dick Richardson and Chris Rootes, 128–45. London: Routledge.

Bennulf, Martin and Sören Holmberg. 1990. 'The Green Breakthrough in Sweden'. *Scandinavian Political Studies* 13, no. 2: 165–82.

Beramendi, Pablo, Silja Häusermann, Herbert Kitschelt, and Hanspeter Kriesi, eds. 2015. *The Politics of Advanced Capitalism*. Cambridge and New York: Cambridge University Press.

Berkhout, Joost, Didier Ruedin, Wouter van der Brug, and Gianni D'Amato. 2015. 'Research Design'. In *The Politicization of Migration*, edited by Wouter van der Brug, Gianni D'Amato, Joost Berkhout, and Didier Ruedin, 19–30. London: Routledge.

Bertelli, Anthony and Peter John. 2013. 'Public Policy Investment: Risk and Return in British Politics'. *British Journal of Political Science* 43, no. 4: 741–73.

Bevan, Shuan. 2019. 'Gone Fishing: The Creation of the Comparative Agendas Project Master Codebook'. In *Comparative Policy Agendas: Theory, Tools, Data*, edited by Frank Baumgartner, Christian Breunig, and Emiliano Grossman, 17–34. Oxford: Oxford University Press.

Bille, Lars. 2007. 'Politisk kronik. 2. halvår 2006'. *Økonomi og Politik* 80, no. 3: 67–76.

Birkland, Thomas A. 1997. *After Disaster: Agenda Setting, Public Policy, and Focusing Events*. Washington DC: Georgetown University Press.

Blank, Robert H. and Viola Burau. 2014. *Comparative Health Policy*, 4th ed. Basingstoke: Palgrave Macmillan.

Böhm, Katharina, Achim Schmid, Ralf Götze, Claudia Landwehr, and Heinz Rothgang. 2013. 'Five Types of OECD Healthcare Systems: Empirical Results of a Deductive Classification'. *Health Policy* 113, no. 3: 258–69.

Bolin, Niklas. 2016. 'Green Parties in Finland and Sweden: Successful Cases of the North?' In *Green Parties in Europe*, edited by Emilie van Haute, 158–76. London: Routledge.

Boomgaarden, Hajo G., Rens Vliegenthart, Claes H. de Vreese, and Andreas T. Schuck. 2010. 'News on the Move: Exogenous Events and News Coverage of the European Union'. *Journal of European Public Policy* 17, no. 4: 506–26.

Borg, Ingwer and Patrick Groenen. 1997. *Modern Multidimensional Scaling: Theory and Applications*. New York: Springer.

Bornschier, Simon. 2010. 'The New Cultural Divide and the Two-Dimensional Political Space in Western Europe'. *West European Politics* 33, no. 3: 419–44.

Boy, Daniel. 2002. 'France'. In *Green Parties in National Governments*, edited by Ferdinand Müller-Rommel and Thomas Poguntke, 63–77. London: Frank Cass.

Boydstun, Amber E., Shaun Bevan, and Herschel F. Thomas. 2014. 'The Importance of Attention Diversity and How to Measure It'. *Policy Studies Journal* 42, no. 2: 173–96.

Brettschneider, Frank. 2004. 'Agenda-Setting, Agenda-Cutting, Agenda-Surfing: Themenmanagement bei der Bundestagswahl 2002'. In *Der versäumte Wechsel*, edited by Herbert Oberreuter, 9–34. München: Olzog.

Budge, Ian. 2015. 'Issue Emphases, Saliency Theory and Issue Ownership: A Historical and Conceptual Analysis'. *West European Politics* 38, no. 4: 761–77.

Budge, Ian and Dennis Farlie. 1983. 'Party Competition: Selective Emphasis or Direct Confrontation? An Alternative View with Data'. In *West European Party Systems: Continuity & Change*, edited by Hans Daalder and Peter Mair, 267–305. London: Sage Publications.

Budge, Ian, Hans-Dieter Klingemann, Andrea Volkens, Judith Bara, and Eric Tanenbaum. 2001. *Mapping Policy Preferences: Estimates for Parties, Electors, and Governments 1945–1998*. Oxford: Oxford University Press.

Bukow, Sebastian. 2016. 'The Green Party in Germany'. In *Green Parties in Europe*, edited by Emilie van Haute, 112–39. London: Routledge.

Bulens, Jo and Kris Deschouwer. 2002. 'Belgium'. In *Green Parties in National Governments*, edited by Ferdinand Müller-Rommel and Thomas Poguntke, 112–32. London: Frank Cass.

Busemeyer, Marius. 2007. 'Determinants of Public Education Spending in 21 OECD Countries, 1980–2001'. *Journal of European Public Policy* 14, no. 4: 582–610.

Busemeyer, Marius. 2009. 'Social Democrats and the New Partisan Politics of Public Investment in Education'. *Journal of European Public Policy* 16, no. 1: 107–26.

Busemeyer, Marius. 2015. *Skills and Inequality: Partisan Politics and the Political Economy of Education Reforms in Western Welfare States*. Cambridge: Cambridge University Press.

Busemeyer, Marius, Simon T. Franzmann, and Julian L. Garritzmann. 2013. 'Who Owns Education? Cleavage Structures in the Partisan Competition over Educational Spending'. *West European Politics* 36, no. 3: 531–46.

Busemeyer, Marius and Christine Trampusch. 2011. 'Comparative Political Science and the Study of Education'. *British Journal of Political Science* 41, no. 2: 413–43.

Cao, Xun, Helen V. Milner, Aseem Prakash, and Hugh Ward. 2014. 'Research Frontiers in Comparative and International Environmental Politics: An Introduction'. *Comparative Political Studies* 47, no. 3: 291–308.

Carmines, Edward G. 1991. 'The Logic of Party Alignments'. *Journal of Theoretical Politics* 3, no. 1: 65–80.

Carmines, Edward G. and James A. Stimson. 1986. 'On the Structure and Sequence of Issue Evolution'. *American Political Science Review* 80, no. 3: 901–20.

Carter, Neil. 2006. 'Party Politicization of the Environment in Britain'. *Party Politics* 12, no. 6: 747–67.

Carter, Neil. 2007. *The Politics of the Environment*, 2nd ed. Cambridge: Cambridge University Press.

Carter, Neil. 2009. 'Vote Blue, Go Green? Cameron's Conservatives and the Environment'. *Political Quarterly* 80, no. 2: 233–42.

Carter, Neil. 2013. 'Greening the Mainstream: Party Politics and the Environment'. *Environmental Politics* 22, no. 1: 73–94.

Christensen, Jørgen Grønnegaard. 2000. 'Governance and Devolution in the Danish School System'. In *The Governance of Schooling*, edited by Margaret A. Arnott and Charles D. Rabb, 198–216. London: Routledge.

Christensen, Love, Stefan Dahlberg, and John Martinsson. 2015. 'Changes and Fluctuations in Issue Ownership: The Case of Sweden, 1979–2010'. *Scandinavian Political Studies* 38, no. 2: 137–57.

Cobb, Roger W. and Charles D. Elder. 1983. *Participation in American Politics*. Baltimore: Johns Hopkins University Press.

Cook, Timothy E. 1998. *Governing with the News: The News Media as a Political Institution*. Chicago: University of Chicago Press.

Cowell-Meyers, Kimberly. 2017. 'The Contagion Effects of the Feminist Initiative in Sweden: Agenda-Setting, Niche Parties and Mainstream Parties'. *Scandinavian Political Studies* 40, no. 4: 481–9.

Cox, Trevor F. and Michael A. Cox. 1994. *Multidimensional Scaling*. London: Chapman & Hall.

Cutler, David M. and Mark McClellan. 2001. 'Is Technological Change in Medicine Worth It?' *Health Affairs* 20, no. 5: 11–29.

Dalton, Russell. 2017. 'Party Representation across Multiple Issue Dimensions'. *Party Politics* 23, no. 6: 609–22.

Dalton, Russell J., David M. Farrell, and Ian McAllister. 2011. *Political Parties and Democratic Linkage: How Parties Organize Democracy*. Oxford: Oxford University Press.

Dalton, Russell J. and Ian McAllister. 2015. 'Random Walk or Planned Excursion? Continuity and Change in the Left–Right Positions of Political Parties'. *Comparative Political Studies* 48, no. 6: 759–87.

Damgaard, Erik and Palle Svensson. 1989. 'Who Governs? Parties and Policies in Denmark'. *European Journal of Political Research* 17, no. 6: 731–45.

de Rynck, Stefaan. 2005. 'Regional Autonomy and Education Policy in Belgium'. *Regional and Federal Studies* 15, no. 4: 485–500.

de Sio, Lorenzo, Andrea de Angelis, and Vincenzo Emanuele. 2017. 'Issue Yield and Party Strategy in Multiparty Competition'. *Comparative Political Studies* 51, no. 9: 1208–38.

de Sio, Lorenzo and Till Weber. 2014. 'Issue Yield: A Model of Party Strategy in Multidimensional Space'. *American Political Science Review* 108, no. 4: 870–85.

de Vreese, Claes and Holi A. Semetko. 2004. 'News Matters: Influences on the Vote in a Referendum Campaign'. *European Journal of Political Research* 43, no. 5: 699–722.

de Vries, Catherine and Sara B. Hobolt. 2012. 'When Dimensions Collide: The Electoral Success of Issue Entrepreneurs'. *European Union Politics* 13, no. 2: 246–68.

de Vries, Catherine and Gary Marks. 2012. 'The Struggle over Dimensionality: A Note on Theory and Empirics'. *European Union Politics* 13, no. 2: 185–93.

de Wilde, Pieter. 2011. 'No Polity for Old Politics? A Framework for Analyzing the Politicization of European Integration'. *Journal of European Integration* 33, no. 5: 559–75.

de Wilde, Pieter, Anna Leupold, and Henning Schmidtke. 2016. 'Introduction: The Differentiated Politicisation of European Governance'. *West European Politics* 39, no. 1: 3–22.

Dearing, James W. and Everett M. Rogers. 1996. *Agenda-Setting*. London: Sage Publications.

Dixon, Ruth, Christian Arndt, Manuel Mullers, Jarmo Vakkuri, Kristina Engblom-Pelkkala, and Christopher Hood. 2013. 'A Lever for Improvement or a Magnet for Blame? Press and Political Responses to International Educational Rankings in Four EU Countries'. *Public Administration* 91, no. 2: 484–505.

Dobbins, Michael and Kerstin Martens. 2012. 'Towards an Education Approach à la Finlandaise? French Education Policy after PISA'. *Journal of Education Policy* 27, no. 1: 23–43.

Dolezal, Martin, Laurenz Ennser-Jedenastik, Wolfgang C. Müller, and Anna Katharina Winkler. 2013. 'How Parties Compete for Votes: A Test of Saliency Theory'. *European Journal of Political Research* 53, no. 1: 57–76.

Egan, Patrick J. 2013. *Partisan Priorities: How Issue Ownership Drives and Distorts American Politics*. Cambridge: Cambridge University Press.

Esping-Andersen, Gøsta. 1990. *The Three Worlds of Welfare Capitalism*. London: Polity Press.

Evans, Geoffrey. 1998. 'Euroscepticism and Conservative Electoral Support: How an Asset Became a Liability'. *British Journal of Political Science* 28, no. 4: 573–90.

Evans, Geoffrey and Anand Menon. 2017. *Brexit and British Politics*. Cambridge: Polity Press.

Ezrow, Lawrence. 2007. 'On the Inverse Relationship between Votes and Proximity for Niche Parties'. *European Journal of Political Research* 47, no. 2: 206–20.

Freeman, Gary P. 1985. 'National Styles and Policy Sectors: Explaining Structured Variation'. *Journal of Public Policy* 5, no. 4: 467–96.

Garritzmann, Julian L. and Kilian Seng. 2016. 'Party Politics and Education Spending: Challenging Some Common Wisdom'. *Journal of European Public Policy* 23, no. 4: 510–30.

Gerlinger, Thomas. 2010. 'Health Care Reform in Germany'. *German Policy Studies* 6, no. 1: 107–42.

Giaimo, Susan. 2002. *Markets & Medicine*. Ann Arbor: University of Michigan Press.

Gingrich, Jane R. 2011. *Making Markets in the Welfare State*. Cambridge: Cambridge University Press.

Grande, Edgar and Swen Hutter. 2016a. 'Introduction: European Integration and the Challenge of Politicisation'. In *Politicising Europe: Integration and Mass Politics*, edited by Swen Hutter, Edgar Grande, and Hanspeter Kriesi, 3–31. Cambridge: Cambridge University Press.

Grande, Edgar and Swen Hutter. 2016b. 'Is the Giant Still Asleep? The Politicisation of European Integration in the National Arena'. In *Politicising Europe: Integration and Mass Politics*, edited by Swen Hutter, Edgar Grande, and Hanspeter Kriesi, 90–111. Cambridge: Cambridge University Press.

Grande, Edgar and Hanspeter Kriesi. 2016. 'Conclusions: The Post-Functionalists Were (Almost) Right'. In *Politicising Europe: Integration and Mass Politics*, edited by Swen Hutter, Edgar Grande, and Hanspeter Kriesi, 279–300. Cambridge: Cambridge University Press.

Grande, Edgar, Tobias Schwarzbözl & Matthias Fatke 2018. "Politicizing immigration in Western Europe", *Journal of European Public Policy*, Advance online publication.

Green, Jane and Will Jennings. 2012. 'Valence as Macro-Competence: An Analysis of Mood in Party Competence Evaluations in Great Britain'. *British Journal of Political Science* 42, no. 2: 311–43.

Green, Jane and Will Jennings. 2017. *The Politics of Competence*. Cambridge: Cambridge University Press.

Greene, Zachary. 2016. 'Competing on the Issues. How Experience in Government and Economic Conditions Influence the Scope of Parties' Policy Messages'. *Party Politics* 22, no. 6: 209–22.

Green-Pedersen, Christoffer. 2006. 'Long-Term Changes in Danish Party Politics? From Class Competition to Issue Competition'. *Scandinavian Political Studies* 29, no. 3: 221–37.

Green-Pedersen, Christoffer. 2007. 'The Growing Importance of Issue Competition: The Changing Nature of Party Competition in Western Europe'. *Political Studies* 55, no. 3: 607–28.

References

Green-Pedersen, Christoffer. 2012. *Partier i nye tider: Den politiske dagsorden i Danmark*. Aarhus: Aarhus University Press.

Green-Pedersen, Christoffer. 2019. 'Issue Attention in West European Party Politics: CAP and CMP Coding Compared'. In *Comparative Policy Agendas: Theory, Tools, Data*. Edited by Frank Baumgartner, Christian Breunig, and Emiliano Grossman, 373–90. Oxford: Oxford University Press.

Green-Pedersen, Christoffer and Carsten Jensen. 2019. 'Electoral Competition and the Welfare State'. *West European Politics* 42, no. 4: 808–23.

Green-Pedersen, Christoffer and Jesper Krogstrup. 2008. 'Immigration as a Political Issue in Denmark and Sweden: How Party Competition Shapes Political Agendas'. *European Journal of Political Research* 47, no. 5: 610–34.

Green-Pedersen, Christoffer and Peter Bjerre Mortensen. 2010. 'Who Sets the Agenda and Who Responds to It in the Danish Parliament?' *European Journal of Political Research* 49, no. 2: 257–81.

Green-Pedersen, Christoffer and Peter Bjerre Mortensen. 2015. 'Avoidance and Engagement: Issue Competition in Multi-Party Systems'. *Political Studies* 63, no. 4: 747–64.

Green-Pedersen, Christoffer and Pontus Odmalm. 2008. 'Going Different Ways? Right-Wing Parties and the Immigrant Issue in Denmark and Sweden'. *Journal of European Public Policy* 15, no. 3: 367–81.

Green-Pedersen, Christoffer and Simon Otjes. 2019. 'A Hot Topic? Immigration on the Agenda in Western Europe'. *Party Politics*. 25, no. 3: 424–434.

Green-Pedersen, Christoffer and Lisbeth H. Thomsen. 2005. 'Bloc Politics vs. Broad Cooperation: The Functioning of Danish Minority Parliamentarism'. *Journal of Legislative Studies* 11, no. 2: 153–69.

Green-Pedersen, Christoffer and Kees van Kersbergen. 2002. 'The Politics of the "Third Way": The Transformation of Social Democracy in Denmark and the Netherlands'. *Party Politics* 8, no. 5: 507–24.

Green-Pedersen, Christoffer and Stefaan Walgrave, eds. 2014. *Agenda Setting, Policies, and Political Systems: A Comparative Approach*. Chicago: University of Chicago Press.

Green-Pedersen, Christoffer and John Wilkerson. 2006. 'How Agenda-Setting Attributes Shape Politics: Basic Dilemmas, Problem Attention and Health Politics Developments in Denmark and the US'. *Journal of European Public Policy* 13, no. 7: 1039–52.

Grek, Sotiria. 2009. 'Governing by Numbers: The PISA "Effect" in Europe'. *Journal of Education Policy* 24, no. 1: 23–37.

Grossmann, Matt. 2012. 'The Variable Politics of the Policy Process: Issue-Area Differences and Comparative Networks'. *Journal of Politics* 75, no. 1: 65–79.

Gustafsson, Line R. 2012. *What Did You Learn in School Today?* Aarhus: Politica.

Hacker, Jacob S. 2004. 'Review Article: Dismantling the Health Care State?' *British Journal of Political Science* 34, no. 4: 693–724.

Hacker, Jacob S. and Paul Pierson. 2014. 'After the "Master Theory": Downs, Schattschneider, and the Rebirth of Policy-Focused Analysis'. *Perspectives on Politics* 12, no. 3: 643–62.

Hansen, Martin Ejnar. 2008. 'Back to the Archives? A Critique of the Danish Part of the Manifesto Database'. *Scandinavian Political Studies* 31, no. 2: 201–16.

Häusermann, Silja and Hanspeter Kriesi. 2015. 'What Do Voters Want?' In *The Politics of Advanced Capitalism*, edited by Pablo Beramendi, Silja Häusermann, Herbert Kitschelt, and Hanspeter Kriesi, 202–30. Cambridge: Cambridge University Press.

Helbling, Marc and Anke Tresch. 2011. 'Measuring Party Positions and Issue Salience from Media Coverage: Discussing and Cross-Validating New Indicators'. *Electoral Studies* 30, no. 1: 174–83.

Hellström, Jonas and Magnus Blomgren. 2016. 'Party Debate over Europe in National Election Campaigns: Electoral Disunity and Party Cohesion'. *European Journal of Political Research* 55, no. 2: 265–82.

Hertner, Isabelle. 2015. 'Is it Always Up to the Leadership? European Policy-Making in the Labour Party, Parti Socialiste (PS) and Sozialdemokratische Partei Deutschlands (SPD)'. *Party Politics* 21, no. 3: 470–80.

Hillygus, Sunshine and Todd G. Shields. 2009. *The Persuadable Voter: Wedge Issues in Presidential Campaigns*. Princeton: Princeton University Press.

Hinnfors, Jonas, Adrea Spehar, and Gregg Bucken-Knapp. 2012. 'The Missing Factor: Why Social Democracy Can Lead to Restrictive Immigration Policy'. *Journal of European Public Policy* 19, no. 4: 585–603.

Hobolt, Sara B. 2009. *Europe in Question: Referendums on European Integration*. Oxford: Oxford University Press.

Hobolt, Sara B. and Catherine de Vries. 2015. 'Issue Entrepreneurship and Multiparty Competition'. *Comparative Political Studies* 48, no. 9: 1159–85.

Hobolt, Sara B. and Catherine de Vries. 2016. 'Public Support for European Integration'. *Annual Review of Political Science* 19: 413–32.

Hobolt, Sara B. and James Tilley. 2016. 'Fleeing the Centre: The Rise of Challenger Parties in the Aftermath of the Euro Crisis'. *West European Politics* 39, no. 5: 971–91.

Hoeglinger, Dominic. 2016. *Politicizing European Integration: Struggling with the Awakening Giant*. London: Palgrave Macmillan.

Holian, David. 2004. 'He's Stealing My Issues! Clinton's Crime Rhetoric and the Dynamics of Issue Ownership'. *Political Behavior* 26, no. 2: 95–124.

Hooghe, Liesbet and Gary Marks. 2009. 'Postfunctionalist Theory of European Integration: From Permissive Consensus to Constraining Dissensus'. *British Journal of Political Science* 39, no. 1: 1–23.

Hooghe, Liesbet and Gary Marks. 2018. 'Cleavage Theory Meets Europe's Crises: Lipset, Rokkan, and the Transnational Cleavage'. *Journal of European Public Policy* 25, no. 1: 109–35.

Hooghe, Liesbet, Gary Marks, and Carole J. Wilson. 2002. 'Does Left/Right Structure Party Positions on European Integration?' *Comparative Political Studies* 35, no. 8: 965–89.

Hutter, Swen. 2016. 'Methodological Appendix: Measuring Politicisation, Benchmarks and Data'. In *Politicising Europe: Integration and Mass Politics*, edited by Swen Hutter, Edgar Grande, and Hanspeter Kriesi, 301–13. Cambridge: Cambridge University Press.

Hutter, Swen, Daniela Braun, and Alena Kerscher. 2016a. 'Constitutive Issues as Driving Forces of Politicisation?' In *Politicising Europe: Integration and Mass Politics*, edited by Swen Hutter, Edgar Grande, and Hanspeter Kriesi, 137–55. Cambridge: Cambridge University Press.

Hutter, Swen and Edgard Grande. 2014. 'Politicizing Europe in the National Electoral Arena: A Comparative Analysis of Five West European Countries, 1970–2010'. *Journal of Common Market Studies* 52, no. 5: 1002–18.

Hutter, Swen, Edgar Grande, and Hanspeter Kriesi, eds. 2016b. *Politicising Europe: Integration and Mass Politics*. Cambridge: Cambridge University Press.

Ivarsflaten, Elisabeth. 2005. 'Threatened by Diversity: Why Restrictive Asylum and Immigration Policies Appeal to West Europeans'. *International Journal of Public Opinion Research* 15, no. 1: 21–45.

Iversen, Torben and John D. Stephens. 2008. 'Partisan Politics, the Welfare State and Three Worlds of Human Capital Formation'. *Comparative Political Studies* 41, no. 4–5: 600–37.

Jahn, Detlef. 1993. 'The Rise and Decline of New Politics and the Greens in Sweden and Germany'. *European Journal of Political Research* 24, no. 2: 177–94.

Jahn, Detlef. 2016. *The Politics of Environmental Performance*. Cambridge: Cambridge University Press.

Jakobi, Anja P. 2011. 'Political Parties and the Institutionalization of Education: A Comparative Analysis of Party Manifestos'. *Comparative Education Review* 55, no. 2: 189–209.

Janda, Kenneth, Robert Harmel, Christine Edens, and Patricia Goff. 1995. 'Changes in Party Identity: Evidence from Party Manifestos'. *Party Politics* 1, no. 2: 171–96.

Jensen, Carsten. 2011a. 'Marketization via Compensation: Health Care and the Politics of the Right in Advanced Industrialized Nations'. *British Journal of Political Science* 41, no. 4: 907–26.

Jensen, Carsten. 2011b. 'Focusing Events, Policy Dictators and the Dynamics of Reform'. *Policy Studies* 32, no. 2: 143–58.

Jensen, Carsten. 2011c. 'Capitalist Systems, De-Industrialization and the Politics of Public Education'. *Comparative Political Studies* 44, no. 4: 412–35.

Jensen, Carsten and Michael Bang Petersen. 2017. 'The Deservingness Heuristic and the Politics of Health Care'. *American Journal of Political Science* 61, no. 1: 68–83.

Jones, Bryan D. and Frank R. Baumgartner. 2005. *The Politics of Attention: How Government Prioritizes Problems*. Chicago: University of Chicago Press.

Jordan, Jason. 2010. "Institutional Feedback and Support for the Welfare State: The Case of National Health Care". *Comparative Political Studies* 43, no. 7: 862–885.

Jordan, Jason. 2011. "Health Care Politics in the Age of Retrenchment". *Journal of Social Policy* 40, no. 1:113–134.

Katz, Richard and Peter Mair. 1995. 'Changing Models of Party Organization and Party Democracy'. *Party Politics* 1, no. 1: 5–28.

Katz, Richard S. and Peter Mair. 2018. *Democracy and the Cartelization of Political Parties*. Oxford: Oxford University Press.

Kavanagh, Dennis. 1997. 'The Labour Campaign'. In *Britain Votes, 1997*, edited by Pippa Norris and Neil T. Galvin, 25–33. Oxford: Oxford University Press.

Kavanagh, Dennis, David Richards, Martin Smith, and Andrew Geddes. 2006. *British Politics*, 5th ed. Oxford: Oxford University Press.

Kingdon, John W. 1995. *Agendas, Alternatives, and Public Policies*. New York: HarperCollins.

Kitschelt, Herbert. 1994. *The Transformation of Social Democracy*. Cambridge: Cambridge University Press.
Kitschelt, Herbert. 1995. *The Radical Right in Western Europe*. Cambridge: Cambridge University Press.
Kitschelt, Herbert. 2000. 'Citizens, Politicians and Party Cartelization'. *European Journal of Political Research* 37, no. 2: 149–79.
Kitschelt, Herbert. 2007. 'Party Systems'. In *The Oxford Handbook of Comparative Politics*, edited by Carles Boix and Susan Stokes, 522–54. Oxford: Oxford University Press.
Kitschelt, Herbert and Staf Hellemans. 1990. 'The Left–Right Semantics and the New Politics of Cleavage'. *Comparative Political Studies* 23, no. 2: 210–38.
Kitschelt, Herbert and Philipp Rehm. 2015. 'Party Alignments: Change and Continuity'. In *The Politics of Advanced Capitalism*, edited by Pablo Beramendi, Silja Häusermann, Herbert Kitschelt, and Hanspeter Kriesi, 179–201. Cambridge and New York: Cambridge University Press.
Klein, Rudolph. 2007. 'The New Model NHS: Performance, Perceptions and Expectations'. *British Medical Bulletin* 81–82: 39–50.
Klein, Rudolph. 2013. *The New Politics of the NHS*, 7th ed. Oxford: Blackwell.
Klüver, Heike and Jae-Jae Spoon. 2014. 'Who Responds? Voters, Parties and Issue Attention'. *British Journal of Political Science* 46, no. 3: 633–54.
Knill, Christoph, Marc Debus, and Stephan Heichel. 2010. 'Do Parties Matter in Internationalised Policy Areas? The Impact of Political Parties on Environmental Policy Outputs in 18 OECD Countries, 1970–2000'. *European Journal of Political Research* 49, no. 3: 301–36.
Knodel, Philipp and Heiko Walkenhorst. 2010. 'What's England Got Do with It? British Underestimation of International Initiatives in Education Policy'. In *Transformation of Education Policy*, edited by Kerstin Martens, Alexander-Kenneth Nagel, Michael Windzio, and Ansgar Weyman, 132–52. Basingstoke: Palgrave Macmillan.
Kraft, Jonas. 2017. 'Political Parties and Public Investments: A Comparative Analysis of 22 Western Countries'. *West European Politics* 41, no. 1: 128–46.
Kriesi, Hanspeter. 2016. 'The Politicization of European Integration'. *Journal of Common Market Studies* 54, no. 1: 32–47.
Kriesi, Hanspeter, Edgar Grande, Martin Dolezal, Marc Helbinger, Dominic Höglinger, Swen Hutter, and Bruno Wüest. 2012. *Political Conflict in Western Europe*. Cambridge: Cambridge University Press.
Kriesi, Hanspeter, Edgar Grande, Romian Lachat, Martin Dolezal, Simon Bornschier, and Timotheus Frey. 2008. *West European Politics in the Age of Globalization*. Cambridge: Cambridge University Press.
Kriesi, Hanspeter, Ruud Koopmans, Jan Willem Duyvendak, and Marco Giugni. 1995. *New Social Movements in Western Europe: A Comparative Analysis*. Minneapolis: University of Minnesota Press.
Kruskal, Joseph and Myron Wish. 1978. *Multidimensional Scaling*. London: Sage Publicaions.
Langsæther, Peter Egge and Rune Stubager. 2019. 'Old Wine in New Bottles? Reassessing the Effects of Globalization on Political Preferences in Western Europe'. *European Journal of Political research*, Advance online publication.

References

Laver, Michael. 1989. 'Party Competition and Party System Change: The Interaction of Coalition Bargaining and Electoral Competition'. *Journal of Theoretical Politics* 1, no. 3: 301–24.

Lawson, Kay. 1980. *Political Parties and Linkage: A Comparative Perspective*. New Haven: Yale University Press.

Lawton, Denis. 2005. *Education and Labour Party Ideologies 1900–2001 and Beyond*. London: Routledge.

Layman, Geoffrey and Thomas Carsey. 2002. 'Party Polarization and "Conflict Extension" in the American Electorate'. *American Journal of Political Science* 46, no. 4: 786–802.

Lehmann, Pola and Malisa Zobel. 2018. "Positions and saliency of immigration in party manifestos: A novel dataset using crowd coding." *European Journal of Political Research* 57, no. 4: 1056–1083.

Leinaweaver, Justin and Robert Thomson. 2016. 'Greener Governments: Partisan Ideologies, Executive Institutions, and Environmental Policies'. *Environmental Politics* 25, no. 4: 633–60.

Lieberman, Evan S. 2005. 'Nested Analysis as a Mixed-Method Strategy for Comparative Research'. *American Political Science Review* 99, no. 3: 435–52.

Lindaman, Kara and Donald P. Haider-Markel. 2002. 'Issue Evolution, Political Parties, and the Culture Wars'. *Political Research Quarterly* 55, no. 1: 91–110.

Lipset, Seymour M. and Stein Rokkan, eds. 1967. *Party Systems & Voter Alignments*. New York: Free Press.

Liu, Xinsheng, Eric Lindquist, and Arnold Vedlitz. 2011. 'Explaining Media and Congressional Attention to Global Climate Change, 1969–2005: An Empirical Test of Agenda-Setting Theory'. *Political Research Quarterly* 64, no. 2: 405–19.

Lohneis, Hans Werner. 1983. 'The West German Election of 1983'. *West European Politics* 6, no. 4: 246–51.

McCombs, Maxwell and Jian-Hua Zhu. 1995. 'Capacity, Diversity, and Volatility of the Public Agenda: Trends from 1954–1994'. *Public Opinion Quarterly* 59, no. 4: 495–517.

Mair, Peter. 1997. *Party System Change*. Oxford: Clarendon Press.

Mair, Peter. 2001. 'The Green Challenge and Political Competition: How Typical Is the German Experience?' *German Politics* 10, no. 2: 99–116.

Mair, Peter. 2006. 'Cleavages'. In *Handbook of Party Politics*, edited by Richard Katz and William Crotty, 371–5. London: Sage Publications.

Mair, Peter. 2013. *Ruling the Void*. London: Verso.

Malunat, Bernd M. 1987. 'Umweltpolitik im Spiegel der Partiprogramme'. *Aus Politik und Zeitgeschichte* 29, 29–42.

Marmor, Theodore and Claus Wendt. 2012. 'Conceptual Frameworks for Comparing Healthcare Politics and Policy'. *Health Policy* 107, no. 1: 11–20.

Meguid, Bonnie. 2005. 'The Role of Mainstream Party Strategy in Niche Party Success'. *American Political Science Review* 99, no. 3: 347–59.

Meguid, Bonnie. 2008. *Party Competition between Unequals: Strategies and Electoral Fortunes in Western Europe*. Cambridge: Cambridge University Press.

Meijers, Mauritz. 2017. 'Contagious Euroscepticism: The Impact of Eurosceptic Support on Mainstream Party Positions on European Integration'. *Party Politics* 23, no. 4: 413–23.

Meyer, Thomas M. and Bernhard Miller. 2015. 'The Niche Party Concept and its Measurement'. *Party Politics* 21, no. 2: 259–71.

Meyer, Thomas M. and Markus Wagner. 2013. 'Mainstream or Niche? Vote-Seeking Incentives and the Programmatic Strategies of Political Parties'. *Comparative Political Studies* 46, no. 10: 1246–72.

Meyer, Thomas M. and Markus Wagner. 2015. 'Issue Engagement in Election Campaigns: The Impact of Electoral Incentives and Organizational Constraints'. *Political Science Research and Methods* 4, no. 3: 555–71.

Moe, Terry and Susan Wiborg. 2017. 'Introduction'. In *The Comparative Politics of Education: Teacher Unions and Education Systems Around the World*, edited by Terry M. Moe and Susanne Wiborg, 1–23. New York: Cambridge University Press.

Mortensen, Peter Bjerre. 2013. '(De-)Centralization and Attribution of Blame and Credit'. *Local Government Studies* 39, no. 2: 163–81.

Mortensen, Peter Bjerre and Christoffer Green-Pedersen. 2015. 'Institutional Effects of Changes in Political Attention: Explaining Organizational Changes in the Top Bureaucracy'. *Journal of Public Administration Research and Theory* 25, no. 1: 165–89.

Mortensen, Peter Bjerre, Christoffer Green-Pedersen, Gerard Breeman, Laura Bonafont Chaques, Will Jennings, Peter John, Anna Palau, and Arco Timmermans. 2011. 'Comparing Government Agendas: Executive Speeches in the Netherlands, United Kingdom and Denmark'. *Comparative Political Studies* 44, no. 8: 973–1000.

Mudde, Cas. 2013. 'Three Decades of Populist Radical Right Parties in Western Europe: So What?' *European Journal of Political Research* 52, no. 1: 1–19.

Müller-Rommel, Ferdinand and Thomas Poguntke, eds. 2002. *Green Parties in National Governments*. London: Frank Cass.

Niemann, Dennis. 2010. 'Turn the Tide: New Horizons in German Education Policymaking through IO Influence'. In *Transformation of Education Policy*, edited by Kerstin Martens, Alexander-Kenneth Nagel, Michael Windzio, and Ansgar Weyman, 77–104. Basingstoke: Palgrave Macmillan.

Norris, Pippa and Ronald Inglehart. 2019. *Cultural Backlash. Trump, Brexit, and Authoritarian Populism*. Cambridge: Cambridge University Press.

Odmalm, Pontus and Tim Bale. 2015. 'Immigration into the Mainstream: Conflicting Ideological Streams, Strategic Reasoning and Party Competition'. *Acta Politica* 50, no. 4: 365–78.

Odmalm, Pontus and Betsy Super. 2014. 'Getting the Balance Right? Party Competition on Immigration and Conflicting Ideological "Pulls"'. *Scandinavian Political Studies* 37, no. 3: 301–22.

OECD. 2017a. *International Migration Outlook, 2017*. Accessed 2 February 2018.

OECD. 2017b. *Quarterly GDP* (indicator). doi:10.1787/b86d1fc8-en. Accessed 3 August 2017.

OECD. 2017c. *Annual Labour Force Statistics*. Accessed 13 September 2017.

OECD. 2017d. *Patents by Main Technology and by International Patent Classification* (IPC). Accessed 15 September 2017.

OECD. 2018. *Foreign Population* (indicator). doi:10.1787/16a914e3-en. Accessed 17 September 2018.

Okunade, Albert A. and Vasudeva N. Murthy. 2002. 'Technology as a "Major Driver" of Health Care Costs: A Cointegration Analysis of the Newhouse Conjecture'. *Journal of Health Economics* 21, no. 1: 147–59.

Otjes, Simon and Alexia Katsanidou. 2017. 'Beyond Kriesiland: EU Integration as a Super Issue after the Eurocrisis'. *European Journal of Political Research* 56, no. 2: 301–19.

Panebianco, Angelo. 1988. *Political Parties: Organization and Power*. Cambridge: Cambridge University Press.

Pedersen, Mogens N. 1996. 'Euro-Parties and European Parties: New Arenas, New Challenges and New Strategies'. In *The European Union: How Democratic Is It?*, edited by Svein S. Andersen and Kjell A. Eliassen, 15–40. London: Sage Publications.

Peters, Guy. 2005. 'The Problem of Policy Problems'. *Journal of Comparative Policy Analysis* 7, no. 4: 349–70.

Petrocik, J. R. 1996. 'Issue Ownership in Presidential Elections, with a 1980 Case Study'. *American Journal of Political Science* 40, no. 3: 825–50.

Pfaff, Martin. 2009. 'Germany: Evidence, Policy, and Politics in Health Care Reform'. In *Comparative Studies and the Politics of Modern Medical Care*, edited by Theodore Marmor, Richard Freeman, and Kieke G. H. Okam, 88–119. New Haven: Yale University Press.

Pierson, Paul. 1994. *Dismantling the Welfare State*. Cambridge: Cambridge University Press.

Poguntke, Thomas. 1999. 'The Winner Takes All: The FDP in 1982–1983—Maximizing Votes, Office, and Policy?' In *Policy, Office or Votes*, edited by Wolfgang Müller and Kaare Strøm, 216–36. Cambridge: Cambridge University Press.

Premfors, Rune. 1998. 'Reshaping the Democratic State: Swedish Experience in a Comparative Perspective'. *Public Administration* 76, no. 1: 141–59.

Prosser, Christopher. 2016. 'Dimensionality, Ideology and Party Positions towards European Integration'. *West European Politics* 39, no. 4: 731–54.

Rahat, Gideon and Ofer Kenig. 2018. *From Party Politics to Personalized Politics*. Oxford: Oxford University Press.

Rauh, Christian, Antje Kirschner, and Roland Kappe. 2011. 'Political Parties and Higher Education Spending: Who Favours Redistribution?' *West European Politics* 34, no. 6: 1185–206.

Repetto, Robert, ed. 2006. *Punctuated Equilibrium and the Dynamics of U.S. Environmental Policy*. New Haven: Yale University Press.

Richardson, Dick and Chris Rootes, eds. 1995. *The Green Challenge: The Development of Green Parties in Europe*. London: Routledge.

Riker, William. 1996. *The Strategy of Rhetoric: Campaigning for the American Constitution*. New Haven: Yale University Press.

Ringarp, Johanna and Martin Rothland. 2010. 'Is the Grass always Greener? The Effect of the PISA Results on Education Debates in Sweden and Germany'. *European Educational Research* 9, no. 3: 422–30.

Rittel, Horst W. J. and Melvin M. Webber. 1973. 'Dilemmas in a General Theory of Planning'. *Policy Sciences* 4, no. 2: 155–69.

Robertson, David B. 1976. *A Theory of Party Competition*. London: John Wiley & Sons.

Rohrschneider, Robert. 1993. 'New Party versus Old Left Realignments: Environmental Attitudes, Party Policies, and Partisan Affiliations in Four West European Countries'. *Journal of Politics* 55, no. 3: 682–701.

Rüdig, Wolfgang. 2002. 'Germany'. In *Green Parties in National Governments*, edited by Ferdinand Müller-Rommel and Thomas Poguntke, 79–111. London: Frank Cass.

Schain, Martin A. 2006. 'The Extreme Right and Immigration Policy Making: Measuring Direct and Indirect Effects'. *West European Politics* 29, no. 2: 270–89.

Schattschneider, Elmer E. 1960. *The Semi-Sovereign People: A Realist's Guide to Democracy in America*. New York: Holt.

Schumacher, Gijs, Catherine E. de Vries, and Barbara Vis. 2013. 'Why Do Parties Change Position? Party Organization and Environmental Incentives'. *Journal of Politics* 75, no. 2: 464–77.

Schumacher, Gijs, Marc de Wardt, Barbara Vis, and Michael Baggesen-Klitgaard. 2015. 'How Aspiration to Office Moderates the Impact of Government Participation on Party Platform Change'. *American Journal of Political Science* 59, no. 4: 1040–54.

Seeberg, Henrik Bech. 2013a. 'The Opposition's Policy Influence through Issue Politicisation'. *Journal of Public Policy* 33, no. 1: 89–107.

Seeberg, Henrik Bech. 2013b. *The Power of the Loser: Opposition Policy Influence through Agenda-Setting*. Aarhus: Politica.

Seeberg, Henrik Bech. 2016. 'Opposition Policy Influence through Agenda-Setting: The Environment in Denmark, 1993–2009'. *Scandinavian Political Studies* 39, no. 2: 185–206.

Seeberg, Henrik Bech. 2017. 'How Stable is Political Parties' Issue Ownership? A Cross-Time, Cross-National Analysis'. *Political Studies* 65, no. 2: 475–92.

Senninger, Roman. 2016. 'Issue Expansion and Selective Scrutiny: How Opposition Parties Used Parliamentary Questions about the European Union in the National Arena from 1973 to 2013'. *European Union Politics* 18, no. 2: 283–306.

Sides, John and Jack Citrin. 2007. 'European Opinion about Immigration: The Role of Identities, Interests and Information'. *British Journal of Political Science* 37, no. 3: 477–504.

Sigelman, Lee and Emmett H. Buell. 2004. 'Avoidance or Engagement? Issue Convergence in US Presidential Campaigns, 1960–2000'. *American Journal of Political Science* 48, no. 4: 650–61.

Sitter, Nick. 2001. 'The Politics of Opposition and European Integration in Scandinavia: Is Euro-Scepticism a Government–Opposition Dynamic?' *West European Politics* 24, no. 1: 22–39.

Somer-Topcu, Zeynep. 2009. 'Timely Decisions: The Effects of Past National Elections on Party Policy'. *Journal of Politics* 71, no. 1: 238–48.

Soroka, Stuart. 2002. *Agenda-Setting Dynamics in Canada*. Vancouver: University of British Columbia Press.

Spoon, Jae-Jae. 2011. *Political Survival of Small Parties in Europe*. Ann Arbor: University of Michigan Press.

Spoon, Jay, Sara B. Hobolt, and Catherine de Vries. 2014. 'Going Green: Explaining Issue Competition on the Environment'. *European Journal of Political Research* 53, no. 2: 363–80.

Steenbergen, Marco R. and David J. Scott. 2004. 'Contesting Europe? The Salience of European Integration as a Party Issue'. In *European Integration and Political Conflict*, edited by Gary Marks and Marco R. Steenbergen, 165–212. Cambridge: Cambridge University Press.

Stevens, Daniel. 2013. 'Issue Evolution in Britain: The Debate on European Union Integration, 1964–2010'. *European Journal of Political Research* 52, no. 4: 536–57.

Stoll, Heather. 2010. 'Elite-Level Conflict Salience and Dimensionality in Western Europe: Concepts and Findings'. *West European Politics* 33, no. 3: 445–73.

Strøm, Kaare. 1990. 'A Behavioral Theory of Competitive Political Parties'. *American Journal of Political Science* 34, no. 2: 565–98.

Stubager, Rune. 2009. 'Education-Based Group Identity and Consciousness in the Authoritarian–Libertarian Value Conflict'. *European Journal of Political Research* 48, no. 2: 204–33.

Stubager, Rune. 2010. 'The Development of the Education Cleavage: Denmark as a Critical Case'. *West European Politics* 33, no. 3: 505–33.

Stubager, Rune, Kasper Møller Hansen, Kristoffer Callesen, Andreas Leed, and Christine Enevoldsen. 2016. *Danske Vælgere, 1971–2015: En oversigt over udviklingen i vælgernes holdninger mv*. Aarhus: Institut for Statskundskab.

Stubager, Rune and Henrik Seeberg. 2016. 'What Can a Party Say? How Parties' Communication Can Influence Voters' Issue Ownership Perceptions'. *Electoral Studies* 44, no. 1: 162–71.

Stubager, Rune and Rune Slothuus. 2013. 'What Are the Sources of Political Parties' Issue Ownership? Testing Four Explanations at the Individual Level'. *Political Behavior* 35, no. 3: 567–88.

Szczerbiak, Aleks and Paul Taggart. 2008. *Opposing Europe? The Comparative Party Politics of Euroscepticism*, vol. 2. Oxford: Oxford University Press.

Taggart, Paul and Aleks Szczerbiak. 2002. 'The Party Politics of Euroscepticism in EU Member and Candidate States'. SEI Working Paper 51, University of Sussex. <https://www.sussex.ac.uk/webteam/gateway/file.php?name=sei-working-paper-no-51.pdf&site=266of>.

Talshir, Gayil. 2002. *The Political Ideology of Green Parties*. London: Routledge.

Tavits, Margit. 2008. 'Policy Positions, Issue Importance and Party Competition in New Democracies'. *Comparative Political Studies* 41, no. 1: 48–72.

Tavits, Margit and Joshua D. Potter. 2015. 'The Effect of Inequality and Identity on Party Strategies'. *American Journal of Political Science* 59, no. 3: 744–58.

Thesen, Gunnar. 2013. 'When Good News is Scarce and Bad News is Good: Government Responsibilities and Opposition Possibilities in Political Agenda-Setting'. *European Journal of Political Research* 52, no. 3: 364–89.

Tromp, Bart. 1989. 'Party Strategies and System Change in the Netherlands'. *West European Politics* 12, no. 4: 82–97.

van de Wardt, Marc. 2015. 'Desperate Needs, Desperate Deeds: Why Mainstream Parties Respond to the Issues of Niche Parties'. *West European Politics* 38, no. 1: 93–122.

van de Wardt, Marc, Cathriene de Vries, and Sara B. Hobolt. 2014. 'Exploiting the Cracks: Wedge Issues in Multiparty Competition'. *Journal of Politics* 76, no. 4: 986–99.

van der Brug, Wouter. 2000. 'Politieke Problemen, Prioriteiten en Partijkeuze'. In *Politieke Veranderingen in Nederland 1971–1998: Kiezers en de Smalle Marges van de Politiek*, edited by Jacques J. A. Thomassen, Kees Aarts, and Hendrik van der Kolk, 187–202. Entchede: SDU Uitgevers.

van der Brug, Wouter, Gianni D'Amato, Joost Berkhout, and Didier Ruedin. 2015. *The Politicization of Migration.* London: Routledge.

van der Brug, Wouter and Joust van Spanje. 2009. 'Immigration, Europe, and the New Cultural Dimension'. *European Journal of Political Research* 48, no. 3: 309–34.

van der Eijk, Cees and Mark Franklin. 2007. 'The Sleeping Giant Potential for Political Mobilization of Disaffection with European Integration'. In *European Elections and Domestic Politics*, edited by Wouter van der Brug and Cees van der Eijk, 189–208. Notre Dame: University of Notre Dame Press.

van Haute, Emilie, ed. 2016. *Green Parties in Europe*. London: Routledge.

van Heck, Sjoerd. 2018. 'Appealing Broadly or Narrowing Down? The Impact of Government Experience and Party Organization on the Scope of Parties' Issue Agendas'. *Party Politics*, 24, no. 4: 347–57.

van Heerden, Sjordje, Sara L. de Lange, Wouter van der Brug, and Fennema Meindert. 2013. 'The Immigration and Integration Debate in the Netherlands: Discursive and Programmatic Reactions to the Rise of Anti-Immigration Parties'. *Journal of Ethnic and Migration Studies* 40, no. 1: 119–36.

van Kersbergen, Kees. 1997. 'Between Collectivism and Individualism: The Politics of the Centre'. In *The Politics of Problem Solving in Post-War Democracies*, edited by Hans Keman, 113–40. London: Macmillan.

van Kersbergen, Kees and Andre Krouwel. 2008. 'A Double-Edged Sword! The Dutch Centre Right and the "Foreigners Issue"'. *Journal of European Public Policy* 15, no. 3: 398–414.

van Spanje, Joost. 2010. 'Contagious Parties: Anti-Immigration Parties and Their Impact on Other Parties' Immigration Stances in Contemporary Western Europe'. *Party Politics* 16, no. 5: 563–86.

Vangoidsenhoven, Guido and Jean-Benoit Pilet. 2015. 'The Politicization of Immigration in Belgium'. In *The Politicization of Migration*, edited by Wouter van der Brug, Gianni D'Amato, Joost Berkhout, and Didier Roudin, 52–74. London: Routledge.

Vanhuysse, Pieter and Achim Goerres, eds. 2012. *Ageing Populations in Post-Industrial Democracies.* London: Routledge.

Vedung, Erik. 1988. 'The Swedish Five-Party Syndrome and the Environmentalists'. In *When Parties Fail*, edited by Kay Lawson and Peter H. Merkl, 76–109. Princeton: Princeton University Press.

Vliegenthart, Rens and Stefaan Walgrave. 2011. 'Content Matters: The Dynamics of Parliamentary Questioning in Belgium and Denmark'. *Comparative Political Studies* 44, no. 8: 1031–59.

Vliegenthart, Rens, Stefaan Walgrave, and Connie Meppelink. 2011. 'Inter-Party Agenda-Setting in the Belgian Parliament: The Role of Party Characteristics and Competition'. *Political Studies* 59, no. 2: 368–88.

Volkens, Andreas, Judith Bara, Ian Budge, Michael D. McDonald, and Hans-Dieter Klingemann. 2013. *Mapping Policy Preferences from Texts III*. Oxford: Oxford University Press.

Wagner, Markus. 2012a. 'Defining and Measuring Niche Parties'. *Party Politics* 18, no. 6: 845–64.

Wagner, Markus. 2012b. 'When Do Parties Emphasize Extreme Positions? How Incentives for Policy Differentiation Influence Issue Importance'. *European Journal of Political Research* 51, no. 1: 64–88.

Walgrave, Stefaan, Jonas Lefevere, and Anke Tresch. 2012. 'The Associative Dimension of Issue Ownership'. *Public Opinion Quarterly* 76, no. 4: 771–82.

Walgrave, Stefaan, Jonas Lefevere, and Anke Tresch. 2015. 'The Conceptualisation and Measurement of Issue Ownership'. *West European Politics* 38, no. 4: 778–96.

Walgrave, Stefaan and Michiel Nuytemans. 2009. 'Friction and Party Manifesto Change in 25 Countries, 1945–98'. *American Journal of Political Science* 53, no. 1: 190–206.

Walgrave Stefaan and Frederic Varone. 2008. 'Punctuated Equilibrium and Agenda-Setting: Bringing Parties Back In: Policy Change after the Dutroux Crisis in Belgium'. *Governance* 21, no. 3: 365–95.

Ward, Dalston, Jeong Hyun Kim, Margit Tavits, and Matt Graham. 2015. 'How Economic Integration Affects Party Competition'. *Comparative Political Studies* 48, no. 10: 1227–59.

Weaver, Kent. 1986. 'The Politics of Blame Avoidance'. *Journal of Public Policy* 6, no. 4: 371–98.

Webb, Paul. 2000. *The Modern British Party System*. London: Sage Publications.

Wiborg, Susanne. 2015. 'Privatizing Education: Free School Policy in Sweden and England'. *Comparative Education Review* 59, no. 3: 473–98.

Index

Note: Tables and figures are indicated by an italic "*t*" and "*f*" following the page number.

Abou-Chadi, T. 4, 20, 22, 33, 79–80, 82, 86, 91–2, 114, 118, 123–4, 133–4, 174–5, 177
Adams, J. 1, 19, 71, 177
agenda-setting 6–7, 24–8, 31–4, 37–8, 45, 53, 66, 78, 115, 173
agricultural
   employment 152n.9
   policy 115, 119n.2
   products/production 26–7, 115, 118–19
agriculture 46*t*, 50, 66n.12, 118–19
Akkerman, T. 86, 95
Albright, J. 44–5, 52, 54–7
Alonso, S. 86
Andersen, J. G. 95, 116, 118, 129, 132
animal rights 29–30, 50, 119n.2
Ansell, B. W. 135–6, 138–9
Aragonès, E. 18
Arndt, C. 17
asylum 3, *see also* immigration, refugees
Austria 53–4, 172
authoritarian/libertarian distinction 12, 14–15

Bakker, R. 43
Bale, T. 82, 85–7, 94–5
Bardi, L. 10, 28, 171–2, 178–9
Bartolini, S. 11–12
Baumgartner, F. R. 6, 23–8, 32–3, 37, 45–6, 53, 56–7, 72, 111–12, 115, 184–5
Bawn, K. 171–2
Bélanger, E. 3, 18
Belgium 6, 8, 47–9, 51, 51*t*, 53–4, 60, 62, 64, 69, 73–5, 73*t*, 76*f*, 90n.4 –91nn.6,10, 96, 108n.8, 111–12, 112*t*, 119, 121n.4–2n.6, 121*t*, 127–8, 130, 133–4, 139–41, 141n.5, 142*t*, 144, 150, 158n.3, 159–61, 159*t*, 160n.5, 162n.14, 168, 172–4, 183

Bennulf, M. 128–9
Beramendi, P. 3–4, 11, 13–14, 29, 64n.11, 151–2
Berkhout, J. 82–3
Bertelli, A. 30, 185–6
Bevan, S. 45–6, 87–8
Bhopal disaster 115–16
Bille, L. 129
biodiversity 114, 118–19
Birkland, T. A. 32–3
Blair, T. 148, 151, 164–5
blame avoidance 153–5, 163–4, 167–8, 174
Blank, R. H. 153–4, 157
Böhm, K. 155, 162–3, 165
Bolin, N. 128–9
Boomgaarden, H. G. 100
Borg, I. 72
Bornschier, S. 13–14
bottom-up
   approach 3–5, 10–14, 12n.1, 16–17, 22–4, 39, 71, 179, 181, 183, *see also* sociological approach
   perspective 3–7, 39, 182
bottom-up vs. top-down linkage 181
Boy, D. 131
Boydstun, A. E. 28
Brettschneider, F. 42
Brexit 97n.17, 100, 111–12, 184
Brown, G. 163–4
Budge, I. 6, 18, 41, 44–5, 178–9
Buell, E. H. 18–19
Bukow, S. 126–7
Bulens, J. 127–8
Burau, V. 153–7
Busemeyer, M. 135–6, 138–9, 143
business 46*t*, 57–8, 58*f*, 66n.12, 69–70, 73–7, 86–7, 115–16, 118–19, 170

Cameron, D. 111
Cao, X. 118
capitalism 116–18, 132
capitalist/worker cleavage 11–12
Carmines, E. G. 10–11, 17–18
Carsey, T. 17
cartel
  approach 5–6
  dynamics 186
  perspective 184
  version of a top-down perspective 184–5
Carter, N. 114, 116–18, 131
challenger parties 19–20, 29–30
Chapel Hill Expert Survey (CHES) 14n.2, 43, 157n.2
Chernobyl disaster 115–16, 122*t*, 123–5, 124n.11, 128–9, 132, 173–4
Christensen, J. G. 144, 146
Christian Democratic parties 2, 19–21, 51, 91n.6, 108n.7, 117–18, 127–8, 130, 143n.8
citizenship 27, 82–3, 87–8
Citrin, J. 84
class-based political parties 1
class politics 69, 170
class-related issues 7
class voting 10
cleavages 11–14, 16–17, 39–40, 171, 182
climate change 38
coalitions 20–1, 48, 80, 93–4, 103, 117, 125–7, 130, 163–4, 167, 171–8, 186
  building 2, 4–5, 8–9, 21, 29, 34–5, 48, 80, 84–5, 130, 178, 186
  considerations 2, 4–5, 8, 20–1, 29–31, 34–5, 39, 59, 78–86, 92–3, 95–8, 101–2, 114, 116, 125, 131–4, 137–8, 151, 154, 156, 172, 176–9
  formation 48, 84, 127–8
  governments 1, 42–3, 48, 93–4
  incentives 3–4, 8, 39–40, 78–9, 87, 93, 97, 99, 101–3, 115, 117–18, 127–33, 136, 156, 176–7, 182–4
Cobb, R. W. 24–5, 32–3, 78
codebooks 45–6, 45n.3, 49, 87–8, 105, 118–19

coding 6–7, 44–6, 49, 56–7, 105, 105n.1, 119n.2, 139n.2
Cold War 171
Comparative Agendas Project (CAP) 6, 41, 44–5, 45n.3, 47, 53n.2, 56n.5, 58n.10, 105, 118–19, 139–40, 145–6, 157–8
Comparative Manifesto Project (CMP) 6–7, 18, 41, 44–5, 47, 52, 53n.2, 54–7, 54n.3, 105, 110n.14, 119n.2, 124n.11, 138n.1, 139n.2, 140, 157n.2
conflict
  dimensions 4, 12–13, 19–20, 23, 26–7, 64, 68–9, 78, 137
  structure 3–5, 12–16, 39–40
Cook, T. E. 36
core parties 138–9, 152
country-fixed effects 89–91, 90*t*, 92n.11, 107–8, 120–2, 141, 160
Cowell-Meyers, K. 62, 171
Cox, M. A. 72
Cox, T. F. 72
crime and justice 25–6, 46*t*, 53*f*, 59, 60*f*, 62, 64, 66, 69–70, 73–7, 83, 100, 172–4
cross-national
  differences 69, 80, 119–20, 124–5, 144, 156, 159–60, 162
  perspective 87
  variation 4–5, 8, 22, 38, 43–4, 64, 82, 87, 92–3, 101–2, 109, 137, 141, 172
culture 46*t*, 66n.12, 138n.1
Cutler, D. M. 154–5

Dalton, R. J. 5, 10, 15–16, 177, 181
Danish Union of Teachers 144
data sources 41–5, 47, 110n.14, 157n.2
Dearing, J. W. 28
defence 13–14, 26–7, 46*t*, 50n.10, 58–9, 59*f*, 64, 66, 68–9, 75, 171
deindustrialization 143–4, 143*t*
demarcation vs. integration 12–15
democracies 3, 181
democratization 47–8

Index

Denmark 3, 6, 8, 43–4, 47–50, 51*t*, 52–9, 56*f*, 60–2, 64, 67*t*, 69, 73–5, 74*f*, 80, 84–5, 89, 89*t*, 90n.4 –91nn.6, 10, 92–8, 92n.15, 94*t*, 105–8, 105n.1, 108n.8, 111–13, 112*t*, 116–17, 119–20, 121*t*, 121n.4, 122nn.6–7, 124nn.9, 12, 129–33, 141, 141n.5, 142*t*, 144–6, 145*f*, 145*t*, 147–52, 152n.9, 156n.1, 159–60, 159*t*, 160nn.5, 7, 161nn.8, 10, 162, 171–2, 175–80, 183, 185–7
de Rynck, S. 150
Deschouwer, K. 127–8
de Sio, L. 178–9
de Vreese, C. 100–1
de Vries, C. 3–4, 10, 17, 19–20, 41, 43, 100–1, 103
de Wilde, P. 99, 103–4
disease 26–7, 158
Dixon, R. 149–51
Dobbins, M. 149–50
Dolezal, M. 4, 18–19
Dutroux crisis 62, 173–4

East European countries 47–8, 171–2
economics 6, 57n.9
   crisis 23
   growth 143–4
   issues 7, 19, 68–9
   see also macroeconomics, non-economic issues
economy 6–7, 13, 14n.2, 25–6, 42–3, 46*t*, 47–8, 50, 57–8, 66–70, 73–7, 105n.1, 123–4, 138–9, 143–4
education 1–2, 46*t*, 136
   failure 146–8, 150
   issue incentives 136
   party politics 138
   performance 137
   policy 8, 135–6, 139n.2, 144, 150
   problem development 144
   quality 136–7
   research 139–40, 144n.13
   secondary education 135–6, 139–40, 145–6, 148–50
   services 135, 137
   spending 143–4
   systems 135, 150
   see also primary schools
Education Reform Bill 148–9
Egan, P. J. 18
Elder, C. D. 24–33, 78
elderly 153–4, 157–8, 161–2
elections 3, 6, 8–9, 34–5, 47–50, 53–4, 66, 89, 89*t*, 90*t*, 91–2, 94–7, 97n.17, 105–6, 105n.1, 106n.3, 108n.8, 109–10, 111n.15, 119–20, 121*t*, 121n.4, 122n.7, 123–4, 126–9, 128*t*, 141, 141n.5, 142*t*, 144, 146*t*, 148, 152n.9, 159–60, 160n.5, 161nn.8, 10–11, 163–4, 171–4, 180
   campaigns 39, 42–4
   issue percentages 67*t*
   manifesto data 80–1
   programmes 88–91, 88*t*, 109*t*, 120*t*, 140*t*, 159*t*
electorate 1–5, 13–19, 28, 30, 34–6, 39, 79–80, 85, 101, 110n.14, 136, 156, 161–4, 168, 178–87
elites 6, 11–12
   actors 181
   approach 11, 184
   behaviour 10–11
   competition approach 24
   control 6
   dynamic 37
   level 17
   mobilization of social conflicts 22–3
   perspective 6, 10–11
   struggle 26
endangered species 114, 118–19
energy 26–7, 44–5, 46*t*, 66n.12, 128–9
   policy 115, 118–19
environment 1–2, 46*t*, 114
   as a policy area 114
   cross-national difference 124–5
   issue incentives 115
environmental
   attention 115, 119, 122*t*, 123–4, 126*t*, 128*t*, 130*t*, 133–4
   crisis 132

environmental (*cont.*)
  disasters 100
  effects 118–19
  index 123*f*
  issues 116–18, 127–9, 133–4, 174n.2
  performance 32–3, 115, 117–18, 122–5, 122*t*, 124n.11, 128n.15, 132, 136–7
  policies 105, 114–16, 118, 129, 153–4
  problems 2, 23, 114–18, 128n.15, 173–5
environmentalism 116
Esping-Andersen, G. 68–9
euro 112–13
  crisis 13, 182
European Commission 99–100, 103
European Council 100
European integration 1–4, 7–8, 12–16, 19–21, 23, 27, 31–4, 43, 46, 46*t*, 54n.3, 58n.10, 59–60, 60*f*, 61*f*, 64, 66, 69–72, 78–9, 99–109, 106*f*, 107*t*, 109*t*, 110–13, 171–2, 174–7, 179–80, 182, 184, 186
European Union (EU) 1–2, 27, 46*t*, 66, 73, 75, 99–112, 111n.15, 121*t*
Euroscepticism 1, 15–16, 101–4, 110, 112–13
Eurosceptic parties 101–3, 107–9, 112–13, 112*t*
Evans, G. 110–11
executive speeches 41–3
expert surveys 14n.2, 41, 43
Exxon Valdez oil spill 115–16
Ezrow, L. 20, 35, 177

Farlie, D. 18, 44–5
financial crisis 13, 20, 47, 57–8, 109–10, 170, 179–80, 182
Finland 53–4
Flanders 96, 127–8
Flemish parties 47n.7, 51, 90n.4, 91n.10, 108n.8, 121n.4, 124n.12, 141n.5, 160n.5
Fonseca, S. C. da 86
foreign affairs 46*t*, 66, 73–5

foreign policy 58–9, 59*f*, 64, 69, 94, 101, 171, 174
France 6, 19, 47–51, 51*t*, 54, 57–60, 64, 73–5, 73*t*, 75*f*, 85, 90n.5–91nn.6, 8, 10, 97, 111, 112*t*, 119, 121*t*, 122n.5, 131–2, 137, 139–41, 142*t*, 149–51, 158n.3, 159–60, 162, 167, 175, 178, 185, 186n.4
Franklin, M. 103–4
Freeman, G. P. 174
Fukushima disaster 173–4
functional equivalents 15–16, 43–4, 71–2

GAL (green/alternative/libertarian) pole 13
GAL/TAN distinction 14–15
Garritzmann, J. L. 138
Gerlinger, T. 165–7
Germany 1, 6, 8–9, 19–20, 42, 47–51, 51*t*, 52–60, 56*f*, 62, 64, 72–3, 73*t*, 75–7, 77*f*, 90n.4, 91nn.6, 10, 97–8, 108nn.7–8, 111–12, 112*t*, 117, 119–20, 121*t*, 121n.4, 122n.7, 124–8, 126*t*, 130–4, 141, 142*t*, 150–2, 150*f*, 159–62, 160n.5, 162n.14, 165–7, 166*f*, 166*t*, 169, 171, 175–8, 183, 185–7
Giaimo, S. 163, 165
Gingrich, J. R. 137, 156–7
globalization 3–4, 10, 12–15, 17, 98, 180
global warming 118–19
Goerres, A. 161–2
Grande, E. 99, 103–4, 107–10, 174
Greece 47–8
Greene, Z. 21–2
Green, J. 18, 79–80, 156
Green parties 12, 15, 19, 29–31, 35, 50, 103, 112*t*, 114, 116–18, 122nn.5–6, 124, 126–33, 143n.8, 174nn.1–2, 182
Green-Pedersen, C. 6–7, 18–22, 24–5, 27–30, 36, 38, 41–5, 49, 52–6, 68–9, 84–5, 89–91, 93, 96–7, 99, 103–5, 108, 129–31, 139n.2, 143–4, 151–2, 154–5, 157, 161–3, 170, 178–9
Grek, S. 150

Groenen, P. 72
Grossmann, M. 32, 34, 78, 173
Gustafsson, L. R. 145–8

Hacker, J. S. 157, 173
Haider-Markel, D. P. 17
Hansen, M. E. 43–4
Häusermann, S. 14–15
health care 3, 6–8, 25–7, 32–4, 36–7, 46*t*, 64, 65*f*, 68–9, 73–9, 153–63, 158*f*, 159*t*, 160*t*, 164–8, 164*f*, 165*t*, 166*f*, 166*t*, 170, 172–6, 178–80, 182, 184–5
Helbling, M. 41–2
Hellemans, S. 12
Hertner, I. 99–100
Hillygus, D.S. 20–1
Hinnfors, J. 86–7
Hobolt, S. 4, 19–20, 29–30, 41, 100–1, 103
Hoeglinger, D. 99–100, 103–4, 109
Holian, D. 18
Holmberg, S. 128–9
Hooghe, L. 1, 3–5, 11, 13–14, 16–17, 22–3, 39–40, 59–60, 98–104, 106–7, 109, 111–12, 170–1, 179–80, 182
hospitals 25–7, 163–5
housing 44–5, 46*t*, 66n.12, 73–5, 83
human capital 143–4, 151
Hutter, S. 66, 99–100, 103–4, 106–7, 109–10

identity 11–12, 83
immigration 1–9, 13–16, 19–20, 23, 27, 29–32, 44–6, 46*t*, 48, 50, 59–62, 60*f*, 62*f*, 64, 66, 69–79, 82–93, 88*f*, 88*t*, 89*t*, 90*t*, 94–8, 94*t*, 96*t*, 101, 108, 114, 116–17, 151–2, 171–2, 174–80, 182, 184–6, *see also* asylum, refugees
inequality 15–17, 44–5
inflation 6
institutional
 factors 118
 features 36
 policies 33–4
 setup 178
 structures 25n.1

institutionalization 11–13, 16–17
integration, *see* European integration
integration vs. demarcation 12–15
international
 affairs 54, 57–9, 66
 agreements 118–19
 approach 86–7
 issues 73
 tests 145–6
investment 13–14, 64n.11, 138–9, 152, 168, 174
investment vs. consumption 13
Ireland 53–4
issue agendas 5, 16, 20–2, 24, 36–7, 43–5, 54–6, 169
issue attention 6–7, 22–3, 28, 37–9, 41–5, 69, 72, 177
issue characteristics 2, 4–5, 7–8, 22, 31–2, 34–5, 38–9, 78–80, 83–4, 99–101, 115–16, 132, 135–9, 153–6, 167–8, 172–5, 178
issue competition 2, 4–8, 17–24, 26–34, 41–5, 47–9, 53, 71–2, 101, 128–9, 157, 175–9, 183–5
issue content 1–7, 10–13, 17, 22–4, 38, 42, 44–5, 52, 54, 64, 169–72, 179–81
issue entrepreneurs 19–20, 99, 103, 107, 110, 133, 151–2, 174n.2, 182
issue evolution 17, 19–20
issue incentive model 2–8, 11, 18, 21, 23–4, 26, 29, 31, 35–6, 38–9, 41, 71, 78–80, 82–4, 97–100, 102–4, 110, 114–18, 124–5, 132–9, 151, 153–4, 156, 167–9, 172, 175–85
issue overlap 18–19, 36–7
issue ownership 2, 18–19, 21, 31, 34–5, 39, 78–80, 83–5, 89–91, 93–5, 101–2, 107–9, 114–16, 125–6, 136–9, 144, 146, 148–51, 154, 156, 162–5, 167n.18, 168, 172, 174–9, 183–4
issue politics 10, 44–5, 157, 170, 175
issue saliency 42, 99, 104
issue typologies 32, 78, 173
issue voting 3, 15–16, 52
issue yield 19n.3, 178–9
Italy 47–8, 171–2

Ivarsflaten, E. 84
Iversen, T. 138, 143–4

Jahn, D. 114–15, 118, 122–6, 123*f*
Jakobi, A. P. 135, 138–40, 143–4
Janda, K. 102–3
Jennings, W. 18, 79–80, 156
Jensen, C. 68–9, 138, 143–6, 151–2, 154–5, 157, 161–2, 170
John, P. 30, 185–6
Jones, B. D. 6, 23–7, 32–3, 37, 45, 53, 56–7, 72, 111–12, 115, 184–5
journalistic criteria 36, 42

Katz, R. S. 1, 5, 10, 184, 186–7
Kavanagh, D. 148, 163
Kingdon, J. W. 24–5, 32–3, 37
Kitschelt, H. 5, 10–12, 14–15, 22–3, 28, 183–4
Klein, R. 163–4
Klüver, H. 30
Knill, C. 118
knowledge society 2, 8, 135, 138–9, 143n.10, 151
Kraft, J. 138–9, 152, 168, 174
Kriesi, H. 1–5, 7, 10–15, 39, 41, 59–60, 64, 70–2, 98, 103–4, 107–10, 170–2, 174, 179–80, 182
Krogstrup, J. 20–1, 44–5, 96–7
Krouwel, A. 95
Kruskal, J. 72
Kruskal Stress Measure 72–3, 73*t*
Kyoto Protocol 118–19

labour 46*t*, 58*f*, 66, 70, 73–7, 79–80
labour market 2–3, 13–14, 43–5, 50n.10, 57–8, 68–9, 135–6, 139, 143–4, 153–4, 170
Langsaether, P. E. 14–15, 180
Laver, M. 34–5
law and order 13–14
Lawson, K. 5, 181
Lawton, D. 148–9
Layman, G. 17
left–right
  attention 43–4

  bloc 117
  conflict 4, 14–15, 54–6, 68–9, 99–100, 116, 137
  differences 165–7
  dimension 23, 27, 34–5, 68–70, 78–9, 84, 116, 137, 156, 176–7
  divide 95, 137
  ideology 176
  orientation 51
  party competition 171
  related issues 55*f*, 57, 59, 66, 68–70, 78, 178
  scale 39–40, 116–17, 137–8, 180
  structure 2, 14n.2, 80, 93, 116, 183–4
left-wing
  alliances 143*t*
  bloc 94–5, 117, 125, 128–30, 144
  coalition 117–18, 126–7
  issue ownership 114, 116, 156, 175–6
  opposition 94
  orientation 84–5
  parties 26–7, 107–8, 114, 116–18, 120–2, 122*t*, 127–9, 130n.17, 131–4, 137–8, 144, 147–8, 156, 160, 160*t*, 174
legislatures 27–8, 30, 36–7
Leinaweaver, J. 118
libertarian/authoritarian distinction 12, 14–15
libertarian vs. authoritarian conflict 12
Lieberman, E. S. 80–1
Lindaman, K. 17
Lipset, S. M. 11–14, 16–17, 22–3, 39–40
Liu, X. 32–3, 36, 89–91, 108
local and regional affairs 46, 46*t*, 73–5
Lohneis, H. W. 126

Maastricht Treaty 124, 173–4
macroeconomics 3, 13–14, 38, 57–8, 58*f*, 70, 116–17, 125–6, 170
Macron, E. 186n.4
mainstream parties 2–5, 8–9, 19–21, 24, 29–35, 39, 49–51, 51*t*, 59, 69, 78–80, 82–7, 89–98, 89*t*, 100–10, 107*t*, 114–18, 120–2, 122*t*, 125, 127–34, 136–9, 141–4, 143*t*, 146–56, 160, 160*t*, 161n.9, 165–9, 172–8, 182–7

Index

Mair, P. 1, 5, 10–12, 28, 39–40, 117, 126–7, 171–2, 178–9, 184, 186–7
Malunat, B. M. 125–6
manifestos 6–7, 18, 41–6, 48–50, 53–69, 53*f*, 54*f*, 80–1, 105, 107n.4, 109, 111, 119, 124n.12, 127n.14, 128n.16, 141–2, 178–9
Marks, G. 1, 3–5, 10–11, 13–14, 16–17, 22–3, 39–40, 59–60, 98–104, 106–7, 109, 111–12, 170–1, 179–80, 182–4
Marmor, T. 157
Martens, K. 149–50
McAllister, I. 177
McClellan, M. 154–5
McCombs, M. 28, 53
media 1, 31–3, 36–8, 41–3, 83, 85, 100, 110n.14, 115–18, 149–50, 155, 163–4, 175
Meguid, B. M. 1, 3, 18–20, 82, 86, 118, 122–3, 127–8
Meijers, M. 107–8
Menon, A. 111
Meyer, T. M. 4, 18–19
Middle East 171
Miller, B. 19
Moe, T. 135, 138–9
Mortensen, P. B. 6–7, 18–19, 22, 27–30, 36, 38, 41–3, 49, 89–91, 108, 154–5, 178–9
Mudde, C. 86
Müller-Rommel, F. 118
multidimensional scaling (MDS) 7, 72–3, 74*f*, 75*f*, 76*f*, 77*f*, 78, 179–80
Murthy, V. N. 154–5

NATO 171
Netherlands 1, 6, 20–1, 29–30, 42–4, 47–51, 51*t*, 54, 57–60, 62, 73*t*, 75–7, 77*f*, 80, 86–7, 89, 89*t*, 90n.5, 91nn.6, 10, 93, 95–6, 96*t*, 107–8, 111, 112*t*, 113, 116–17, 119–20, 121*t*, 122–5, 122n.5, 130–1, 130*t*, 133–4, 140n.3, 141, 142*t*, 149–50, 158n.3, 159–60, 159*t*, 161n.11, 162n.14, 169, 171, 174, 183, 185–6

new politics 7, 10, 12–14, 17, 59, 60*f*, 116, 171, 178
niche parties 1–5, 8–9, 19–21, 29–31, 35–7, 39, 48, 50, 69, 79–82, 103, 114, 135, 137, 153, 156, 168–70, 174n.1, 176–7, 180, 182–3, 185–7
Niemann, D. 150
non-economic issues 17, 19, 44–5, 59, 68–9, 123–4, 180–1
Norris, P. 59, 170, 180–1
Norway 53–4
nuclear
  energy 26–7, 128–9
  missiles 171
  power 115, 119n.2
Nuytemans, M. 186

Odmalm, P. 82, 84–7, 93
OECD 2n.1, 91n.8, 115, 124n.8, 146, 152n.9, 161nn.8, 10
Okunade, A. A. 154–5
OLS models 89–91, 120–2, 141, 160
Otjes, S. 93

Panebianco, A. 102–3
Paris Agreement 118–19
parliamentary
  activities 41, 45–6
  data 42–3, 57n.7
  debates 41, 57n.7
  influence 126
  questions 42–3, 89n.3, 105
  representation 128–9, 149n.16, 161n.11
  system 93
particularism 13–15
party competition 3–4, 6–7, 14–15, 17–20, 22–3, 25–6, 30, 38–9, 41–3, 47–8, 59–60, 64, 68–9, 71–2, 78, 81–2, 87, 102–3, 108, 110–12, 118, 119n.2, 125, 139n.2, 150–3, 157, 164–5, 167, 171, 174–5, 177, 179–84

party system agenda 1–9, 26, 28–9, 31–2, 35–9, 41–2, 47–50, 52–4, 56–60, 62–6, 68–9, 71–2, 78–82, 89, 91–3, 94*t*, 95, 96*t*, 97–9, 101, 103–12, 114, 117–19, 124, 126*t*, 127–33, 127n.14, 128*t*, 130*t*, 141, 144, 145*t*, 146–7, 146*t*, 148–53, 148*t*, 158–9, 161n.11, 166*t*, 169–75, 178–87
party system attention 2, 6–8, 24, 26, 32, 35–6, 38, 59–62, 64, 66, 71, 84–5, 87, 88*f*, 89, 89*t*, 97n.17, 106*f*, 107, 110, 118, 121*t*, 122–5, 132, 140–1, 140*f*, 142*t*, 144, 151–2, 154, 158–60, 158*f*, 159*t*, 162–3, 164*f*, 166*f*, 167–8, 170–5, 177–80, 182–3, 186
Pedersen, M. N. 102–3
personal rights 46*t*, 59, 60*f*, 62–4, 63*f*, 66, 70, 75, 158n.3, 171
Petersen, M. B. 154
Peters, G. 33
Petrocik, J. R. 18
Pfaff, M. 165–7
Pierson, P. 155, 163, 173
Pilet, J.-B. 48, 96
Poguntke, T. 118, 126
pollution 33–4, 114–16, 118–19, 122–3
Portugal 47–8
Potter, J. D. 17, 44–5, 180–1
Premfors, R. 146–7
primary schools 2, 144, 146–52, 168
Prime Minister 30–1, 51, 96, 127–8
problem characteristics 32–5, 38, 79–80, 83, 100–1, 136, 139, 151, 153–4, 173–5
problem information 2, 32–5, 37–8, 57–8, 78–80, 83–5, 91–2, 97–8, 100–1, 115–16, 122–5, 132, 136–7, 144, 154, 173–5, 178
Programme for International Student Assessment (PISA) 2, 145–7, 145n.14, 149–51, 173–5
Prosser, C. 101–2
public
  agenda 36–7
  attention 37n.4
  attitudes 112

  awareness 146
  budget 6
  debates 82, 150–1
  health 153–8
  influence 111–12
  lands 118–19
  money 155
  opinion 25, 84, 100–1
  pensions 26–7
  regulation 154

Rauh, C. 138
refugees 3, 27, 82–3, 87–8, 91n.8, 185–6, *see also* asylum, immigration
regression
  analyses 22, 80–1, 176
  approach 162
  estimates 107*t*, 122*t*, 143*t*, 160*t*
  framework 80–1, 125
  model 107
Rehm, P. 5, 183–4
religion 11–12, 43, 62
Repetto, R. 114
Richardson, D. 118
right-wing
  bloc 117, 128–32, 144
  governments 96–7, 125, 129, 138
  parties 4, 10, 12–13, 15–16, 19, 29–30, 36–7, 51, 82, 84–7, 89–92, 90*t*, 93–8, 101–4, 107–9, 107*t*, 114, 116–18, 130, 133–4, 137–8, 143*t*, 147–8, 169, 174–6, 182–3, 185–7
Riker, W. 17
Ringarp, J. 146–7, 150
Rittel, H. W. J. 33, 84
Robertson, D. B. 18, 44–5
Rogers, E. M. 28
Rohrschneider, R. 116
Rokkan, S. 11–14, 16–17, 22–3, 39–40
Rootes, C. 118
Rothland, M. 146–7, 150
Rüdig, W. 126–7

Schain, M. A. 86
Schattschneider, E. E. 10–11, 17, 25

Index

Schumacher, G. 23, 30, 177
Scott, D. J. 28n.2, 49–50, 110n.14
second conflict 3–4, 13–14, 16, 23, 64, 99–100, 151–2, 180
second dimension 4, 6–8, 10, 12–17, 59–60, 64, 70–3, 75–8, 82, 84, 170–1, 179–82
Seeberg, H. B. 18, 34, 38, 79–80, 101, 116, 125–6, 129, 137, 148–51, 156, 162–5, 176
Semetko, H. A. 100–1
Seng, K. 138
Senninger, R. 99–100, 105
Shields, T. G. 20–1
Sides, J. 84
Sigelman, L. 18–19
Sitter, N. 101
Slothuus, R. 18
social conflict 1, 10–12, 14–17, 22–3, 39
Social Democratic parties 2, 8, 12, 30, 35, 51, 86–7, 94–5, 116–17, 125, 127–8, 130–3, 139, 160
Social Liberal parties 84–5, 93–5, 116–18, 120–2, 122t, 125–6, 129–33, 138–9, 143–4, 143t, 145t, 146–7, 151–2, 168, 174n.2
social policy 7, 13–14, 46t, 66–70, 68f, 153–4, 170
sociological approach 10–13, *see also* bottom-up approach
Somer-Topcu, Z. 102–3, 177
Soroka, S. 32–3, 78, 115–16, 136
Southern European countries 47–8
Spain 47–8
Spoon, J.-J. 4, 20, 22, 30, 44–5, 114, 123–4, 133
state–market issues 14n.2, 70, 73–5, 93
Steenbergen, M. R. 28n.2, 49
Stephens, J. D. 138, 143–4
Stevens, D. 17
Stimson, J. A. 10–11, 17
Stoll, H. 14–15
Strøm, K. 29
Stubager, R. 12–15, 18, 79–80, 144, 171, 180
Super, B. 84–7

Sweden 1, 3, 6, 47–9, 51t, 57–8, 60, 62, 64, 72–5, 73t, 74f, 84–5, 89n.3, 91–3, 96–7, 105n.1, 106n.3, 108n.8, 110, 112t, 117–20, 121t, 121n.4, 122–5, 124n.12, 128–34, 128t, 141, 141nn.5–6, 143t, 144, 146–50, 146t, 147f, 152n.9, 156n.1, 159–60, 159t, 160t, 161nn.8, 10, 162, 171, 174n.2, 175–7, 185–6
Switzerland 53–4, 110, 172
systemic saliency 28n.2, 49
Szczerbiak, A. 112–13

Taggart, P. 112–13
Talshir, G. 116, 118, 132
TAN/GAL distinction 14–15
TAN (traditional/authority/national) pole 13
Tavits, M. 17, 21–2, 44–5, 180–1
technological
  advances/progress 136–7, 153–5, 157, 162–3
  change 155–6
  development 161–2, 167, 173–4
technology 8, 46t, 66n.12, 75, 156–8, 161n.8, 167–8
territories/former colonies 46, 46t, 66n.12
Thatcher, M. 163
Thesen, G. 38
Tilley, J. 19–20, 29–30
Tobago 146
Tobit model 92n.13, 108n.9, 124n.13, 142n.7, 162n.13
top-down approach/perspective 3–7, 10–11, 17–18, 22–4, 39, 179, 181–5
Trampusch, C. 135, 138
transnational
  cleavage 171
  conflict 13–14, 98
  issues 179–80
transportation 7, 26–7, 46t, 66n.12, 73–7
Tresch, A. 41–2
Trinidad 146
Tromp, B. 130–1
Turkey 42, 99–100

UK 6, 19, 43–4, 47–50, 51*t*, 54, 57–60, 62, 73–5, 73*t*, 76*f*, 85, 87, 90n.5, 91nn.6, 10, 97–8, 101–2, 105n.1, 110–11, 110n.14, 112*t*, 118–19, 121*t*, 122nn.6–7, 124n.9, 131–2, 140n.3, 141, 144, 145n.14, 148–51, 148*t*, 149*f*, 152n.9, 156n.1, 159–60, 159*t*, 161nn.8, 10, 162–8, 164*f*, 165*t*, 174–6, 178, 182, 184
unemployment 6, 32–4, 90*t*, 91–2, 100, 136–8
unique landscapes and natural reserves 114, 118–19
universalism 13–15
US 17, 26–7, 45–6, 171–2

valence 32–3, 115, 133–8, 138n.1, 151, 153–6, 168, 173–4, 176, 178
van der Brug, W. 14–15, 72, 82, 84, 86–7, 91–2, 101–2, 130–1, 180
van der Eijk, C. 103–4
van de Wardt, M. 4, 20, 41, 43, 94, 103, 176–7
Vangoidsenhoven, G. 48, 96
van Haute, E. 118
van Heck, S. 21–2, 30
van Heerden, S. 86
Vanhuysse, P. 161–2
van Kersbergen, K. 51, 95, 130–1

van Spanje, J. 14–15, 72, 84, 86, 101–2, 180
Varone, F. 62, 173–4
Vedung, E. 128–9
Venezuela 146
Vliegenthart, R. 41–3
Volkens, A. 41

Wagner, M. 4, 18–19, 21, 30
Walgrave, S. 6–7, 18, 24–5, 28, 41–3, 62, 79–80, 173–4, 177, 186
Wallonia 96, 127–8
Ward, D. 17, 44–5, 52, 59, 180–1
water 114, 118–19, 122–3, 136–7
Weaver, K. 154–5
Webber, M. M. 33, 84
Webb, P. 148
Weber, T. 19n.3, 178–9
wedge issue 2, 20–1, 34–5, 94, 103, 110, 126, 128–32, 137, 156, 176–7
welfare state 3, 8, 14n.2, 30, 68–9, 84–5, 138, 157, 170, 176
Wendt, C. 157
Wiborg, S. 135, 138–9, 146–7
Wilders, G. 96
Wilkerson, J. D. 157, 161
Wish, M. 72

Zhu, J.-H. 28, 53